Your German Exchange

D0278164

This comprehensive vocabulary and phrase
book is one of a new series of books
written specifically to help students
of all ages
on foreign exchanges.

Helen & Nigel Harrison

YOUR GERMAN EXCHANGE

Yarker Publishing

First published in Great Britain in 1997 by
Yarker Publishing
Gordon House
276 Banbury Road
Summertown
Oxford
OX2 7ED

Printed in Great Britain by
Redwood Books

British Library Cataloguing-in-Publication Data
A catalogue record for this book is available from
the British Library

ISBN 1-901609-01-4

ACKNOWLEDGEMENTS

Grateful thanks to
Daniel Hartlaub who translated the text
and to Stefan Davies
for his assistance in checking the text.

Acknowledgement also to
Waddingtons Games Limited &
McDonald's Restaurants Limited

CONTENTS

Contents

Contents

Contents

Contents

Contents

THE EXCHANGE
DER AUSTAUSCH

ARRIVING   *ANKOMMEN*

MEETING THE FAMILY   *DIE FAMILIE KENNENLERNEN*

Hello!	*Hallo!*
I'm…	*Ich bin…*
Are you Madame / Monsieur..?	*Sind Sie Herr / Frau…?*
Thank you for coming to meet me.	*Danke, daß Sie mich abgeholt haben.*
I recognized you from the photos you sent me.	*Ich erkenne Sie wieder von den Fotos, die sie mir geschickt haben.*
I'm very pleased to meet you.	*Ich freue mich, Sie kennenzulernen.*
This is a present for you from my family.	*Hier ist ein Geschenk für Sie von meiner Familie.*
It's really good to see you again.	*Es ist wirklich schön, Euch/Sie wieder zu sehen.*

THEY MAY SAY TO YOU   *SIE KÖNNTEN ZU DIR SAGEN*

Did you have a good journey?	*Hattest Du eine gute Reise?*
What was the flight like?	*Wie war der Flug?*
What was the crossing like?	*Wie war die Überfahrt?*
Would you like to go to the toilet?	*Willst Du auf die Toilette gehen?*
Would you like something to eat or drink?	*Möchtest Du etwas essen oder trinken?*
Are you hungry / thirsty?	*Hast Du Hunger / Durst?*
Are you tired?	*Bist Du müde?*

ARRIVING cont.   *ANKOMMEN Forts.*

THEY MAY SAY TO YOU cont.   *SIE KÖNNTEN DIR SAGEN Forts.*

I'll show you round the house.	*Ich zeige Dir das Haus / die Wohnung.*
I'll show you your room.	*Ich zeige Dir dein Zimmer.*
Do you want to unpack now or later?	*Möchtest Du jetzt gleich auspacken, oder später?*
Would you like to ring your family to say you have arrived safely?	*Möchtest Du Deine Familie anrufen, um Sie zu sagen, daß Du gut angekommen bist?*
Shall I dial the number for you?	*Soll ich die Nummer für Dich wählen?*

YOU MIGHT WANT TO SAY	*DU KÖNNTEST ZU / IHNEN SAGEN*
Yes, the journey was fine, thank you.	*Ja danke, ich hatte eine gute Reise.*
No, it was a dreadful journey.	*Nein, die Reise war schrecklich.*
We got held up.	*Wir sind aufgehalten worden.*
The flight was very late leaving.	*Der Flug hatte sehr viel Verspätung.*
The flight was bumpy.	*Der Flug war sehr unruhig.*
The crossing was rough.	*Die Überfahrt war sehr stürmisch.*
I was seasick.	*Ich wurde seekrank.*

ARRIVING cont.	ANKOMMEN Forts.
YOU MIGHT WANT TO SAY cont.	***DU KÖNNTEST IHNEN SAGEN Forts.***

Could I ring my parents, please?	*Könnte ich bitte meine Eltern anrufen?*
I like your house / your room.	*Mir gefällt Euer/Ihr Haus / Eure/Ihre Wohnung / Euer/Ihr Zimmer.*
Where is the loo / toilet?	*Wo ist das Klo?*
Could I have a wash, please?	*Kann ich mich bitte waschen?*
Could I have a drink of water, please?	*Kann ich bitte ein Glas Wasser haben?*

UNPACKING **AUSPACKEN**

Shall I unpack my case now?	*Soll ich jetzt meinen Koffer auspacken?*
Where shall I put my clothes?	*Wo soll ich meine Kleider hintun?*
You can use this half of the wardrobe.	*Du kannst diese Seite vom Schrank benutzen.*
These drawers are for you.	*Diese Schubladen sind für Dich.*

SLEEPING ARRANGEMENTS **SCHLAFVORBEREITUNGEN**

I hope you don't mind sharing a room with me?	*Hoffentlich macht es Dir nichts aus, das Zimmer mit mir zu teilen?*
Do you prefer to have a room on your own or be with me?	*Willst Du lieber ein Zimmer für Dich alleine haben oder mit mir teilen?*

ARRIVING cont.   *ANKOMMEN Forts.*

SLEEPING   *SCHLAFVORBEREITUNGEN*
ARRANGEMENTS cont.   *Forts.*

This is your bed.	*Das ist Dein Bett.*
Do you prefer a duvet or blankets?	*Willst Du lieber ein Federbett oder eine Wolldecke?*
Would you like another pillow?	*Willst Du noch ein Kissen?*
Would you like the window open?	*Schläfst Du bei offenem Fenster?*
Do you prefer the window shut?	*Schläfst Du lieber bei geschlossenem Fenster?*

NEEDING SOMETHING   *ETWAS BRAUCHEN*

Do you need anything?	*Brauchst Du irgend etwas?*
Do you want something?	*Möchtest Du etwas?*
Have you got..?	*Hast Du/Haben Sie...*
• any more hangers?	• *noch ein paar Kleiderbügel?*
• a towel?	• *ein Handtuch?*
I forgot to bring …	*Ich habe...*
• an alarm clock.	• *meinen Wecker vergessen*
• a hairdryer	• *meinen Fön vergessen*
• a comb	• *meinen Kamm vergessen*
• my toothbrush	• *meine Zahnbürste vergessen*
Could I borrow..?	*Könnte ich mir...leihen?*

ARRIVING - DAILY ROUTINE cont.

ANKOMMEN - TAGESABLAUF Forts.

What time do you usually get up?	*Wann stehst Du normalerweise auf?*
Will you wake me when you get up?	*Kannst Du mich wecken wenn Du aufstehst?*
What time shall I set my alarm for?	*Auf wieviel Uhr soll ich meinen Wecker stellen?*
Would you like to lie in tomorrow?	*Würdest Du morgen gerne etwas länger schlafen?*
I'm really tired. Could I sleep until I waken tomorrow?	*Ich bin sehr müde. Kann ich morgen ausschlafen?*
We have to get up early tomorrow because we are going out.	*Wir müssen morgen früh aufstehen, weil wir weggehen wollen.*
What time do you have breakfast?	*Um wieviel Uhr frühstückst Du normalerweise?*
What do you like for breakfast?	*Was ißt Du gerne zum Frühstück?*
I usually have toast and cereal.	*Normalerweise esse ich Toastbrot und Müsli/Cornflakes*
What time do you have dinner?	*Um wieviel Uhr eßt Ihr zu Abend?*

NIGHT-TIME

SCHLAFGEWOHNHEITEN

What time do you usually go to bed?	*Wann gehst Du normalerweise ins Bett?*
You look tired.	*Du siehst müde aus.*
Would you like to go to bed?	*Würdest du gerne ins Bett gehen?*
I am really tired.	*Ich bin sehr müde.*
I would like to go to bed now.	*Ich würde jetzt gerne ins Bett gehen.*
Can I stay up a little longer, please?	*Kann ich bitte etwas länger aufbleiben?*
Can I read in bed for a bit, please?	*Kann ich bitte vor dem Einschlafen noch etwas lesen?*

DAILY ROUTINE cont.   *TAGESABLAUF Forts.*

LIGHTS ON OR OFF?   *LIGHT AN- ODER*
                               AUSLASSEN?

Could you leave the light on, please?	Können Sie / kannst Du das Licht bitte anlassen?
Do you like a light on at night?	Soll ich das Licht die Nacht über anlassen?
I prefer to sleep in the dark.	Ich schlafe lieber im Dunkeln.
I get nervous without a light.	Ich werde leicht nervös ohne Licht.
I am frightened of the dark.	Ich fürchte mich vor der Dunkelheit.
Would you like this nightlight left on all night?	Soll ich die Nachttischlampe die ganze Nacht über anlassen?

TOO HOT OR TOO COLD?   *ZU WARM ODER ZU KALT?*

Are you warm enough?	Ist Dir warm genug?
Would you like an extra blanket?	Möchtest Du gerne noch eine Decke haben?
Yes please / No thank you.	Ja bitte / Nein danke.
Are you too hot?	Ist Dir zu warm?
Would you like a thinner duvet?	Möchtest Du eine dünnere Bettdecke haben?
Would you like a hot water bottle?	Möchtest Du eine Wärmflasche haben?
Could I have a hot water bottle, please?	Könnte ich bitte eine Wärmflasche haben?
Would you like me to put the electric blanket on before you go to bed?	Soll ich die Heizdecke anschalten, bevor Du ins Bett gehst?
Don't forget to turn the electric blanket off before you get into bed.	Vergiß nicht die Heizdecke auszuschalten, bevor Du ins Bett gehst.

DAILY ROUTINE cont.	**TAGESABLAUF Forts.**

PROBLEMS AT NIGHT / PROBLEME IN DER NACHT

PROBLEMS AT NIGHT	PROBLEME IN DER NACHT
Call me if you want anything in the night.	*Weck' mich auf, wenn Du etwas brauchst in der Nacht.*
I had a nightmare.	*Ich hatte einen Alptraum.*
I had a dream.	*Ich habe geträumt.*
I can't get to sleep.	*Ich kann nicht einschlafen.*
I was scared.	*Ich hatte Angst.*
I heard a noise.	*Ich habe ein Geräusch gehört.*
I don't want to be on my own.	*Ich mag nicht alleine sein.*
I am missing home.	*Ich vermisse mein Zuhause. / Ich habe heimweh.*
Could I have a drink of water, please?	*Kann ich bitte ein Glas Wasser haben?*

DECIDING WHERE TO GO FOR A DAY OUT / ÜBERLEGEN WAS MAN TAGSÜBER MACHT

DECIDING WHERE TO GO FOR A DAY OUT	ÜBERLEGEN WAS MAN TAGSÜBER MACHT
What would you like to do today?	*Was möchtest Du heute gerne machen?*
We thought we would go out somewhere.	*Wir haben uns überlegt, etwas zu unternehmen.*
Would you like to do some sightseeing?	*Möchtest Du gerne etwas besichtigen?*
Would you like to go to…?	*Würdest Du gerne…gehen?*
Have you ever been there before?	*Bist Du da schon einmal gewesen?*
Would you like to visit…?	*Würdest Du gerne …besuchen?*
It will be a long day.	*Es wird ein langer Tag werden.*

19

DAILY ROUTINE cont.

TAGESABLAUF Forts.

DECIDING WHERE TO GO FOR A DAY OUT cont.

ÜBERLEGEN WAS MAN TAGSÜBER MACHT Forts.

How long will it take?	*Wie lange wird es dauern?*
What time would we have to get up ?	*Um wieviel Uhr müßten wir aufstehen?*
What time will we need to leave?	*Um wieviel Uhr müssen wir losgehen?*
What time would we get back?	*Um wieviel Uhr wären wir zurück?*
Do you feel up to doing that?	*Hast Du Lust darauf?*
We thought we would go out for a meal.	*Wir haben uns überlegt, essen zu gehen.*
Would you like to go shopping?	*Würdest Du gerne einkaufen gehen?*
Is there anything you need to buy?	*Gibt es irgend etwas, was Du Dir gerne kaufen möchtest?*

WHAT TO TAKE WITH YOU.

WAS DU MITNEHMEN SOLLTEST

Bring your camera, if you have one.	*Nimm Deinen Fotoapparat mit, falls Du einen hast.*
What should I wear?	*Was soll ich anziehen?*
Wear old clothes / smart clothes.	*Ziehe alte / schicke Kleider an..*
Wear walking shoes.	*Ziehe Laufschuhe an.*
Wear comfortable shoes.	*Ziehe bequeme Schuhe an.*
Wear boots.	*Ziehe Stiefel an.*
Bring a mack or a coat.	*Nimm einen Regenmantel oder eine Jacke mit.*
Bring your money.	*Nimm Geld mit.*

SPEAKING PROBLEMS

CAN YOU SPEAK SLOWER, PLEASE?

SPRACHPROBLEME

KÖNNTEST DU / KÖNNTEN SIE BITTE ETWAS LANGSAMER SPRECHEN?

I don't understand what you said.	*Ich habe nicht verstanden, was Du gesagt hast / Sie gesagt haben.*
Can you repeat that please?	*Könntest Du / Könnten Sie das bitte nocheinmal sagen?*
Pardon?	*Entschuldigung? / Wie bitte?*
Can you talk really slowly, please?	*Könntest Du / Könnten Sie bitte ganz langsam sprechen?*

HOW DO YOU SPELL THAT?

WIE BUCHSTABIERT MAN DAS?

Can you write that down for me, please?	*Könntest Du / Könnten Sie mir das bitte aufschreiben?*
How do you pronounce this word?	*Wie spricht man dieses Wort aus?*

LACK OF VOCABULARY

EINEN GERINGEN WORTSCHATZ HABEN

I do not know the word in German.	*Ich kenne das Wort in deutsch nicht.*
I've forgotten the German word.	*Ich habe das deutsche Wort vergessen.*
What's that called in German?	*Wie heißt das auf Deutsch?*
Have you a dictionary?	*Hast Du / haben Sie ein Wörterbuch?*
I need to look a word up in the dictionary.	*Ich muß ein Wort im Wörterbuch nachschlagen.*
What does that mean?	*Was heißt das?*
I can only say a few words.	*Ich kann nur ein paar Wörter sagen.*
You are really fluent.	*Du sprichst wirklich fließend.*
I am beginning to understand more.	*Ich fange an, mehr zu verstehen.*
I am nervous of speaking.	*Ich bin unsicher beim Sprechen.*

SPEAKING PROBLEMS cont.   *SPRACHPROBLEME Forts.*

ASKING TO BE CORRECTED   *SICH VERBESSERN LASSEN*

Will you correct my mistakes, please?	*Würdest Du meine Fehler bitte verbessern?*
Was that right?	*War das richtig?*
What was wrong?	*Was war falsch?*
Was my pronunciation wrong?	*War meine Aussprache falsch?*

NOT GETTING ENOUGH PRACTICE AT SPEAKING GERMAN   *ZU WENIG ÜBUNG BEIM DEUTSCHSPRECHEN*

Can we speak in English for an hour and then German for an hour?	*Können wir eine Stunde lang Englisch und dann eine Stunde lang Deutsch sprechen?*
Shall we play this game in German?	*Sollen wir dieses Spiel auf Deutsch spielen?*
We could play it in English next time.	*Das nächste Mal können wir es dann auf Englisch spielen.*
Can you teach me how to play a German card game in German?	*Kannst Du mir auf Deutsch beibringen, wie man ein deutsches Kartenspiel spielt?*
I know I am rather slow but I would like to practise my German a bit more.	*Ich weiß, es geht etwas langsam, aber ich würde mein Deutsch gerne verbessern..*
I know it's annoying for you when I try to speak German but I won't get any better unless I try.	*Sicher findest Du es lästig, wenn ich Deutsch spreche, aber wenn ich nicht übe, werde ich nie besser.*

GENERAL PROBLEMS   *ALLGEMEINE PROBLEME*

HOMESICKNESS   *HEIMWEH*

You are very kind but I am feeling homesick.	*Du bist/Sie sind sehr nett, aber ich habe Heimweh.*
I am missing home.	*Ich vermisse mein Zuhause.*
I am missing my parents - could I possibly ring them up?	*Ich vermisse meine Eltern, kann ich sie vielleicht anrufen?*
If I ring them, they will ring me straight back.	*Wenn ich sie anrufe, rufen sie mich sofort zurück.*
I am sorry to cry. I am happy really. It's just a bit of a strain speaking German.	*Es tut mir leid, daß ich weine. Es geht mir wirklich gut. Es is nur etwas anstrengend, immer Deutsch zu sprechen.*
I will be O.K. in a minute.	*Es geht mir gleich wieder gut.*

WANTING TO BE ALONE   *ALLEIN SEIN WOLLEN*

Do you mind if I go to my room to write some letters?	*Würde es Ihnen/Dir etwas ausmachen, wenn ich in mein Zimmer gehe und ein paar Briefe schreibe?*
I would really like to write to my family to tell them what I have been doing.	*Ich muß unbedingt meiner Familie schreiben, was ich hier schon alles erlebt habe.*
I am in the middle of a good book at the moment and would like to read for a bit, if that's O.K.?	*Ich lese gerade ein sehr gutes Buch. Wenn es Ihnen/Dir nichts ausmacht, würde ich gerne noch ein wenig weiterlesen.*
Could I go to sleep for half an hour? I am feeling tired.	*Könnte ich mich für eine halbe Stunde hinlegen. Ich bin etwas müde.*

GENERAL PROBLEMS cont. *ALLGEMEINE PROBLEME Forts.*

TIREDNESS *MÜDIGKEIT*

I feel rather tired and would prefer to have a quiet day, if you don't mind.	*Ich bin ziemlich müde. Wenn es Dir nichts ausmacht, würde ich lieber einen ruhigen Tag verbringen.*
Could we just stay at home and watch a video or something?	*Könnten wir nicht einfach zuhause bleiben und uns einen Video anschauen, oder so?*

FINDING THE FOOD STRANGE *DAS ESSEN SELTSAM FINDEN*

Could I try just a tiny bit, please?	*Kann ich bitte nur ganz wenig probieren.*
I am not very hungry at the moment.	*Ich habe momentan keinen großen Hunger.*
I don't usually eat very much.	*Ich esse nie sehr viel.*
Could I possibly have my meat cooked a bit longer, please?	*Kann ich mein Fleisch bitte etwas länger durchgebraten haben?*
Do you have any... that I could eat? (See "Food" - p 167-187)	*Hast du / Haben sie.....das ich essen könnte?*

LEAVING   *ABREISEN*

SAYING YOUR THANKS   *SICH BEDANKEN*

Thank you.	***Dankeschön.***
Thank you for having me to stay.	*Vielen Dank, daß ich bei Dir / Euch sein durfte.*
I've had a lovely time.	*Ich hatte eine wunderschöne Zeit.*
You have been very kind.	*Sie waren / Du warst / Ihr wart / sehr nett zu mir.*
Thank you for taking me to see so much.	*Vielen Dank dafür, daß ich so Interessantes sehen konnte.*
I particularly enjoyed going to..	*Besonders toll fand ich...*
You really helped me to improve my German.	*Sie haben / Du hast / Ihr habt / mir sehr dabei geholfen, mein Deutsch zu verbessern.*

FUTURE PLANS   *ZUKUNFTSPLÄNE*

I will phone you when I get home.	***Ich rufe Sie / Dich / Euch an sobald ich Zuhause bin.***
Write to me.	*Schreiben Sie / Schreib'/ Schreibt mir.*
I hope I'll see you next year.	*Hoffentlich sehen wir uns nächstes Jahr wieder.*
Would you like to come to stay in England?	*Würden Sie / Würdest Du / Würdet Ihr auch einmal nach England kommen?*

THE HOME
DAS ZUHAUSE

HOUSES AND FLATS
HÄUSER UND WOHNUNGEN

TYPES OF HOUSES — *HAUSARTEN*

a flat	*eine Wohnung*
a terraced house	*ein Terrassenhaus / Reihenhaus*
a semi-detached house	*eine Doppelhaushälfte*
a detached house	*ein Einzelhaus*
a cottage	*ein Bauernhaus*
old	*alt*
eighteenth / nineteenth century	*achtzehntes / neunzehntes Jahrhundert*
modern	*modern*
ultra-modern	*ultramodern*
homely	*gemütlich*
smart	*gepflegt*
stylish	*modisch / stilvoll*
charming	*charmant / reizend*

THE OUTSIDE OF THE HOUSE — *DAS HAUS - DIE AUSSENSEITE*

the gate	*das Tor*
the entrance	*der Eingang*
the drive	*die Einfahrt*
the path	*der Weg*
the front / back door	*die Haustür / Hintertür*
the front / back garden	*der Vorgarten /der Garten*
the chimney	*der Schornstein*
the roof	*das Dach*
the windows	*die Fenster*

INSIDE THE HOUSE

IM INNEREN DES HAUSES

the basement	*das Kellergeschoß*
a cellar	*ein Keller*

the ground floor	*das Erdgeschoß*
the porch	*das Portal*
the lobby	*das Vorzimmer*
the hall	*der Flur / die Diele*
the living room	*das Wohnzimmer*
the dining room	*das Eßzimmer*
the study	*das Arbeitszimmer*
the kitchen	*die Küche*
the utility room	*die Waschküche*
the downstairs loo	*das unten Klo*
the cloakroom	*die Garderobe*

the stairs	*die Treppen*
the staircase	*der Treppenaufgang / das Treppenhaus*
downstairs	*unten*
upstairs	*oben*
to go downstairs / upstairs	*nach unten / nach oben gehen*

the lift	*der Fahrstuhl / der Aufzug*
to press the button	*den Knopf drücken*
Which floor do you want?	*In welches Stockwerk möchten Sie bitte?*
The first / second / third / fourth floor, please.	*Den ersten / zweiten / dritten / vierten Stock, bitte.*
The fifth / sixth / seventh / eighth floor, please.	*Den fünften / sechsten / siebenten / achten Stock, bitte.*

INSIDE THE HOUSE cont.

IM INNERN DES HAUSES Forts.

the first floor	***der erste Stock***
the main bedroom	*das Elternschlafzimmer*
the spare bedroom	*das Gästezimmer*
my parents' room	*das Zimmer meiner Eltern*
my room	*mein Zimmer*
your room	*dein Zimmer*
the toilet	*die Toilette*
the bathroom / the shower	*das Badezimmer / die Dusche*

the attic	***der Dachboden***
the playroom	*das Kinderzimmer*
the junk room	*der Abstellraum*
the games room	*das Spielzimmer*

INDIVIDUAL ROOMS   *EINZELNE RÄUME*

THE LIVING ROOM   *DAS WOHNZIMMER*

For comprehensive details on using the equipment see Sections on "T.V..,
Video & Radio" (145-151), "Music" (153-158), "Contacting people by phone"
(335-339) & "Reading" (159-166)

FURNITURE	*MÖBEL*
an armchair	***ein Sessel***
to sit in	*sitzen im*
to relax	*sich entspannen*
to get up from	*aufstehen*
to plump up the cushion	*das Sofakissen aufschütteln*
a sofa	***ein Sofa***
to put your feet up	*die Füße hochlegen*

THE LIVING ROOM   *DAS WOHNZIMMER*

a rocking chair	*ein Schaukelstuhl*
to rock	*schaukeln*
a book case	*ein Bücherregal*
a shelf	*ein Regalt*
to read (See "Reading" 159-166)	*Lesen*
a table	*ein Tisch*
an occasional table	*ein (niedriger) Wohnzimmertisch*
a flower vase	*eine Blumenvase*
a card table	*ein Kartentisch*
to play cards	*Karten spielen*
(See "Games - Cards" 96-113)	

CLOCKS   *UHREN*

a grandfather clock	*eine Standuhr*
to wind up / to strike the hour	*aufziehen/ die volle Stunde schlagen*
a cuckoo clock / a digital clock	*eine Kuckucksuhr/eine Digitaluhr*
What time is it?	*Wieviel Uhr ist es? / Wie spöt ist es?*
Is the clock fast / slow?	*Geht die Uhr vor / nach?*
It's ten minutes fast / slow.	*Sie geht zehn Minuten vor / nach.*

LIGHTING   *BELEUCHTUNG*

lamps	*Lampen (f)*
to turn on / off	*anschalten / ausschalten*
a standard lamp	*eine Stehlampe*
a lampshade	*ein Lampenschirm*
a central light	*eine Deckenbeleuchtung*
wall lights	*Wandleuchten (f)*
a dimmer switch	*ein Dimmer-Schalter / ein Helligkeitsregler*
to dim the lights	*die Lichter dämpfen*

THE LIVING ROOM cont.   *DAS WOHNZIMMER Forts.*

LIGHTING cont.   *BELEUCHTUNG Forts.*

a candlestick	***ein Kerzenleuchter***
a candle	*eine Kerze*
to light	*anzünden*
a match	*ein Streichholz*
by candlelight	*bei Kerzenlicht*
to blow out	*ausblasen*

EQUIPMENT   *GERÄTE*

(See "T.V., Video & Radio" 145-151)

the radio	***das Radio***
to turn on / off	*einschalten / ausschalten*
to listen to	*hören*
the television	***der Fernseher***
to turn on / off	*einschalten / ausschalten*
to watch	*fernsehen*
the video player	***der Videorecorder***
to record a programme	*eine Sendung aufnehmen*
to hire a video	*ein Video ausleihen*
to watch a video	*ein Video anschauen*
the hi-fi (See "Music" 153-158)	***die Hi-Fi-Anlage***
the record player	*der Plattenspieler*
a record	*eine Schallplatte*
the cassette player	*das Kassettendeck / das Tape-Deck / der Kassettenrecorder*
a cassette	*eine Kassette*
the C.D. player	*der C.D.-Spieler*
a C.D.	*eine C.D.*
to listen to	*anhören*
to turn up / to turn down	*lauter / leiser stellen*

THE LIVING ROOM cont   *DAS WOHNZIMMER Forts.*

EQUIPMENT cont.   *GERÄTE Forts.*

(For detailed expressions to do with telephones - see 335-339)

THE TELEPHONE	*DAS TELEFON*
to ring (someone)	*anrufen*
to answer	*antworten*
to pick up	*abnehmen*
to use	*benutzen*
an extension	*ein Nebenanschluß*
an answer phone	*ein Anrufbeantworter*
a message	*eine Nachricht*
to listen	*abhören*
to play back	*zurückspielen*

FURNISHING AND DECORATION	*MOBILIAR UND AUSSTATTUNG*
a rug	*ein Läufer / ein Bettvorleger*
a carpet / a fitted carpet	*ein Teppich*
the wallpaper	*die Tapete*
the colour of the paint	*die Wandfarbe*
the curtains	*die Vorhänge*
the blinds	*die Rollos*

THE LIVING ROOM cont

DAS WOHNZIMMER Forts.

THE HEATING

DIE HEIZUNG

Central heating	*Zentralheizung (f)*
to turn the heating on / off	*die Heizung anstellen / abstellen*
to turn the thermostat up / down	*den Thermostat hoch / niedrig stellen*
Is the heating on?	*Ist die Heizung an?*
to feel the radiator	*den Heizkörper anfühlen*
Do you mind if we turn the heating on / off / up / down?	*Macht es dir was aus, wenn wir die Heizung anstellen / abstellen / hoch / niedrig stellen?*
a fireplace	*ein offener Kamin*
to light the fire	*das Feuer anzünden*
a match	*ein Streichholz*
to strike	*anzünden*
a real fire	*ein echter Kamin*
to get it going well	*das Feuer gut hingekommen*
kindling	*Brennholz (n) / Anzündholz*
firelighters	*Feueranzünder (m)*
old newspapers	*altes Zeitungspapier*
logs	*Holzscheite (n)*
coal	*Kohle (f)*
a pair of tongs	*Feuerzange (f)*
a poker	*Feuerhaken (m) / Schürhaken*
to sit by the fire	*beim Feuer sitzen*
to toast crumpets	*Brot (n) rösten*
a toasting fork	*eine Röstgabel*
to burn	*brennen*
an electric fire	*eine Elektroheizung*
a gas fire	*eine Gasheizung*
to turn on / off	*an-/ ausschalten*

THE DINING ROOM   *DAS ESSZIMMER*

THE DINING TABLE   *DER EßTISCH*

the chairs	*die Stühle*

LAYING THE TABLE   *DEN TISCH DECKEN*

Would you like me to lay the table for you?

How many people shall I lay for?

Soll ich den Tisch für Dich / Sie eindecken?

Für wieviel Leute soll ich eindecken?

Where do you keep..?

- the table mats
- a tablecloth
- napkins

Wo bewahrst Du / bewahrt Ihr / bewahren Sie....

- *die Tischsets*
- *die Tischdecke....*
- *die Servietten.... .....auf?*

What cutlery do we need?
- knives
- forks
- soup spoons
- fish knives and forks
- dessert spoons and forks
- teaspoons
- serving spoons

Welches Besteck brauchen wir?
- *Messer (n)*
- *Gabeln (f)*
- *Suppenlöffel (m)*
- *Fischmesser und -gabeln*
- *Dessertlöffel und -gabeln*
- *Teelöffel*
- *Servierlöffel*

What crockery shall I put out?

- dinner plates
- side plates
- dishes
- serving plates

Welches Geschirr soll ich nehmen?

- *Eßteller (m)*
- *Salatteller*
- *Schüsseln (f)*
- *Servierteller*

THE DINING ROOM cont.	DAS ESSZIMMER Forts.

LAYING THE TABLE cont.	DEN TISCH DECKEN Forts.

What glasses do we need?	Welche Gläser (n) brauchen wir?
• water glasses	• Wassergläser
• a jug of water	• ein Wasserkrug
• red wine glasses	• Rotweingläser
• white wine glasses	• Weißweingläser
• champagne glasses	• Sektgläser

Do you want..?	Brauchst Du.? / Brauchen Sie..?
salt and pepper	Salz (n) und Pfeffer (m)
mustard	Senf (m)
butter	Butter (f)
preserves	Marmelade (f)
marmalade	Orangenmarmelade
cereals	Müsli (n) / Cornflakes
fruit juice	Fruchtsaft (m)
sugar	Zucker (m)
milk	Milch (f)
cream	Sahne (f)

Do you want candles?	Willst Du Kerzen? / Wollen Sie Kerzen?
a candelabra	ein Kerzenleuchter
a candle	eine Kerze
to light	anzünden
a match	ein Streichholz
to blow out	ausblasen

CLEARING THE TABLE.	DEN TISCH ABRÄUMEN
Would you like me to clear the table?	Soll ich den Tisch abräumen?
Where shall I put..?	Wo soll ich....hintun?
Where do you keep..?	Wo bewahrt ihr / bewahren Sie....auf?

THE DINING TABLE cont.   *DER EßTISCH Forts.*

SEATING ARRANGEMENTS	*SITZORDNUNG*
Would you like to sit there?	*Möchtest Du Dich gerne dort hinsetzen?*
Sit next to me.	*Setz' Dich neben mich.*
Sit opposite me.	*Setz' Dich mir gegenüber.*
Sit anywhere.	*Setz' Dich irgendwo hin.*

THE STUDY   *DAS ARBEITSZIMMER*

For comprehensive details on using the equipment see "Computers" 131-138, "Computer Games" 139-144 and "Contacting people by phone" 335-339.

a desk	***ein Schreibtisch***
a drawer	*eine Schublade*
the desk top	*die Schreibtischplatte*
a desk lamp	*eine Schreibtischlampe*
an anglepoise lamp	*eine Klemmlampe*
a calculator	*ein Taschenrechner*
a diary	*ein Terminkalender*
an address book	*ein Adreßbuch*
a blotter	*ein Tintenlöscher*
a pen holder	*ein Federhalter*
a paperweight	*ein Briefbeschwerer*
a telephone (See 335-339)	*ein Telefon*
a chair	***ein Stuhl***
to sit down	*sich setzen*
to get up	*aufstehen*

THE STUDY cont.	*DAS ARBEITSZIMMER Forts.*

a bookcase	***ein Bücherregal***
a bookshelf	*ein Bücherbrett*
a book	*ein Buch*
to read (See 159-166)	*lesen*
a typewriter (See 133-137)	*eine Schreibmaschine*
a computer (See 131-138)	*ein Computer*

THE KITCHEN   *DIE KÜCHE*

THE COOKER   *DER HERD*

gas	***Gas***
to turn on / off	*anstellen / abstellen*
to turn up / down	*hoch / niedrig stellen // aufdrehen / abdrehen*
to light	*anzünden*
a match	*ein Streichholz*
automatic	*automatischer Gasanzünder*
electricity	***Elektrizität***
halogen	*eine Elektroplatte*
a ceramic hob	*eine Herdplatte aus Keramik*
a microwave	***eine Mikrowelle***
to microwave	*die Mikrowelle benutzen*
to heat up	*erhitzen*
to defrost	*auftauen*
to set the timer for five minutes	*die Schaltuhr auf fünf Minuten stellen*

THE KITCHEN cont. *DIE KÜCHE Forts.*

THE COOKER cont. *DER HERD Forts.*

THE OVEN	*DER BACKOFEN*
the oven door	*die Ofentür*
to open	*öffnen*
to shut	*schließen*
temperature	*Temperatur*
to adjust	*einstellen*
high / medium / low	*hoch / mittel / niedrig*
degrees	*Stufen / Grad*
Fahrenheit	*Fahrenheit*
Centigrade	*Celsius*
Gas Mark Four	*Gas herd Stufe vier*
a shelf	*eine Ofenschiene*
top / middle / bottom	*obere / mittlere / untere*
a glass door	*eine Glasofentür*
an oven light	*Die Ofenbeleuchtung*
cooking time	*Backzeit*
an auto-timer	*eine automatische Schaltuhr*
a minute timer	*eine Minuten- Schaltuhr*
to set	*(ein-) stellen*

THE HOB	*DIE KOCHMULDE*
a ring	*eine Kochplatte*
front / back	*vordere / hintere*
left / right	*linke / rechte*

THE KITCHEN cont.   *DIE KÜCHE Forts.*

OVEN UTENSILS	*OFENGERÄTE*
a casserole	*eine Kasserolle*
a roasting dish	*eine Bratpfanne*
an oven tin	*ein Ofenblech*
a round tin	*ein Rundblech*
an oblong tin	*ein rechteckiges Blech*
a cake tin	*ein Kuchenblech*
a bun tray	*eine Gebäckform*
a loaf tin	*eine Brotform*
a deep tin	*ein Tiefblech*
an oven glove	*ein Ofenhandschuh / ein Topflappen*

COOKING VERBS abc)	*KOCHVOKABULAR*
to bake	*backen*
to be nearly ready	*es ist fast gar*
to boil	*kochen*
to casserole	*schmoren*
to check	*abschmecken*
to cook	*kochen*
to cover	*zudecken*
to heat gently / quickly	*langsam / schnell erhitzen*
to put on	*aufsetzen*
to roast	*braten*
to see if it's done	*nachschauen ob's fertig ist*
to simmer	*brodeln / sieden*
to take off	*herunternehmen/ von feuer nehmen*

EQUIPMENT	*GERÄTE*
a saucepan / a lid	*ein Topf / ein Deckel*
large / medium / small	*groß / mittel / klein*
to cover partially	*teilweise zudecken*
to cover / to uncover	*zudecken / abdecken*

THE KITCHEN cont.   *DIE KÜCHE Forts.*

EQUIPMENT cont.   *GERÄTE Forts.*

a frying pan	*eine Bratpfanne*
a fish slice	*ein (Braten-)Wender*
a wooden spoon	*ein Holzlöffel / Kochlöffel*
to stir	*(um-) rühren*
a wok	*ein Wok*
to stir fry	*unter ständigem Rühren anbraten*

THE SINK   *DIE SPÜLE*

the bowl	*das Becken*
the draining board	*das Abtropfbrett / Abtropffläche*
the taps	**die Wasserhähne**
hot / cold	*heiß / kalt*
a mixer tap	*eine Mischbatterie*
to turn on / off	*aufdrehen / zudrehen*
too hot	*zu heiß*
not hot enough	*nicht heiß genug*
to fill the sink with water	*das Spülbecken mit Wasser füllen*
washing up liquid	**Spülmittel**
to squirt	*spritzen*
bubbles	*Schaum*
grease / greasy	*Fett / fettig*
clean / dirty	*sauber / schmutzig*
to rinse off	*nachspülen*
sink equipment	**Spülgeräte**
a brush / a sponge	*eine Bürste / ein Schwamm*
a wire wool pad	*ein Topfkratzer*
a dishcloth	*ein Spüllappen*
to brush / to rub	*bürsten / scheuern*
to scour / to wash	*schrubben / spülen*

THE KITCHEN cont.

DIE KÜCHE Forts.

DRYING DISHES

GESCHIRR TROCKNEN

to drain	*abtropfen lassen*
a rack	*ein Abtropfgestell*
a cutlery basket	*ein Besteckkorb*
to leave to dry	*abtrocknen lassen*
to dry	*trocknen*
a tea towel	*ein Küchenhandtuch*
to put away	*wegräumen*
to stack	*stapeln*

THE FRIDGE

DER KÜHLSCHRANK

to refrigerate	*kühlen*
the fridge door	*die Kühlschranktür*
a bottle rack	*ein Flaschenfach*
an egg rack	*ein Eierfach*
a salad drawer	*ein Gemüsefach*
an ice compartment	*ein Eisfach*
an ice cube tray	*ein Eiswürfelbehälter*
ice cubes	*Eiswürfel*
a shelf	*ein Fach*

THE FREEZER

DIE TIEFKÜHLTRUHE

to freeze	*einfrieren*
to defrost	*abtauen*
to thaw out	*auftauen*
to melt	*schmelzen*
the fast freeze button	*der Schnellgefrierknopf*
maximum / minimum	*Maximum / Minimum*

THE KITCHEN cont.   *DIE KÜCHE Forts.*

THE DISHWASHER   *DIE GESCHIRRSPÜLMASCHINE*

to load / unload	*einräumen / ausräumen*
to stack	*stapeln*
to turn on / off	*an- ausstellen*
a drawer	*ein Geschirrkorb*
a cutlery basket	*ein Besteckkorb*
dishwasher powder/salt/rinse aid	*Geschirrspülmittel / Salz/ Klarspüler*

DISHWASHER PROGRAMMES   *SPÜHLMASCHINEN-PROGRAMME*

a normal wash	*ein Normalprogramm*
a quick wash	*ein Kurzprogramm*
a delicates programme	*ein Schonprogramm*
a long wash	*ein Vor- und Hauptspülgang*
rinse and hold	*Spülen und anhalten*

KITCHEN WASTE   *KÜCHENABFÄLLE*

the waste bin	*der Abfalleimer*
to empty	*ausleeren*
to be full	*voll sein*
a dustbin	*ein Mülleimer*
a waste disposal unit	*ein Müllschlucker*

THE KITCHEN cont.   *DIE KÜCHE Forts.*

KITCHEN CUPBOARDS   *KÜCHENSCHRÄNKE*

a wall unit	*ein Oberschrank*
a base unit	*ein Unterschrank*
a carousel	*ein Drehschrank*
the work surfaces	***die Arbeitsflächen***
kitchen paper	*Küchenpapier*
a knife rack	*ein Messerblock*
a herb rack	*ein Gewürzständer*
a crockery cupboard	***ein Geschirrschrank***
a dinner plate	*ein Eßteller*
a side plate	*ein Salatteller*
a cup	*eine Tasse*
a saucer	*eine Untertasse*
a soup bowl	*ein Suppenteller / eine -tasse*
a dish	*eine Schüssel*
an egg cup	*ein Eierbecher*
a serving dish	*eine Servierschüssel*
a milk jug	*ein Milchkrug*
a sugar bowl	*eine Zuckerdose*
a butter dish	*eine Butterdose*
a glass cupboard	***ein Gläserschrank***
a tumbler	*ein Becherglas*
a wine glass	*ein Weinglas*
a glass jug	*ein Glaskrug*

KITCHEN CUPBOARDS cont. *KÜCHENSCHRÄNKE Forts*

a cutlery drawer	*eine Besteckschublade*
a knife / a fork	*ein Messer / eine Gabel*
a spoon	*ein Löffel*
a teaspoon	*ein Teelöffel*
a dessertspoon	*ein Dessertlöffel*
a tablespoon	*ein Eßlöffel*
a serving spoon	*ein Servierlöffel*
a soup ladle	*eine Suppenkelle*
a measuring spoon	*ein Meßlöffel*

a kitchen tool drawer	*eine Schublade für Küchengeräte*
a can opener	*ein Dosenöffner*
a bottle opener	*ein Flaschenöffner*
a potato peeler	*ein Kartoffelschäler*
a sharp knife	*ein scharfes Messer*
a bread knife	*ein Brotmesser*
a potato masher	*ein Kartoffelstampfer*
a lemon zester	*ein Zestenreißer*
a fish slice	*eine Fischkelle / ein Wender*
kitchen tongs	*Küchenzangen*
a whisk / a balloon whisk	*ein Rührbesen / ein Schneebesen*
a spatula	*eine Teigspachtel*
a garlic press	*eine Knoblauchpresse*
a skewer	*ein Fleischspieß*

OTHER KITCHEN EQUIPMENT *ANDERE KÜCHENGERÄTE*

The kettle	*Der Wasserkessel*
an electric kettle	*ein elektrischer Wasserkessel*
an automatic kettle	*ein Wasserkessel mit Automatik*
to turn on / off	*an- ausstellen*
to boil / to pour	*kochen / ausgießen*

OTHER KITCHEN EQUIPMENT cont.	*ANDERE KÜCHENGERÄTE Forts.*

The bread bin	*Der Brotkasten*
the bread board	*das Brotschneidebrett*
the bread knife	*das Brotmesser*
to cut	*schneiden*
to butter	*mit Butter bestreichen*
to soften	*weich machen*
too hard	*zu hart*
a butter dish	*ein Butterteller*
a butter knife	*ein Buttermesser*
to melt	*schmelzen*
a loaf of bread	*ein Laib Brot*
a slice of bread	*eine Scheibe Brot*
crumbs	*Brotkrümel*

The toaster	*Der Toaster*
to make toast	*toasten*
to set the toaster	*den Toaster anstellen*

A pastry board	*Ein Nudelbrett*
a rolling pin	*ein Nudelholz*
cutters	*Ausstechformen*

A coffee grinder	*Eine Kaffeemühle*
coffee beans	*Kaffeebohnen*
to grind	*mahlen*
a coffee maker	*eine Kaffeemaschine*
filter paper	*Filterpapier*
a plunger	*ein Tauchsieder*

OTHER KITCHEN
EQUIPMENT cont.

ANDERE KÜCHENGERÄTE
Forts.

Scales	*Küchenwaagen*
to weigh	*wiegen*
to measure	*messen*
to balance	*ausbalancieren /*
	ins Gleichgewicht bringen
weights	*Gewichte*

A food processor	*Ein Mixer*
a goblet	*Behälter*
a lid	*ein Deckel*
to liquidize	*flüssig machen*
fast / slow	*schnell / langsam*
to purée	*pürieren*
to chop	*zerkleinern*
to mix	*mixen/mischen*
to blend	*vermischen / einrühren*

Smaller equipment	*Kleinere Geräte*
an electric hand whisk	*ein elektrisches Handrührgerät*
a salt mill	*eine Salzmühle*
a pepper mill	*eine Pfeffermühle*
a lemon squeezer	*eine Zitronenpresse*
a sieve	*ein Sieb*
a colander	*ein Durchschlagsieb*
a steamer	*ein Dampfkochtopf*
a salad spinner	*ein Salattrockner*
a measuring jug	*ein Meßbecher*
a pestle and mortar	*ein Stößel und Mörser*

THE UTILITY ROOM

WASHING, DRYING & IRONING CLOTHES

DIE WASCHKÜCHE

KLEIDER WASCHEN, TROCKNEN & BÜGELN

Dirty clothes	*Schmutzigewäsche*
soiled	*verschmutzt*
a stain	*ein Fleck*
stain remover	*Fleckentferner*
to treat quickly	*schnell behandeln*
to pre-soak	*einweichen*
to bleach	*bleichen*
to scrub	*schrubben*
clean clothes	*saubere Wäsche*

The washing machine	*Die Waschmachine*
to open the door	*die Tür öffnen*
to put the clothes in	*die Wäsche hineintun*
to put the powder in	*das Waschpulver hineingeben*
biological powder	*umweltfreundliches Waschpulver*
non-biological powder	*umweltschädliches Waschpulver*
washing liquid	*Flüssig-Waschmittel*
pre-wash spray	*Vorwasch Spray*
to add conditioner	*Weichspüler hinzugeben*

To choose a cycle	*Einen Waschgang wählen*
to press a button	*eine Programmtaste drücken*
to turn a dial	*den Programmwähler drehen*
Type of wash (abc)	*Verschiedene Waschgänge*
boil / coloured	*Buntwäsche / Kaltwäsche*
cool / hot	*Kochwäsche/ Pflegeleichte Wäsche*
rinse	*Spülgang*
white	*Weißwäsche*
woollens	*Wollwäsche*

WASHING, DRYING & IRONING CLOTHES cont.

WASCHEN, TROCKNEN & KLEIDER BÜGELN Forts.

Type of spin	*Verschiedene Schleuderprogramme*
short	*Kurzschleudern*
long	*Langschleudern*

DRYING CLOTHES

WÄSCHE TROCKNEN

Outside	*Im Freien*
a washing line	*eine Wäscheleine*
a prop	*ein Wäschepfahl*
to peg	*anklammern*
a peg	*eine Wäscheklammer*
a peg bag	*ein Wäscheklammerbeutel*
a linen basket	*ein Wäschekorb*
to dry	*trocknen*
to put out	*herausnehmen*
to take in	*hineintragen*
It's raining.	*Es regnet*

Inside	*Im Haus*
an airer	*ein Trockenständer*
a clothes horse	*ein Wäscheständer*
by the fire	*am Kamin*
on a radiator	*auf der Heizung*

In the tumble drier	*Im Wäsche-Trockner*
to put the clothes in	*die Wäsche hineingeben*
to take them out	*die Wäsche herausnehmen*
to set them timer	*die Schaltuhr einstellen*
hot / cool	*heiß / kalt*
to add a conditioning sheet	*ein Weichmachertuch hinzufügen*
to prevent static	*Elektrostatik verhindern*
to clean the grill	*das Flusensieb reinigen*
to remove the fluff	*die Flusen entfernen*

IRONING CLOTHES   *KLEIDER BÜGELN*

The ironing board	*das Bügelbrett*
to put up	*aufstellen*
to take down	*zusammenklappen*
the iron	*das Bügeleisen*
to iron	*bügeln*
to do the ironing	*die Kleider wäsche bügeln*

A steam iron	*Ein Dampfbügeleisen*
to fill with water	*mit Wasser auffüllen*
to run out of water	*kein Wasser mehr haben*
to squirt	*besprühen*
to steam	*dämpfen*

The temperature of the iron	*Die Bügeltemperatur*
a cool / warm / hot iron	*ein kaltes / warmes / heißes Bügeleisen*
too cold / too hot	*zu kalt / zu heiß*
to scorch	*versengen*
a burn	*eine verbrannte Stelle*

The ironing	*Die gebügelten Kleider*
creased	*zerrknittert*
crumpled	*zerdrückt*
to fold	*zusammenlegen*
to smooth out	*glätten*
to turn the clothes the right way out	*die Kleider nach der richtigen Seite wenden*
inside out	*von innen nach außen*
to air	*lüften*

DOING THE CLEANING   *SAUBERMACHEN*

Vacuuming	***Staubsaugen***
a vacuum cleaner	*ein Staubsauger*
to undo the flex	*die Kabelschnur herausziehen*
to plug in	*einstecken*
a power point	*eine Steckdose*
to switch on	*einschalten*
a carpet	*ein Teppich*
a solid floor	*ein Fußboden*
an upright cleaner	*ein Handstaubsauger*
a cylinder cleaner	*ein Bodenstaubsauger*
to empty the dustbag	*den Staubbeutel ausleeren*

Cleaning tools for the vacuum	***Bestandteile des Staubsaugers***
a thin nozzle	*eine schmale Düse*
a soft / hard brush	*eine weiche / harte Bürste*
a wide brush	*eine breite Bürste*
the hose	*der Saugschlauch*
to suck up	*aufsaugen*
poor / good suction	*wenig / viel Saugkraft*

Brushing	***Kehren***
a broom	*ein Besen*
a soft / hard brush	*ein weicher / harter Handkehrer*
a dustpan	*eine Kehrschaufel*
to sweep up	*zusammenkehren*
a pile	*ein Haufen*
to collect	*aufnehmen / aufsammeln*
to throw away	*Wegwerfen*
dust	*Staub (m)*
dirt	*Schmutz (m)*

DOING THE CLEANING cont.   *SAUBERMACHEN Forts*

Washing surfaces	*Fußboden putzen*
a bucket	*ein Eimer*
water	*Wasser (n)*
cleaning agent	*Putzmittel (n)*
disinfectant	*Desinfektionsmittel (n)*
to disinfect	*desinfizieren*
a spray	*ein Spray*
to spray	*sprühen / sprayen*
a sponge	*ein Schwamm*
to soak	*vollsaugen / aufsaugen*
to squeeze	*ausdrücken*
to wring out	*auswringen*
to wipe	*wischen*
to rub	*reiben*
a mop	*ein Wischmop*
a scrubbing brush	*eine Scheuerbürste*
to scrub	*scheuern*

Polishing	*Staubwischen & Polieren*
a duster	*ein Staubtuch*
to dust	*abstauben*
the dust	*der Staub*
a cobweb	*ein Spinnennetz / eine Spinnwebe*
to polish	*polieren*
polish	*Politur (f)*
spray polish	*Politur aufsprühen*
a tin of polish	*eine Dose mit Politor*
furniture polish	*Möbelpolitur*
floor polish	*Bodenpolitur / Bohnerwachs*
beeswax	*Bienenwachs (n)*
to apply lightly	*dünn auftragen*
to make something shine	*etwas zum Glänzen bringen*
to buff up	*auf Hochglanz bringen*
to clean the silver / the brass	*das Silber / Messing putzen*

DOING THE CLEANING cont.   *SAUBERMACHEN Forts*

CLEANING THE BATHROOM   *DAS BAD SAUBERMACHEN*

Cleaning the loo	*Das Klo saubermachen / putzen*
a lavatory brush	*eine Klobürste*
lavatory cleaner	*WC-Reiniger (m)*
to squirt	*spritzen*
to wipe	*wischen*
to flush the toilet	*die Klospülung ziehen / drücken*
to put out more loo rolls	*mehr Klopapierrollen aufstellen*
Cleaning...	*Putzen...*
the basin	*das Waschbecken*
the bath	*die Badewanne*
the mirrors	*den Spiegel*
the shelves	*die Regale*

REMOVING RUBBISH   *DEN MÜLL WEGBRINGEN*

To empty ...	*Ausleeren....*
the ashtrays	*die Aschenbecher*
the waste bins	*die Abfalleimer*
to put the dustbins out	*die Mülleimer raustellen / raussetzen*
to take the bottles to a bottle bank	*die Flaschen zu einem Flaschencontainer bringen*
to recycle	*recyclen / wieder aufbereiten*

OFFERING TO HELP　　　　*HILFE ANBIETEN*

Can I help you with the...?	*Kann ich Dir beim....helfen?*
cooking - See 173-183	*kochen*
Shall we get ourselves a snack?	*Sollen wir uns einen Imbiß holen?*
Shall I cook my favourite recipe?	*Soll ich mein Lieblingsessen kochen?*
Shall I make a cake?	*Soll ich einen Kuchen backen?*
Shall I make some biscuits?	*Soll ich Plätzchen backen?*
housework - See 50-52	*Hausarbeiten*
Can I help you with the cleaning?	*Kann ich Dir beim Saubermachen helfen?*
Ironing - See 49	*Bügeln*
Would you like me to do the ironing?	*Soll ich die wäsche bügeln?*
washing up - See 40-41	*Abwaschen*
dusting - See 51	*Abstauben*
Shall I dust the living room?	*Soll ich das Wohnzimmer abstauben?*
shopping - See 20	*Einkaufen*
Is there anything you want from the shops?	*Kann ich Dir etwas vom Einkaufen mitbringen?*
Do you want to give me a list?	*Willst Du mir eine Einkaufsliste mitgeben?*

WOULD YOU LIKE ME TO...?   *MÖCHTEST DU DASS ICH...?*

post your letters - see 332-334	*Deine Briefe einwerfe.*
dry the dishes - see 41	*das Geschirr abtrockne*
lay / clear the table - see 34-35	*den Tisch decke /abräume*
load / unload the dishwasher - 42	*die Spülmaschine ein/ ausräume*
make some toast - see 45	*Toast mache*
make the beds - see 55	*die Betten mache*
put the kettle on - see 44	*den Wasserkocher anstelle /*
	Wasserkessel aufsetze
tidy up	*aufräume*
vacuum - see 50	*staubsauge*
do the laundry - see 47-49	*die Wäsche wasche*
walk the dog - see 234	*den Hund ausführe*
mow the lawn - see 70	*den Rasen mähe*

THE BEDROOM   *DAS SCHLAFZIMMER*

Types of bed	***Bettentypen***
a single bed	*ein Einzelbett*
a double bed	*ein Doppelbett*
bunk beds	*Stockbetten*
to climb the ladder	*die Leiter hochsteigen*
to get down	*runtersteigen*
to choose	*aussuchen*
the top / bottom bunk	*das obere / untere Bett*
a camp bed	*ein Feldbett*
an inflatable mattress	*eine Luftmatratze*

THE BEDROOM cont.   *DAS SCHLAFZIMMER Forts.*

The bed linen	*Die Bettwäsche*
to make the beds	*die Betten machen*
to throw over	*beziehen*
to put on	*auflegen*
to straighten	*glätten*
to tuck	*feststecken*
to turn down	*aufdecken*
to change the bed	*die Bettwäsche wechseln*
A sheet	*Ein Bettlaken*
the bottom / the top sheet	*das Bett- Umschlaglaken*
a single / double sheet	*ein Einzelbett- Doppelbettlaken*
an undersheet	*ein Matratzenschoner*
A pillow / a pillow case	*Ein Kissen / ein Kissenbezug*
to plump up	*aufschütteln*
Bed covers	*Bettdecken*
a duvet	*ein Federbett*
a duvet cover	*ein Bettbezug*
a blanket	*eine Wolldecke / Bettdecke*
How many blankets do you like?	*Wieviele Decken möchtest Du?*

BEDROOM FURNITURE   *SCHLAFZIMMERMÖBEL*

The bedside table	*Der Nachttisch*
a bedside lamp	*eine Nachttischlampe*
to turn on / off	*an- ausschalten*
to need a new bulb	*eine neue Birne brauchen*

THE BEDROOM cont.   *DAS SCHLAFZIMMER Forts.*

An alarm clock	*Ein Wecker*
to set the alarm	*den Wecker stellen*
to go off	*losgehen*
to switch off the alarm	*den Wecker ausstellen*
What time shall I set the alarm?	*Auf wieviel Uhr soll ich den Wecker stellen?*
What time do you want to get up tomorrow?	*Um wieviel Uhr möchtest Du morgen aufstehen?*
Will you wake me, please?	*Kannst Du mich bitte aufwecken?*
to wind the clock	*die Uhr aufziehen*
to sleep through the alarm	*den Wecker nicht hören*

The wardrobe	*Der Kleiderschrank*
a double / single wardrobe	*ein Doppel-/ Einzelschrank*
a hanger	*ein Kleiderbügel*
a skirt hanger / a coat hanger	*ein Rockbügel / ein Kleiderbügel*
a rail	*eine Kleiderstange*
to hang up	*aufhängen*
full hanging / half hanging	*voll / halb behängt*

A chest of drawers	*Eine Kommode*
the top / middle / bottom drawer	*die obere / mittlere / untere Schublade*
to open / to shut	*öffnen / schließen*

A dressing table / a stool / to sit	*Eine Frisierkommode / ein Stuhl / sitzen*
a mirror	*ein Spiegel*
to look at one's reflection in	*sich im Spiegel anschauen / sein Spiegelbild betrachten*
to look good / to look terrible	*gut / schlecht aussehen*

THE BEDROOM cont.   *DAS SCHLAFZIMMER Forts.*

Doing one's hair	*Sich frisieren / Sich die Haare machen*
a hair brush	*eine Haarbürste*
to do one's hair	*sich seine Haare zurechtmachen*
to brush one's hair	*sich seine Haare bürsten*
a comb	*ein Kamm*
to comb one's hair	*sich seine Haare kämmen*

THE WINDOW	*DAS FENSTER*
to open / shut the window	*das Fenster öffnen / schließen*
to air the room	*das Zimmer lüften*
to draw the curtains	*die Vorhänge zuziehen*
to open the curtains	*die Vorhänge aufziehen*
to lower the blind	*die Rollos herunterlassen*
to raise the blind	*die Rollos hochziehen*

THE BATHROOM   *DAS BADEZIMMER*

Having a bath	*Ein Bad nehmen*
to get undressed / to have a bath	*sich ausziehen / ein Bad nehmen*
to put the plug in	*den Stöpsel reintun / zustöpseln*
to run the bath	*das Bad einlaufen lassen*
to turn on the taps	*die Wasserhähne aufdrehen*
hot / cold / a mixer tap	*heiß / kalt / ein Mischhahn*
to add bubble bath	*Badeschaum hinzugeben*
bath oil / bath salts	*Badeöl / Badesalz*
essential oil	*ätherische Öle*
to get in the bath	*in die Badewanne steigen*
to use a shower cap	*eine Duschkappe benutzen*
to sit down / to lie down	*sich hinsetzen / sich hinlegen*
to immerse oneself	*in das Wasser eintauchen*

HAVING A BATH cont.   *EIN BAD NEHMEN Forts.*

Washing oneself	*Sich waschen*
soap	*Seife*
a flannel	*ein Waschlappen*
a loofah	*ein Luffaschwamm*
a pumice stone	*ein Bimsstein*
a back brush	*eine Rückenbürste*
to have a long soak	*ein langes Bad nehmen*

Staying in the bath too long	*Zu lange Baden*
to hurry up	*sich beeilen*
How long are you going to be?	*Wie lange brauchst Du noch?*
I would like to use the bathroom soon.	*Ich möchte bald ins Badezimmer*

Getting out	*Raussteigen*
to stand up / to get out	*aufstehen / heraussteigen*
to pull out the plug	*den Stöpsel rausziehen*
to wash out the bath	*die Badewanne saubermachen*
a bath mat	*eine Badematte*

Drying oneself	*Abtrocknen*
to dry oneself / a towel	*sich abtrocknen / ein Handtuch*
a towel rail	*ein Handtuchhalter*
a heated towel rail	*eine beheizte Handtuchstange*
a bath towel / a hand towel	*ein Badetuch / ein Handtuch*
dry / wet	*trocken / naß*
clean / dirty	*sauber / schmutzig*

USING THE BATHROOM
cont.

DAS BADEZIMMER
BENUTZEN Forts

Talcum powder and deodorant	*Körperpuder und Deodorant*
a powder puff	*eine Puderquaste*
to put on	*auftragen*
anti-perspirant	*Antitranspirant / Schweißhemmer*
a spray	*ein Spray*
a roll-on	*ein Roller*
a gel	*ein Gel*

Getting dressed	*Anziehen*
to get dressed	*sich anziehen*
a bathrobe	*ein Bademantel*
a dressing gown	*ein Morgenmantel*

Using the basin	*Das Waschbecken benutzen*
to wash one's hands	*sich seine Hände waschen*
to wash one's face	*sich sein Gesicht waschen*
to open one's toiletry bag	*Waschbeutel*
to look in the mirror	*in den Spiegel gucken*

Cleaning one's teeth	*Zähne putzen*
to clean one's teeth	*sich die Zähne putzen*
a tube of toothpaste	*eine Zahnpastatube*
to squeeze	*herausdrücken*
a toothbrush	*eine Zahnbürste*
soft / medium / hard	*weiche / mittel / hart*
natural bristle / nylon	*Natur- Nylonborsten*
to brush	*putzen*
to rinse out the mouth	*sich den Mund ausspülen*
to gargle	*gurgeln*
to use mouthwash	*Mundwasser benutzen*

USING THE BATHROOM cont.	DAS BADEZIMMER BENUTZEN Forts
Shaving	***Rasieren***
to shave	*sich rasieren*
an electric razor	*ein Rasierapparat*
to plug in	*anschließen*
to turn on / off	*an- ausschalten*
a razor / a razor blade	*ein Naßrasierer / eine Rasierklinge*
shaving soap / cream / brush	*Rasierseife -schaum -pinsel*
to lather	*sich einseifen*
to nick	*sich schneiden*
to bleed / to stop bleeding	*bluten / aufhören zu bluten*
to rinse off	*sich abspülen*
to use aftershave	*Aftershave benutzen*
to splash on	*sich auftragen*
to trim one's beard	*seinen Bart stutzen*

Having a shower	***Duschen***
the shower	*die Dusche*
to take a shower	*eine Dusche nehmen*
to shut the curtain	*den Duschvorhang schließen*
to shut the shower door	*die Duschkabinentür schließen*
to turn on the shower	*die Dusche anstellen*
to adjust the temperature	*die Temperatur einstellen*
to wash oneself	*sich waschen*

Washing one's hair	***Haare waschen***
to wash one's hair	*sich seine Haare waschen*
shampoo	*Shampoo*
for dry / normal / greasy hair	*für trockenes / normales / fettiges Haar*
dandruff shampoo	*Anti-Schuppen Shampoo*
to apply / to rub in	*auftragen / einreiben*
to lather	*aufschäumen*
to rinse / conditioner	*ausspülen / Haarschnellkur*

USING THE BATHROOM cont.   DAS BADEZIMMER BENUTZEN Forts

Drying one's hair	*Haaretrocknen*
to dry one's hair	*seine Haare trocknen*
to rub with a towel	*mit dem Handtuch rubbeln*
to put one's hair in a turban	*einen Turban um die Haare wickeln*
to use a hairdryer	*einen Fön benutzen*
to borrow a hairdryer	*sich einen Fön ausleihen*
to put on mousse / spray	*Haarcreme / Haarspray auftragen*
firm / medium / light control	*fester / medium / leichter Halt*
to blow dry	*trocken fönen*
to straighten	*glätten*
to curl	*wellen*

Using the loo	*Das Klo benutzen*
the toilet	*die Toilette*
to need the loo	*auf's Klo müssen*
to go to the loo	*auf's Klo gehen*
to put the seat up / down	*den Klodeckel auf- zumachen*
loo roll	*Klopapier'*
We have run out of loo roll.	*Wir haben kein Klopapier mehr.*
Is there any more loo roll, please?	*Gibt es noch Klopapier?*
to flush the loo	*die Klospühlung ziehen*
the bidet	*das Bidet*

Other objects on the bathroom shelf	*Andere Gegenstände im Badezimmerregal*
cotton wool	*Watte*
tissues	*Wattetücher*
cotton wool buds	*Ohrstäbchen*

USING THE BATHROOM cont.	DAS BADEZIMMER BENUTZEN Forts
FOR WOMEN	*FÜR FRAUEN*

Perfume	*Parfüm*
to put on	*auftragen*
toilet water	*Toilettenwasser*
a spray / an atomiser	*ein Spray / ein Zerstäuber*
a bottle	*eine Flasche*

Personal hygiene	*Körperpflege*
sanitary towels	*Damenbinden*
tampons	*Tampons*
depilatory cream	*Enthaarungscreme*

Make-up / cosmetics	*Make-up / Kosmetika*
a make-up bag	*ein Schminktasche*
to put on make-up	*sich schminken*

Make-up for the face	*Make-up*
foundation	*Grundmake-up*
blusher	*Rouge*
concealer	*Absdeckstift*
powder	*Puder*
to dot / spread evenly / smooth	*auftupfen / gleichmäßig verteilen / glätten*

For the lips	*Für die Lippen*
a tube of lipstick	*eine Lippenstifttube*
a lip brush	*ein Lippenpinsel*
lip outliner	*ein Lippenkonturenstift*
lip gloss / a lip salve	*ein Lip-Gloss / Lippenbalsam*
a pencil	*ein Stift*
to outline / to fill in	*umranden / ausfüllen*

USING THE BATHROOM cont.

FOR WOMEN cont.

MAKE-UP

DAS BADEZIMMER BENUTZEN Forts

FÜR FRAUEN Forts.

KOSMETIKA

For the eyes	*Für die Augen*
eyeliner	*Eyeliner*
eyeshadow	*Lidschatten*
mascara	*Wimperntusche*

For the eyebrows	*Für die Augenbrauen*
a pair of tweezers	*eine Pinzette*
to pluck	*zupfen*
to shape / to brush	*formen/ bürsten*

Taking make-up off	*Abschminken*
to apply	*auftragen*
make-up remover	*Make-up Entferner*
cotton wool	*Watte*
to wipe	*wischen*
to remove	*entfernen*
eye make-up remover pads	*Augen- Abschmink-Pads*
to cleanse	*reinigen*
cleansing lotion	*Reinigungslotion*
to tone	*abtönen*
to nourish	*eincremen*
cream	*Creme*
a night / day cream	*eine Nacht-/Tagescreme*

THE GARDEN
DER GARTEN

TYPES OF GARDEN · *GARTENTYPEN*

a cottage garden	*ein Bauerngarten*
a herb garden	*ein Gewürzgarten*
a kitchen garden	*ein Gemüsegarten*
a knot garden	*ein Blütengarten*
an orchard	*ein Obstgarten*
a wild flower garden	*ein Wildblumengarten*
a public garden	*eine öffentliche Gartenanlage*
a park	*ein Park*

DESCRIBING GARDENS · *BESCHREIBUNG DER GÄRTEN*

large / small	*Groß / klein*
formal / wild	*angelegt / wild*
pretty	*hübsch*
untidy	*unordentlich*
overgrown	*überwachsen*

COMMON GARDEN CONTENTS · DER GARTEN BEINHALTET

A flower bed	***Ein Blumenbeet***
a flower	*eine Blume*
a bud	*eine Knospe*
a plant	*eine Pflanze*
a weed	*Unkraut*

A lawn	***Ein Rasen***
a border	*eine Umrandung*
a path	*ein Weg*
a seat	*ein Stuhl*

GARDENS cont.

GÄRTEN Forts.

Trees	*Bäume*
a tree	*ein Baum*
a trunk	*ein Baumstamm*
a branch	*ein Ast*
a twig	*ein Zweig*
a leaf	*ein Blatt*
a bush	*ein Strauch*

OTHER GARDEN FEATURES

ANDERE GARTENMERKMALE

a greenhouse	*ein Gewächshaus*
a conservatory	*ein Wintergarten*
a pond	*ein Teich*
a fountain	*ein Springbrunnen*
a wall	*eine Mauer*
a fence	*ein Zaun*
a hedge	*eine Hecke*

COMMON FLOWERS (abc)

ALLGEMEIN BEKANNTE BLUMEN

carnation	*Nelke (f)*	narcissus	*Osterglocke (f)*
daffodil	*Narzisse (f)*	rose	*Rose (f)*
geranium	*Geranie (f)*	snowdrop	*Schneeglökchen(n)*
lavender	*Lavendel (n)*	tulip	*Tulpe (f)*
lily of the valley	*Maiglökchen (f)*		

COMMON WILD PLANTS (abc)

WILDWACHSENDE PFLANZEN

bluebell	*Glockenblume (f)*	dandelion	*Löwenzahn (m)*
buttercup	*Butterblume (f)*	dock leaf	*Sauerampfer(m)*
cowslip	*Schlüsselblume(f)*	nettle	*Nessel (f)*
daisy	*Gänseblümchen-f*		

GARDENS cont.

GÄRTEN Forts.

COMMON TREES AND BUSHES (abc)

ALLGEMEIN BEKANNTE BÄUME UND STRÄUCHER

ash	*Esche (f)*	hawthorn	*Hagedorn (m)*
beech	*Buche (f)*	holly	*Stechpalme (f)*
birch	*Birke (f)*	oak	*Eiche (f)*
chestnut	*Kastanie (f)*	privet	*Liguster (f)*
elm	*Ulme (f)*	sycamore	*Platane (f)*
fir	*Fichte (f)*	yew	*Eibe (f)*

COMMON ANIMALS (abc)

ALLGEMEIN BEKANNTE TIERE

a bat	*ein Fledermaus*	a molehill	*ein Maulwurfshügel*
a hedgehog	*ein Igel*	a rabbit	*ein Kaninchen*
a mole	*ein Maulwurf*	a squirrel	*ein Eichörnchen*

COMMON INSECTS (abc)

ALLGEMEIN BEKANNTE INSEKTEN

an ant	*eine Ameise*	a fly	*eine Fliege*
a bee	*eine Biene*	a moth	*eine Motte*
a butterfly	*ein Schmetterling*	a spider	*eine Spinne*
a caterpillar	*eine Raupe*	a wasp	*eine Wespe*

COMMON BIRDS (abc)

ALLGEMEIN BEKANNTE VÖGEL

a blackbird	*eine Amsel*	a robin	*ein Rotkehlchen*
a blue tit	*eine Blaumeise*	a rook	*eine Krähe*
a crow	*ein Rabe*	a starling	*ein Star*
a dove	*eine Wildtaube*	a thrush	*eine Drossel*
a magpie	*eine Elster*	a bird table	*ein Futtertisch*
an owl	*eine Eule*	a bird's nest	*ein Vogelnest*
a pigeon	*ein Taube*	an egg	*ein Ei*

GARDENS cont.

GÄRTEN Forts.

GARDEN FURNITURE

GARTENMÖBEL

a garden seat	*ein Gartenstuhl*
a sunbed	*eine Sonnenliege*
a deckchair	*ein Liegestuhl*
a hammock	*eine Hängematte*
a statue	*eine Statue*
an urn	*eine Urne*
a bird table	*ein Vogeltisch*

GARDEN ENTERTAINMENT

GARTENVERGNÜGUNGEN

HAVING A BONFIRE

EIN GARTENFEUER MACHEN

to gather wood	*Holz sammeln*
to find kindling	*Brennholz suchen*
to light	*anzünden*
smoke	*Rauch*
flames	*Flammen*
sparks	*Funken*
to cook jacket potatoes	*Schalenkartoffeln grillen*
the direction of the wind	*die Windrichtung*
to change	*wechseln*
to get out of control	*außer Kontrolle geraten*
to put out	*ausmachen*
a bucket of water	*ein Eimer Wasser*
a hose	*ein Schlauch*

GARDEN ENTERTAINMENT · *GARTENVERGNÜGUNGEN*

HAVING FIREWORKS · *EIN FEUERWERK MACHEN*

to stand well clear	*Abstand halten*
to watch from over there	*von weitem zuschauen*
to light	*anzünden*
a fuse	*ein Zündschnur*
a match	*ein Streichholz*
to go out	*ausgehen*
to leave it alone	*es alleine lassen*
to have another	*noch einmal*
a fireworks display	*eine Feuerwerksvorführung*
a box of fireworks	*eine Feuerwerkskiste*
a sparkler	*eine Wunderkerze*
a catherine wheel	*ein Feuerrad*
a rocket	*eine Rakete*
a Roman candle	*eine Leuchtkugel*

BARBECUES · *GRILLPARTIES*
See "Food" - pages 184-5, 313

GARDEN GAMES · *GARTENSPIELE*

Playing mini golf	***Mini-Golf spielen***
a golf club	*ein Golfschläger*
a golf ball	*ein Golfball*
a hole	*ein Loch*
to pot the ball in one	*den Ball einlochen*
clock golf	*Zeit-Golf*
to strike	*schlagen*

GARDEN ENTERTAINMENT   *GARTENVERGNÜGUNGEN*

Playing croquet	***Krocket spielen***
a croquet mallet	*ein Krocketschläger*
a hoop	*ein Tor*
the central stick	*der zentrale Schläger*
to go straight through	*gerade durchgehen*
to hit the hoop	*das Tor treffen*
to knock someone out of the way	*jemanden aus den Weg hauen*

Playing bowls	***Boule spielen***
to throw	*werfen*
to roll	*rollen*
to hit	*treffen*
to miss	*verfehlen*
to be the nearest	*am nächsten sein*
to be hit out of the way	*weggeschlagen sein*

Trampolining	***Trampolinspringen***
a trampoline	*ein Trampolin*
to bounce	*springen*

GARDENING   *GARTENARBEIT*

The equipment	***Die Arbeitsgeräte***
the garden shed	*der Gartenschuppen*
a wheelbarrow	*eine Schubkarre*
a spade / a fork	*ein Spaten/eine Heugabel*
a trowel	*ein Pflanzenspatel*
a hoe / a rake	*eine Hacke / ein Rechen*
a pair of clippers	*Gartenschere*
a hedge trimmer	*eine Heckenschere*
a broom	*ein Besen*
a dustbin	*ein Mülleimer*

GARDENING cont.   *GARTENARBEIT Forts*

Mowing the lawn	***Den Rasen mähen***
a lawn mower	*ein Rasenmäher*
an electric mower	*ein elektrischer Rasenmäher*
a hand mower / a motor mower	*ein Handmäher / ein Motormäher*
to cut the grass	*den Rasen mähen*
to push / to pull	*drücken / ziehen*
to alter the setting	*die Messereinstellung verändern*
to turn the corner	*um die Ecken mähen*
straight lines	*gerade Bahnen*
to empty the box	*den Kasten ausleeren*
grass cuttings	*Grasabfälle*
The grass needs cutting.	*der Rasen muß gemäht werden*

Doing the weeding	***Unkraut jäten***
a weed	*Unkraut*
to pull out	*jäten*
to uproot	*entwurzeln*

Watering the garden	***Den Garten gießen***
The garden needs watering.	*Der Garten muß gegossen werden*
a watering can	*eine Gießkanne*
to fill	*füllen*
to spray	*gießen*
a hose pipe	*ein Wasserschlauch*
a sprinkler	*ein Sprenger*
an automatic sprinkler	*eine automatische Sprinkleranlage*
to turn on / off	*an- ausstellen*

PETS

HAUSTIERE

A budgerigar	***Ein Wellensittich***
a cage	*ein Käfig*
a perch	*eine Sitzstange*
a swing / to swing	*ein Schaukel / schaukeln*
a mirror / to admire himself	*ein Spiegel / sich bewundern*
a bell / to ring	*eine Glocke / klingeln*

A cat	***Eine Katze***
a kitten	*ein Kätzchen*
a cat basket	*ein Katzenkorb*

A dog	***Ein Hund***
a puppy	*ein Welpe*
a dog kennel	*eine Hundehütte*
to take the dog for a walk - See page	*den Hund ausführen*
to go to dog training classes	*zum Hundetraining gehen*

A dove	***Eine Taube***
a dove cote	*ein Taubenschlag*

A goldfish	***Ein Goldfisch***
a goldfish bowl	*ein Goldfischglas*
water	*Wasser*
to swim around	*herumschwimmen*
weeds	*Wasserpflanzen*
pebbles	*Kieselsteine*
to clean out the tank	*das Aquarium säubern*

PETS cont.   *HAUSTIERE Forts.*

Other pets	*Andere Haustiere*
a guinea pig	*ein Meerschweinchen*
a hamster	*ein Hamster*
a mouse	*eine Maus*
a parrot - to talk	*ein sprechender Papagei*

Useful expressions	*Nützliche Ausdrücke*
Does it bite?	*Beißt er/ sie / es?*
Don't put your finger in the cage.	*Steck Deinen Finger nicht in den Käfig.*
I have to take it to the Vets.	*Ich muß ihn / sie / es zum Tierarzt bringen.*

GAMES
SPIELE

COMMON EXPRESSIONS **ALLGEMEINE AUSDRUCKSWEISEN**

Would you like to play?	**Möchtest Du etwas spielen?**
What would you like to play?	Was möchtest Du gerne spielen?
Do you like playing..?	Spielst Du gerne....?
Shall we have a game of..?	Sollen wir....spielen?

How many can play?	**Wieviele können mitspielen?**
It's a game for two people.	Es können zwei Leute mitspielen.
You need four people to play.	Man braucht vier Leute zum Spielen.
We haven't got enough people.	Wir haben nicht genügend Spieler / Spielerinnen.
We have too many people.	Wir sind zu viele Leute.

You play in teams.	**Man spielt in Teams**
How many are in each team?	Wieviele sind in jedem Team?
Will you be in my team?	Spielst Du in meinem Team?
I'll be in the other team.	Ich spiele im anderen Team.

What do you need to be able to play?	**Was braucht man für das Spiel?**
You need paper and a pencil.	Man braucht Papier und Bleistift.
This pencil is blunt.	Mein Bleistift ist stumpf
My lead has broken.	Mein Stift ist abgebrochen
Have you another pencil?	Hast Du noch einen Bleistift?
Could I have more paper, please?	Kann ich bitte mehr Papier haben?

STARTING GAMES cont.

DAS SPIEL ANFANGEN Forts.

Where shall we play?	*Wo sollen wir spielen?*
Shall we play in..?	*Sollen wir....spielen?*
..my / your room?	*...in meinem / Deinem Zimmer?*
..the living room?	*im Wohnzimmer?*
..on this table? / ..on the floor?	*auf diesem Tisch / auf dem Boden?*

How long does a game take?	*Wie lange dauert das Spiel?*
This game doesn't take long.	*Dieses Spiel dauert nicht lange.*
This game takes too long.	*Dieses Spiel dauert zu lange.*
It takes at least an hour.	*Es dauert mindestens eine Stunde.*
This is a quick game.	*Dies ist ein schnelles Spiel.*

How do you play it?	*Wie geht das Spiel?*
You have to..	*Man muß...*
The object of the game is to..	*Das Ziel des Spiels ist...*
You start here.	*Man fängt hier an.*
You go this way round the board.	*Man spielt in diese Richtung.*

Choose a token	*Eine Spielfigur wählen*
Which token would you like?	*Welche Spielfigur möchtest Du sein?*
Which colour would you like to be?	*Welche Farbe möchtest Du sein?*

What happens if you land here?	*Was passiert, wenn man darauf landet?*
You get another turn.	*Man ist nochmal dran.*
You lose a turn.	*Man muß eine Runde aussetzen.*
You go back three spaces.	*Man muß drei Felder zurückgehen.*
You go forward two spaces.	*Man muß zwei Felder vorrücken.*
You have to go back to the beginning.	*Man muß zum Start zurückgehen.*

GAMES cont.   *SPIELE Forts.*

Where is the finish?	*Wo ist das Ziel?*
You finish here.	*Das Ziel ist hier.*
The first person to finish wins.	*Der Erste im Ziel hat gewonnen.*

Pick up a card.	*Eine Karte nehmen*
What does the card say?	*Was steht auf der Karte?*
I can't read what's on the card.	*Ich kann nicht lesen, was auf der Karte steht.*
What does that mean?	*Was heißt das?*
Show me what I have to do now	*Zeig mir, was ich jetzt machen soll.*
You can keep the card till later.	*Du kannst die Karte für später aufbewahren.*

Money	*Geld*
Who's going to be banker?	*Wer macht die Bank?*
Can I be banker?	*Kann ich die Bank machen?*
Will you be banker?	*Willst Du die Bank machen?*
How much money do you start with?	*Mit wieviel Geld fängt man an?*
You have twenty thousand pounds to start with.	*Du bekommst zwanzigtausend Mark am Anfang.*
Each time you go round you get given....	*Für jede Runde bekommst Du etwas....*

GAMES cont.

SPIELE Forts.

Buying and selling	*Kaufen und Verkaufen*
You can buy a..	*Du kannst...kaufen.*
Do you want to buy it?	*Möchtest Du....kaufen?*
I'd like to buy..	*Ich möchte....kaufen.*
I haven't got enough money.	*Mein Geld reicht nicht.*
How much money do I have to pay?	*Wieviel muß ich bezahlen?*
You have to pay..	*Du mußt....bezahlen.*
Have you change for a fifty pound note?	*Kannst Du mir fünfzig Mark wechseln?*
You didn't give me my change.	*Du hast mir nichts zurückgegeben*
You have to give me / all the other players..	*Du mußt mir / allen anderen Spielern....geben.*
You have to pay a fine.	*Du mußt eine Strafe zahlen.*
You pay ten times what's on the dice.	*Du mußt zehn mal soviel zahlen wie auf den Würfel steht.*

What are the rules?	*Wie sind die Spielregeln?*
Can I read the rules, please?	*Kann ich die Spielregeln lesen?*
It's against the rules.	*Das ist gegen die Regeln.*
That's cheating.	*Du mogelst.*
You can't do that.	*Das kannst Du nicht machen.*

Who starts?	*Wer fängt an?*
The highest starts.	*Die höchste Würfelzahl fängt an.*
The lowest starts.	*Die niedrigste Würfelzahl fängt an.*
You need a six to start.	*Du brauchst eine Sechs um anzufangen.*
You need a double to start.	*Du brauchst einen Pasch um anzufangen.*
Shall we toss a coin to see who starts?	*Sollen wir eine Münze werfen, um zu sehen wer anfängt?*
Heads or tails? It's heads.	*Kopf oder Zahl? Kopf.*

GAMES cont.   *SPIELE Forts.*

Throw the dice.	*Würfeln*
How many dice do you use?	*Mit wievielen Würfeln spielen wir?*
You use two dice.	*Man spielt mit zwei Würfeln.*
You only use one.	*Man braucht nur einen.*
Have you got a shaker?	*Hast du einen Würfelbecher?*
The dice rolled off the table.	*Der Würfel ist vom Tisch gerollt.*
The dice fell on the floor.	*Der Würfel ist auf den Boden gefallen.*
Shake again.	*Du mußt nochmal würfeln*

What did you throw?	*Was hast Du gewürfelt?*
I threw a..	*Ich habe eine...*
..one / two / three	*...Eins / Zwei / Drei*
..four / five / six	*...Vier / Fünf / Sechs ..gewürfelt.*
You have to throw a six.	*Du mußt eine Sechs würfeln.*
You have to throw a double.	*Du mußt einen Pasch würfeln.*
Throw again.	*Würfel nochmal.*

Do you like this game?	*Magst Du das Spiel?*
This game is..	*Das Spiel ist...*
..too difficult / too easy.	*...zu schwierig / zu einfach.*
..rather boring / excellent.	*...etwas langweilig / sehr gut.*

How do you win?	*Wie gewinnt man?*
The winner is the first person to finish.	*Wer als erster im Ziel ist gewinnt.*
The winner is the person with the most..	*Der Spieler mit dem / den meisten...*
..money.	*...Geld*
..points.	*...Punkten ...gewinnt.*
Shall we see who's won?	*Sollen wir sehen, wer gewonnen hat?*
Count up your money.	*Zähle Dein Geld.*
How much money have you got?	*Wieviel Geld hast Du?*
Add up your points.	*Zähle Deine Punkte zusammen.*
How many points have you got?	*Wieviele Punkte hast Du?*

GAMES cont.   *SPIELE Forts.*

Who's won?	***Wer hat gewonnen?***
I've won / You've won.	*Ich habe gewonnen / Du hast gewonnen.*
He's won / She's won.	*Er hat gewonnen / Sie hat gewonnen.*
We've won / They've won.	*Wir haben gewonnen / Sie haben gewonnen.*
Our team won.	*Unser Team hat gewonnen.*
Their team won.	*Deren Team hat gewonnen.*
Well played!	*Gut gespielt!*
Bad luck!	*Pech gehabt!*

Shall we stop now?	***Sollen wir jetzt aufhören?***
Shall we have one more game?	*Sollen wir noch ein Spiel spielen?*
Is there time for another game?	*Haben wir Zeit für noch ein Spiel?*
Shall we play the best of three?	*Sollen wir solange spielen, bis einer aus drei Spielen die meisten gewonnen hat?*
Shall we play something else?	*Sollen wir etwas anderes spielen?*
It's time to stop.	*Wir sollten jetzt aufhören.*
We'd better put it away.	*Wir sollten lieber einpacken.*

MONOPOLY

MONOPOLY

The Board | ***Das Brett***

Go	***Los***
to pass Go	*über Los gehen*
I just passed Go.	*Ich bin gerade über Los gegangen*
Collect two hundred pounds salary as you pass Go.	*Ziehen Sie im Vorübergehen DM viertausend Gehalt ein*
Can I have my salary, please?	*Kann ich bitte mein Gehalt haben?*

In Jail	***Im Gefängnis***
Just Visiting	*Nur zum Besuch*
I am just visiting.	*Ich bin nur zu Besuch hier*
In Jail. / I am in jail.	*Im Gefängnis / Ich bin im Gefängnis*
I've been sent to jail.	*Ich bin ins Gefängnis geschickt worden.*
I have/haven't a card to get out of jail free.	*Ich habe eine/ habe keine Karte, um aus dem Gefängnis frei zu kommen*
I threw doubles three times in succession so I have to go to jail.	*Ich habe dreimal hintereinander einen Pasch gewürfelt, also muß ich ins Gefängnis.*
You need to throw a double to get out.	*Du mußt einen Pasch würfeln, um wieder frei zu kommen.*
Will you sell me your get out of jail free card?	*Verkaufst Du mir Deine "Du kommst aus dem Gefängnis frei" Karte?*
How much do you want for your get out of jail free card?	*Wieviel Geld willst Du für Deine "Du kommst aus dem Gefängnis frei" Karte?*
I will pay the fifty pound fine now.	*Ich bezahle die zweihundert Mark Strafe sofort.*
I have to pay the fifty pound fine now.	*Ich muß die zweihundert Mark Strafe sofort bezahlen.*
I've missed three turns so I can come out this go.	*Weil ich dreimal ausgesetzt habe, komme ich in dieser Runde frei.*

MONOPOLY cont.

MONOPOLY Forts.

Income Tax	*Einkommenssteuer*
Pay two hundred pounds.	*Zahle fünfhundert Mark.*
You pay all taxes to the Bank.	*Du bezahlst alle Steuern an die Bank.*
Super Tax	*Zusatzsteuer*
Pay one hundred pounds.	*Zahle dreihundert Mark.*

Other squares	*Andere Felder*
Free Parking	*Frei Parken*
Go to Jail	*Gehen Sie in das Gefängnis*

The Properties	*Häuser & Hotels*
a street	*eine Straße*
a road	*eine Allee*
a square	*ein Platz*

The Stations	*Die Bahnhöfe*
Rent	*Miete*
If two / three / four stations are owned..	*Wenn man zwei / drei / vier Bahnhöfe besitzt.*

The Utilities	*Wasser- und Elektrizitätswerk*
The Waterworks	*Die Wasserwerke*
The Electricity Company	*Das Elektrizitätswerk*
If one utility is owned, rent is four times amount shown on one die.	*Wenn man eines der Werke besitzt, ist die Miete viermal höher als eine Würfelzahl.*
If both utilities are owned, rent is ten times amount shown on one die.	*Wenn man beide Werke besitzt, ist die Miete zehnmal höher als eine Würfelzahl.*

MONOPOLY cont.   *MONOPOLY Forts.*

THE CARDS   *DIE KARTEN*

The Cards	Die Karten
Property Cards	***Besitzrechtkarten***
a site	*ein Grundstück / eine Straße*
a Title Deed	*ein Besitzrecht*
rent - site only	*Miete-nur für das Grundstück*
rent with one / two / three / four houses	*Miete mit einen / zwei / drei / vier Häuser*
rent with a hotel	*Miete mit einem Hotel*
If a player owns all the sites of any colour group, the rent is doubled on unimproved sites in that group.	*Die Miete verdoppelt sich, wenn ein Spieler alle Straßen einer Farbe besitzt.*
Cost of houses - one hundred pounds each.	*Ein Haus kostet eintausend Mark.*
Cost of hotels - one hundred pounds plus four houses.	*Ein Hotel kostet vier Häuser und eintausend Mark.*
Mortgage value of site.	*Der Hypothekenwert des Grundstückes.*

Chance	***Ereignis***
Pick up a Chance card.	*Ziehe eine Ereigniskarte.*
Take the top card.	*Ziehe die oberste Karte*
Put the used card at the bottom of the pile.	*Schiebe die gebrauchte Karte unter den Stapel.*
What does it say?	*Was steht drauf?*
It says.. (abc)	***Es steht drauf....***
Advance to Go	*Rücke bis auf Los vor.*
Advance to Mayfair.	*Rücke vor bis zur Schlossallee.*
Advance to Pall Mall - If you pass Go collect two hundred pounds.	*Rücke vor bis zur Seestraße. Wenn Du über Los kommst, ziehe DM viertausend ein.*
Bank pays you a dividend of fifty pounds.	*Die Bank zahlt Dir eine Dividende von DM eintausend.*

MONOPOLY cont.　　　　　*MONOPOLY Forts.*

Drunk in charge - Fine twenty pounds.	*Betrunken am Steuer. Zahle DM dreihundert Strafe*
Get out of Jail free - This card may be kept until needed or sold.	*Du kommst aus dem Gefängnis frei. Diese Karte muß behalten werden, bis sie gebraucht oder verkauft wird.*
Go back three spaces.	*Gehe drei Felder zurück.*
Go to Jail. Move directly to Jail. Do not pass Go. Do not collect two hundred pounds.	*Gehe in das Gefängnis. Begib Dich direkt dorthin. Gehe nicht über Los. Ziehe nicht DM viertausend ein.*
Make general repairs on your houses - for each house pay twenty five pounds.	*Lasse alle Deine Häuser renovieren. Zahle an die Bank für jedes Haus DM fünfhundert.*
Speeding fine - fifteen pounds.	*Strafe für zu schnelles Fahren.*
Take a trip to Marylebone Station and if you pass Go collect two hundred pounds.	*Mache einen Ausflug nach dem Süd-Bahnhof, und wenn Du über Los kommst, ziehe DM viertausend ein. DM 300*
You are assessed for street repairs - forty pounds per house, one hundred and fifteen pounds per hotel.	*Du wirst zu Srassenausbesserungsarbeiten herangezogen. Zahle für Deine Häuser und Hotels. DM achthundert je Haus und DM zweitausenddreihundert je Hotel an die Bank.*
Your building loan matures - Receive one hundred and fifty pounds.	*Miete und Anleihezinsenwerden fällig. Die Bank zahlt Dir DM dreitausend.*
You have won a crossword competition - Collect one hundred pounds.	*Du hast in einen Kreuzworträtsel-Wettbewerb gewonnen. Ziehe DM zweitausend ein.*

MONOPOLY cont.   *MONOPOLY Forts.*

Community Chest Cards   *Gemeinschaftskarten*
What does it say?   *Was steht drauf?*

It says.. (abc)   *Es steht drauf...*
Advance to Go.   *Rücke vor bis auf Los.*
Annuity matures - Collect one hundred   *Die Jahresrente wird fällig. Ziehe DM*
pounds.   *zweitausend ein.*
Bank error in your favour - Collect two   *Bank-Irrtum zu Deinen Gunsten. Ziehe*
hundred pounds.   *DM viertausend ein*
Doctor's fee - Pay fifty pounds.   *Arzt- Kosten. Zahle DM eintausend.*
From sale of stock - You get fifty   *Aus Lagerverkäufen erhältst Du DM*
pounds.   *fünfhundert.*
Get out of Jail free - This card may be   *Du kommst aus dem Gefängnis frei.*
kept until needed or sold.   *Diese Karte muss behalten werden, bis*
                                             sie gebraucht oder verkauft wird.
Go back to Old Kent Road.   *Gehe zurück nach der Badstraße.*
Go to Jail. Move directly to Jail. Do   *Gehe in das Gefängnis. Begib Dich*
not pass Go. Do not collect two   *direkt dorthin. Gehe nicht über Los.*
hundred pounds.   *Ziehe nicht DM viertausend ein.*
Income Tax Refund - Collect twenty   *Einkommenssteuer-Rückzahlung. Ziehe*
pounds.   *DM vierhundert ein.*
It is your Birthday - Collect ten pounds   *Es ist Dein Geburtstag. Ziehe von*
from each player.   *jedem Spieler DM eintausend ein.*
Pay a ten pound Fine or take a   *Zahle eine Strafe von DM zweihundert*
"Chance".   *oder nimm eine Ereigniskarte.*
Pay Hospital one hundred pounds.   *Zahle an das Krankenhaus DM*
                                             zweitausend.
Pay your Insurance Premium - fifty   *Zahle deine Versicherungsprämie. DM*
pounds.   *fünfhundert.*
Receive interest on seven per cent   *Du erhältst DM zweitausend Zinsen.*
Preference Shares - twenty five pounds.   *Du erhältst auf Vorzugs-Aktien sieben*
                                             Prozent. Dividende DM neunhundert.
You have won Second Prize in a   *Du hast den zweiten Preis in einer*
Beauty Contest - Collect ten pounds.   *Schönheitskonkurrenz   gewonnen.*
                                             Ziehe DM zweihundert ein.
You inherit one hundred pounds.   *Du erbst DM zweitausend.*

MONOPOLY cont.
The Play

MONOPOLY Forts.
Das Spiel

Choosing the pieces	*Die Spielfiguren wählen*
Which piece do you want to be?	*Welche Spielfigur möchtest Du haben?*
What colour do you want to be?	*Welche Farbe möchtest Du sein?*

Starting a game	*Das Spiel beginnen*
Shake two dice to start.	*Wirf mit zwei Würfeln um anzufangen.*
The player with the highest total starts.	*Der Spieler mit der höchsten Würfelzahl fängt an.*
I start.	*Ich fange an.*
You start.	*Sie fängt an.*
He / she starts.	*Er fängt an.*

Whose turn is it now?	*Wer ist jetzt dran?*
It's my / your / his / her go.	*Ich / Du / er / sie ist dran.*
We are playing clockwise / anticlockwise.	*Wir spielen im Uhrzeigersinn / gegen den Uhrzeigersinn.*
It's not your turn.	*Du bist nicht dran.*
You went out of turn.	*Du hast Deinen Zug verpaßt.*
You'd better miss your next go.	*Du solltest Deinen nächsten Zug besser nicht verpassen.*

Throwing the dice	*Würfeln*
to throw a double	*einen Pasch würfeln*
I threw a double so I throw again.	*Ich habe einen Pasch gewürfelt, also würfele ich nochmal.*
I threw three doubles so I have to go to jail.	*Ich habe dreimal Pasch gewürfelt, also muß ich ins Gefängnis.*
to throw two sixes	*zwei Sechser würfeln*

MONOPOLY cont.   *MONOPOLY Forts.*

Moving the tokens	Die Spielfiguren bewegen
I shook a three so I move three places.	*Ich habe eine Drei gewürfelt, also gehe ich drei Felder vor.*
We can both be on that space at the same time.	*Wir können beide gleichzeitig auf dem Feld stehen.*
I have to advance to Go.	*Ich muß auf Los vorrücken.*
I have to go directly to jail.	*Ich muß direkt ins Gefängnis gehen.*

Landing on squares	Auf Plätze und Straßen landen
I hope you land on my property.	*Ich hoffe, Du landest auf meinem Grundstück.*
Oh no! I just landed on your property.	*Oh nein! Ich bin auf Deinem Grundstück gelandet.*
Does anyone own the property I just landed on?	*Gehört das Grundstück, auf dem ich gerade gelandet bin, irgend jemand?*
It's mine, so you owe me..	*Es ist meins, also schuldest Du mir...*
How much do I have to pay you?	*Wieviel muß ich Dir bezahlen?*
You have to pay me twenty two pounds rent - site only.	*Du mußt mir hundertzwanzig Mark Miete bezahlen- nur für das Grundstück.*
I have three houses, so that's nine hundred pounds you owe me.	*Ich habe drei Häuser, also schuldest Du mir fünftausendvierhundert Mark*
You have landed on my hotel.	*Du bist auf meinem Hotel gelandet.*

Buying property	Grundstücke kaufen
Do you want to buy that?	*Willst Du es kaufen?*
Yes, I'll buy it, please.	*Ja, ich will es kaufen.*
No, I don't think I'll buy it.	*Nein, ich will es nicht kaufen.*
No, I haven't enough money.	*Nein, ich habe nicht genügend Geld.*
Have you any change?	*Kannst Du mir wechseln?*

MONOPOLY cont.	*MONOPOLY Forts.*

Selling property	*Grundstücke verkaufen*
Would you like to sell me..?	*Würdest Du mir ....verkaufen?*
I want to sell these houses back to the bank.	*Ich möchte diese Häuser an die Bank zurück verkaufen.*
You only get half price if you sell property back to the Bank.	*Du bekommst nur den halben Preis für Grundstücke, die Du an die Bank zurück verkaufst.*

Putting houses on	*Häuser bauen*
Houses are green.	*Häuser sind grün*
I want to put a house on here.	*Ich möchte hierdrauf ein Haus bauen.*
I have two houses, so you have to pay me..	*Ich habe zwei Häuser, also mußt Du mir ....bezahlen.*
Could I buy a house, please?	*Kann ich bitte ein Haus kaufen?*
I would like four houses, please.	*Ich möchte bitte vier Häuser.*
You have to put houses evenly over your properties.	*Man muß gleichmäßig seine Straßen bebauen.*
The bank has run out of houses, so you'll have to wait.	*Du mußt warten, weil die Bank keine Häuser mehr hat.*
The bank now has houses again - would you like to bid for them?	*Die Bank hat wieder Häuser- möchtest Du welche ersteigern?*

Putting a hotel on	*Ein Hotel bauen*
Hotels are red.	*Hotels sind rot*
I want to buy a hotel now.	*Ich will jetzt ein Hotel kaufen.*
You can't put a hotel on until you have four houses on each site.	*Du kannst kein Hotel bauen, bevor Du nicht vier Häuser auf jeder Straße hast.*
You give the Bank the four houses and pay the difference for a hotel.	*Du gibst der Bank Deine vier Häuser und bezahlst ihr die Differenz für ein Hotel*
Here are the houses in exchange.	*Hier sind meine Häuser die ich austauschen will.*
I have to pay.....extra.	*Ich muß....zusätzlich bezahlen.*

MONOPOLY cont.

MONOPOLY Forts.

The Banker	*Der Bankhalter*
Do you want to buy it?	*Willst Du es / sie kaufen?*
It costs..	*Es / sie kostet...*
You owe the Bank..	*Dir gehört die Bank.*
Does anyone want to bid for this property?	*Möchte jemand dieses Grundstück ersteigern?*
You are the highest bidder.	*Du bist der Meistbietende.*
I haven't got the right change.	*Ich habe kein Wechselgeld.*
Can someone change this note, please?	*Kann mir bitte jemand diesen Schein wechseln?*
The Bank has run out of money.	*Die Bank hat kein Geld mehr.*
The Bank will have to give you an I.O.U. (an I owe you).	*Die Bank muß Dir einen Schuldschein geben.*

Mortgaging property	*Hypotheken*
I would like to mortgage this, please.	*Ich möchte gerne eine Hypothek aufnehmen.*
The mortgage value is printed on each Title Deed.	*Der Hypothekenwert ist auf der Rückseite jeder Besitzrechtkarte aufgedruckt.*
Turn the card face down to show it's mortgaged.	*Drehe die Karte um, damit Du die Hypothek sehen kannst.*
There is no rent to pay because the property is mortgaged.	*Man muß keine Miete zahlen, weil auf dem Grundstück eine Hypothek ist.*
You have to pay ten per cent when you lift the mortgage.	*Du mußt zehn Prozent zahlen, wenn Du die Hypothek auflöst.*
You can't mortgage houses or hotels.	*Du kannst auf Häuser und Hotels Hypotheken aufnehmen.*
You can't build on mortgaged property.	*Man kann nicht auf einem Grundstück mit Hypothek bauen.*
You have to pay off the mortgage first.	*Du mußt die Hypothek erst zurückzahlen.*

MONOPOLY cont.   *MONOPOLY Forts.*

Being bankrupt	*Bankrott gehen*
I'm afraid I can't pay you.	*Ich fürchte, ich kann Dich nicht auszahlen.*
I haven't any money.	*Ich habe kein Geld.*
I shall have to return my houses/hotels to the Bank.	*Ich muß meine Häuser und Hotels an die Bank zurückgeben.*
You only get half their value if you return them.	*Man bekommt nur den halben Wert, wenn man sie zurück gibt.*
Will you take part cash and part property?	*Würdest Du zur Hälfte Geld und zur Hälfte Grundstücke nehmen.*

Seeing who has won	*Herausfinden wer gewonnen hat*
Shall we stop now and see who has won?	*Sollen wir jetzt aufhören, um zu sehen, wer gewonnen hat.*
Shall we leave the game here and carry on playing later?	*Sollen wir unterbrechen und später weiter spielen?*
Add up all your money.	*Zähle Dein Geld zusammen.*
Add up the value of your property.	*Zähle den Wert Deiner Grundstücke zusammen.*
How much do you own?	*Wieviel besitzt Du?*
I own..	*Ich besitze....*
You have won.	*Du hast gewonnen.*
I think I've won.	*Ich glaube, ich habe gewonnen.*

CLUEDO

THE OBJECT OF THE GAME

CLUEDO

DAS ZIEL DES SPIELS

To solve by elimination and deduction the murder of Dr. Black, the owner of Tudor Close, whose body has been found at the foot of the stairs leading to the cellar at a spot marked "X". The winner is the first player to guess correctly:- • Who the murderer was. • Which weapon was used. • The room in which the crime was committed.	*Der detektivische Spürsinn aller Spieler ist auf die Ermittlungakte gerichtet. Dieser schwarze Umschlag enthält drei geheime Karten, deren Inhalt herauszufinden ist.* • *Eine Karte zeigt den Täter* • *Eine zweite Karte die Tatwaffe* • *Und die dritte Karte den Tatort.*

The spot marked "X"	***Die Stelle, die mit einem "X" markiert ist.***
The stairs leading to the cellars	*die Kellertreppe*
the envelope marked "Murder Cards"	*die Ermittlungsakte*

The three "Murder Cards"	***Die drei geheimen Karten***
the murderer	*der Täter*
the weapon	*die Tatwaffe*
the room in which the crime was committed	*der Tatort*

CLUEDO cont.

CLUEDO Forts.

Selecting the three "Murder Cards"	Die Karten für die "geheime" Ermittlungsakte auswählen
Shuffle the nine room cards well.	Mische die neun Karten mit den Tatorten.
Shuffle the six weapon cards separately.	Mische die sechs Karten mit den Tatwaffen.
Shuffle the six person cards too.	Mische die sechs Karten mit den Tatverdächtigen.
Cut the piles of cards.	Lege die Stapel nebeneinander.
Place the top card of each pile unseen into the Murder Envelope.	Nimm von Jedem der drei Stapel die oberste Karte auf und lege sie verdeckt in den schwarzen Umschlag "Ermittlungsakte".
There should be a room card, a weapon card and a person card.	In der "Ermittlungsakte" sollte eine Karte mit dem Tatort, eine mit der Tatwaffe und eine mit dem Täter liegen.

The people and their pieces	Die Tatverdächtigen und ihre Spielfiguren
Colonel Mustard -Yellow	Oberst von Gatow - Gelb
Professor Plum - Purple	Professor Blum - Violett
The Reverend Green - Green	Reverend Grün - Grün
Mrs. Peacock - Blue	Baronin von Porz - Blau
Miss Scarlett - Red	Fräulein Gloria - Rot
Mrs. White - White	Frau Weiß - Weiß

The Board	Das Brett
the ground floor plan of Tudor Close	der Spielplan -das Erdgeschoß der Villa
start	die Startfelder
a square	ein Feld
a door	eine Tür

CLUEDO cont.   *CLUEDO Forts.*

The rooms	*Die Zimmer*
the lounge	*der Salon*
the dining room	*das Speisezimmer*
the kitchen	*die Küche*
the ballroom	*das Musikzimmer*
the conservatory	*der Wintergarten*
the billiard room	*das Billardzimmer*
the library	*die Bibliothek*
the study	*das Arbeitszimmer*
the hall	*die Halle*

The secret passages	*Die Geheimtüren*
from the study to the kitchen and vice versa	*vom Arbeitszimmer in die Küche und umgekehrt*
from the lounge to the conservatory and vice versa	*vom Salon in den Wintergarten und umgekehrt*
You can use a secret passage instead of throwing the dice.	*Wer eine Geheimtür benutzen will, würfelt nicht.*
Using a secret passage counts as one move.	*Eine Geheimtür benutzen, zählt als ein Spielzug.*

The Weapons	*Die Tatwaffen*
The Candlestick	*Der Leuchter*
The Dagger	*der Dolch*
The Lead Piping	*Das Heizungsrohr*
The Revolver	*Die Pistole*
The Rope	*das Seil*
The Spanner	*Die Rohrzange*
the tokens	*die Spielsteine / die Tatwaffen*

CLUEDO cont.   *CLUEDO Forts.*

"Detective Notes" cards	*"Die Ermittlungs-Karten"*
Suspected Persons	*Die Verdächtigten*
Probable Implements	*Der wahrscheinliche Tathergang*
Suspected Scene of Murder	*Vermuteter Tatort*
Have you got some pencils?	*Hast Du ein paar Bleistifte?*
Could I have a pencil, please?	*Kann ich bitte einen Bleistift haben?*
to tick off	*abhaken*
to cross off	*ausstreichen*
to make a note of	*eine Notiz machen*
to record	*aufzeichnen*
to eliminate from your enquiries	*von seinen Ermittlungen streichen*
Using "Detective Notes" cards	*Die "Ermittlungs-Karten" benutzen*
to query	*verhören*
to get confused	*verwirrt sein*
to forget	*vergessen*
You asked me that before.	*Das hast Du mich schon mal gefragt*

Playing	*Spielen*
Place the pieces on their starting squares.	*Setze die Spielfiguren auf ihre Startfelder.*
Put the weapons in different rooms.	*Verteile die Tatwaffen beliebig auf die Zimmer.*
Draw the three Murder Cards (see above).	*Ziehe die "geheimen" Karten für die "Ermittlungsakte".*
Put the Murder Cards in the Murder Envelope.	*Lege die "geheimen" Karten in die "Ermittlungsakte"*
Put the Murder Envelope on the spot marked "X".	*Lege die "Ermittlungsakte" auf das mit einem "X" markierte Feld.*
Shuffle all the cards together.	*Mische sämtliche Karten.*

CLUEDO cont.

CLUEDO Forts.

Deal out the cards one at a time clockwise round the table.	*Verteile die Karten einzeln reihum an die Spieler.*
Sometimes some players have more cards than others. It is easier for them.	*Es kann vorkommen, daß einige Spieler mehr Karten erhalten als andere. Das ist zu deren Vorteil.*
Each player decides to be one of the murder suspects and uses their token.	*Jeder Spieler übernimmt die Figur, die ihm am nächsten steht.*
Miss Scarlett always moves first.	*Fräulein Gloria fängt immer an.*
Play in a clockwise direction.	*Spiele im Uhrzeigersinn.*
Shake the dice and move your token accordingly.	*Bewege Deine Spielfigur entsprechend der gewürfelten Augenzahl.*
You may not move diagonally.	*Man darf nicht diagonal ziehen.*
You have to enter and leave rooms through the doors or secret passages.	*Man kann die Zimmer durch die Türen oder die Geheimtüren betreten und verlassen.*

Making a suggestion	***Einen Verdacht aussprechen***
When you enter a room, you can make a "suggestion" by calling into that room any other person (who has to go immediately into the room) and any weapon (which is then placed in the room). You cannot use any other room in your suggestion, only the room you are in.	*Wenn man ein Zimmer betritt, kann man einen Verdacht aussprechen. Dies geschieht, indem man eine beliebige Person (die sofort in das Zimmer gehen muß) und eine Tatwaffe (die in das Zimmer gebracht werden muß) benennt. Man kann einen Verdacht nur in dem Zimmer aussprechen, in dem man sich gerade befindet.*

CLUEDO cont.   *CLUEDO Forts.*

A sample suggestion	*Ein Beispiel*
"I suggest that the murder was committed in the Lounge by the Reverend Green with the Spanner."	*"Ich glaube, das Reverend Grün den Mord mit der Rohrzange im Salon begangen hat".*

After the suggestion

Wie ein Verdacht überprüft wird

The player who is making the suggestion, does so to the player on his / her left.

Der linke Nachbar des Spielers, der den Verdacht geäußert hat, beginnt.

This player has to examine his / her cards and if he has one (or more) of the suggested cards he must show one (and one only) of them secretly to the other person. (He should not admit to having more than one of the requested cards.)

Er überprüft alle seine Karten. Besitzt er eine (oder mehrere) der unter Verdacht stehenden Karten, zeigt er sie dem Spieler (aber nur ihm) der den Verdacht ausgesprochen hat. (Besitzt der Spieler mehrere der unter Verdacht stehenden Karten, so zeigt er trotzdem nur eine davon).

If this player has none of the cards, the person to his left is then asked the same question.

Wenn er keine der unter Verdacht stehenden Karten besitzt, ist sein linker Nachbar an der Reihe, an den nun der selbe Verdacht geäußert wird.

As soon as someone has shown one of the suggested cards, that turn is ended and play passes to the next player to the left.

Sobald ein Spieler eine der unter Verdacht stehenden Karten gezeigt hat, ist die Runde des Spielers, der einen Verdacht geäußert hat, vorbei. Nun ist sein linker Nachbar an der Reihe.

Each person tries by a process of elimination to discover the three Murder Cards.

Jeder Spieler versucht durch ein Ausscheidungsverfahren herauszufinden, welche "geheimen" Karten sich in der Ermittlungsakte befinden.

CLUEDO cont.

CLUEDO Forts.

Making an accusation

When a player think he knows what the three Murder Cards are, he can, provided it is his turn (even if he has just made a suggestion), make an Accusation by writing down what he thinks the three cards in the Murder Envelope are and checking with the contents of the Murder Envelope, taking care that no-one else sees the cards.

Erheben einer Anklage

Hat ein Spieler so viele Informationen gesammelt, daß er glaubt den Inhalt der Ermittlungsakte zu kennen, so darf er "Anklage erheben" (vorausgesetzt er ist an der Reihe). Er darf dies auch tun, wenn er gerade einen Verdacht geäußert hat. Dann schreibt der Spieler die drei Karten auf, die er in der Ermittlungsakte vermutet und überprüft den Inhalt der Ermittlungsakte-ohne daß seine Mitspieler Einblick nehmen können.

If the player is not correct, he cannot make any more accusations in the game. He should replace the three cards in the Murder Envelope so that the other players can continue the game. He still has to answer other players' suggestions.

Ist auch nur eine Karte falsch benannt, so schiebt der Spieler die drei Karten wieder in den Umschlag. Der Spieler nimmt weiter am Spiel teil, aber nur noch, um Verdächtigungen, die von anderen Spielern geäußert werden, zu überprüfen. Er selbst kann nicht mehr aktiv werden.

N.B. If a player says he does not hold any of the suggested cards when he in fact **does** hold one, this player has no further turns in the game.

N.B. Wenn ein Spieler behauptet, er besitze keine der unter Verdacht stehenden Karten, obwohl er in Wirklichkeit eine besitzt, darf er am Spiel nicht mehr teilnehmen.

CARD GAMES

KARTENSPIELE

GENERAL EXPRESSIONS

ALLGEMEINE AUSDRUCKSWEISEN

Would you like to play cards?	***Möchtest Du gerne Karten spielen?***
What games do you know?	*Was für Spiele kennst Du?*
What would you like to play?	*Was möchtest Du gerne spielen?*
Can you play..?	*Kannst Du....spielen?*
Shall we play..?	*Sollen wir...spielen?*
I'd like to play..	*Ich möchte...spielen.*
I've forgotten how to play.	*Ich weiß nicht mehr, wie man es spielt.*
Can you remind me how to play?	*Könntest Du mir zeigen, wie man es spielt.*
Can you teach me how to play?	*Kannst Du mir beibringen, wie man es spielt.*

A pack of cards	***Ein Kartenspiel***
Have you got a pack of cards?	*Hast Du ein Kartenspiel?*
I brought a pack of cards with me.	*Ich habe ein Kartenspiel mitgebracht.*
I'll go and get them.	*Ich gehe es holen.*

Is it a full pack?	***Ist das Kartenspiel vollständig?***
Shall we check the pack?	*Sollen wir nachzählen?*
Are there any missing?	*Fehlen welche?*
There is one missing.	*Eine fehlt.*
Have you got another pack?	*Hast Du ein anderes Kartenspiel?*

The different suits	***Die verschiedenen Farben***
clubs	*Kreuz*
diamonds	*Karo*
hearts	*Herz*
spades	*Pik*

CARD GAMES cont.   *KARTENSPIELE Forts.*

The number cards	Die Zahlen
ace	*As*
ace high / ace low	*ein hohes As / ein niedriges As*
the ace of hearts	*Das Herz-As*
two	*eine Zwei*
the two of diamonds	*die Karo-Zwei*
three / four / five / six	*eine Drei / Vier / Fünf / Sechs*
seven / eight / nine / ten	*Sieben / Acht / Neun / Zehn*

The face cards	Die Bilder
Jack	*Bube*
Queen	*Dame*
King	*König*
Joker	*Joker*

PLAYING CARD GAMES   *KARTENSPIELE SPIELEN*

Shuffling	Mischen
Shuffle the cards.	*Mische die Karten.*
I'll shuffle / you shuffle.	*Ich mische / Du mischst.*
Give the cards a good shuffle.	*Mische die Karten gut durch.*
The cards aren't shuffled properly.	*Die Karten sind nicht gut gemischt.*

Cutting	Abheben
to cut	*abheben*
You cut to me.	*Du hebst ab.*
I'll cut to you.	*Ich hebe ab.*

CARD GAMES cont.	*KARTENSPIELE Forts.*

Dealing	*Geben*
It's your deal.	*Du bist dran mit Geben.*
You deal the cards face up / face down.	*Du gibst die Karten offen / verdeckt aus.*
You dealt two cards then.	*Du hast eben zwei Karten ausgegeben.*
You missed one out.	*Du hast eine ausgelassen.*
I'm the dealer this time.	*Ich gebe jetzt.*
I've forgotten where I'm up to.	*Ich habe vergessen, bei wem ich bin.*
Count your cards.	*Zähle Deine Karten.*
I am one short.	*Mir fehlt eine.*
I have one extra.	*Ich habe eine zuviel.*
We'd better re-deal.	*Wir sollten lieber nochmal geben.*

Assessing your hand	*Sein Blatt einschätzen*
I haven't sorted my hand yet.	*Ich habe meine Karten noch nicht sortiert.*
Let me just arrange my cards.	*Laß mich meine Karten noch sortieren*
I've got a good hand this time.	*Dieses Mal habe ich ein gutes Blatt.*
I've got a poor hand again.	*Ich habe schon wieder ein schlechtes Blatt.*

Leading	*Die zuerst ausgespielte Karte*
You lead.	*Du spielst aus.*
It's my / his / her / our / your / their lead.	*Ich spiele aus / er spielt aus / sie spielt aus / Wir spielen aus / Du spielst aus / sie spielen aus.*
She led the three of diamonds.	*Sie hat die Karo-Drei ausgespielt.*
What did you lead?	*Was hast Du ausgespielt?*

Playing one's hand	*Seine Karten ausspielen*
He played an ace.	*Er hat ein As ausgespielt.*
What did he play?	*Was hat er ausgespielt?*
I don't know what to play.	*Ich weiß nicht was ich ausspielen soll?*

CARD GAMES cont.   *KARTENSPIELE Forts.*

Following suit	***Farbe bekennen***
You must follow suit if you can.	*Wenn Du die Farbe hast, mußt Du sie bekennen.*
I can't follow suit.	*Ich kann die Farbe nicht bekennen.*
a strong suit	*eine hohe*
a weak suit	*niedrige Farbe*

Trumping	***Trumpfen***
What are trumps?	*Was ist Trumpf?*
Spades are trumps.	*Pik ist Trumpf.*
The three of trumps.	*Die Drei-Trumpf*
I haven't got any trumps.	*Ich habe keinen Trumpf.*
He was holding all the trumps.	*Er hatte alle Trümpfe.*

Throwing away cards	***Karten abwerfen***
to discard	*ablegen*
the stock pile	*der Abwurfstoß*
I need to throw one away.	*Ich muß eine Karte abwerfen.*
I don't know which to throw away.	*Ich weiß nicht welche Karte ich abwerfen soll?*

Picking up cards	***Karten aufnehmen***
Have you picked up yet?	*Hast Du schon aufgenommen?*
Pick one up off the pile.	*Nimm eine Karte vom Stoß auf.*
What did you pick up?	*Was hast Du aufgenommen?*

Putting cards down	***Karten ablegen***
to put a card face down	*eine Karte verdeckt ablegen*
to put a card face up	*eine Karte offen ablegen*
What did she put down?	*Was hat sie abgelegt?*

CARD GAMES cont. *KARTENSPIELE Forts.*

Missing a turn *Eine Runde verpassen*
I missed my turn. *Ich habe meine Runde verpaßt.*
You missed your turn. *Du hast Deine Runde verpaßt.*
You have to miss a turn. *Du mußt eine Runde aussetzen.*

Passing *Aussetzen*
I can't play anything. *Ich kann nichts ausspielen.*
I shall have to pass. *Ich muß aussetzen.*
I pass. *Ich setze aus.*
She passed. *Sie hat ausgesetzt.*

Winning tricks *Stiche machen*
How many tricks have you won? *Wieviele Stiche hast Du gemacht?*
Well done! *Gut gemacht!*
I just won that trick. *Ich habe nur diesen Stich gemacht.*
I don't think I'm going to win many. *Ich glaube nicht, daß ich viele Stiche machen werde.*
We only need to win another one. *Wir brauchen nur noch einen Stich.*
We need to win seven tricks. *Wir müssen sieben Stiche machen.*

Losing tricks *Stiche abgeben*
How many tricks can we afford to lose? *Wieviele Stiche dürfen wir abgeben?*
How many tricks have we lost? *Wieviele Stiche haben wir abgegeben?*
Sorry! *Tut mir leid!*

CARD GAMES cont.   *KARTENSPIELE Forts.*

Cheating	*Mogeln*
Did you cheat?	*Hast Du gemogelt?*
I never cheat.	*Ich mogel nie.*
You shouldn't cheat.	*Du solltest nicht mogeln.*
Don't look at my cards.	*Schaue mir nicht in die Karten.*
I can see your cards.	*Ich kann Deine Karten sehen.*

Memorising cards	*Sich Karten merken*
to remember	*merken*
to forget	*vergessen*
to count	*zählen*
I can't remember if the Ace has gone.	*Ich habe mir nicht gemerkt, ob das As schon weg ist.*
I have forgotten how many..	*Ich habe vergessen wieviele...*
How many trumps have gone?	*Wieviele Trümpfe sind weg?*
Try to remember the tricks.	*Versuche Dir die Stiche zu merken.*
Count the aces / the trumps.	*Zähl die Asse / die Trümpfe*
Have all the hearts gone?	*Sind alle Herze schon weg?*

WHIST

WHIST

You need:

A fifty two card pack

Four people (two pairs of partners)

Man braucht:

ein Spiel mit zweiundfünfzig Karten

vier Spieler (jeweils zwei in einem Team)

The Object of the Game

To win as many of the thirteen available tricks as possible.

Das Ziel des Spieles

So viele wie möglich von den dreizehn vorhanden Stichen zu gewinnen.

HOW TO PLAY

DER SPIELABLAUF

- The dealer deals out all the cards one by one and face down to each player in turn so that each has thirteen cards.

- He should start by dealing to the person on his left so that the last card is dealt to himself.

- This last card is dealt face up and determines what trumps are.

- The player to the dealer's left starts the play with any card.

- The other players have to follow suit if they can but can trump the trick if they cannot.

- If more than one trump is played, the higher trump wins the trick.

- *Der Geber verteilt verdeckt an jeden Spieler reihum einzeln die Karten, bis jeder dreizehn Karten hat.*

- *Die erste Karte sollte an den Spieler links vom Geber ausgeteilt werden, so daß der Geber die letzte Karte an sich selber austeilt.*

- *Die letzte Karte wird offen aufgelegt und gibt den Trumpf an.*

- *Der Spieler links vom Geber beginnt das Spiel, indem er eine Karte seiner Wahl ausspielt.*

- *Die anderen Spieler müssen die Farbe bekennen; wenn sie die Farbe nicht haben sollten, können sie den Stich abtrumpfen.*

- *Wenn mehrere Trümpfe gespielt werden, gewinnt der höchste Trumpf den Stich.*

HOW TO PLAY WHIST cont.

DER SPIELABLAUF Forts.

- If no trumps are played, the highest card of the suit wins with ace counting high.

- The person who wins the trick leads the first card in the next round.

- *Wenn kein Trumpf gespielt wird, gewinnt die höchste Karte der Farbe, wobei das As am höchsten zählt.*

- *Der Spieler der den Stich gewinnt, spielt die erste Karte in der nächsten Runde aus.*

Scoring

- Each trick over six won by either pair of players counts as one point.

- A game is won when seven points have been won.

Erzielte Punktezahl

- *Jeder Stich, der mehr als sechs ergibt, zählt als ein Punkt für das Team, das den Stich gewonnen hat.*

- *Das Spiel ist beendet, wenn eines der Teams sieben Punkte gewonnen hat.*

RUMMY

ROMMÉ

You need:
A fifty two card pack

Any number of players from two to six.

Man braucht:
ein Spiel mit zweiundfünfzig Karten.

Mindestens drei, höchstens sechs Spieler.

The Object of the Game Rummy
To get rid of all your cards by laying them down on the table in front of you.

Das Ziel des Spieles
Alle Karten loszuwerden, indem man sie vor sich auf den Tisch legt.

RUMMY cont.

ROMMÉ Forts.

Players try to collect and arrange cards in the following ways:	*Spieler versuchen Karten zu sammeln um bestimmte Kombinationen zu bilden. Die Kombinationen können dabei wie folgt aussehen:*
• Three of a kind or four of a kind - e.g. three Aces or four Sixes	• *Drei oder vier gleichwertige Karten-z.B.:drei Asse oder vier Sechser.*
• A sequence of three or more cards of the same suit - e.g. Two, Three, Four, Five of Spades.	• *Eine Sequenz an Karten von gleicher Farbe-z.B. :Zwei, Drei, Vier, Fünf in Pik.*

HOW TO PLAY RUMMY

DER SPIELABLAUF VON ROMMÉ

Cut for dealer who deals to each player:	*Nach dem Mischen wird abgehoben. Dann gibt der Geber die Karten wie folgt aus:*
• ten cards each if there are two players	• *für jeden zehn Karten, wenn zwei Spieler mitspielen.*
• seven cards each if there are three or four players	• *für jeden sieben Karten, wenn drei oder vier mitspielen.*
• six cards each if there are five or six players	• *für jeden sechs Karten, wenn fünf oder sechs mitspielen.*
Place remaining cards face down on the table to form a stock pile.	*Die restlichen Karten werden als Abhebestoß verdeckt auf den Tisch gelegt.*
Turn up the top card of the stock pile and lay it face up beside the stock pile to form a waste pile.	*Die erste Karte vom Abhebestoß wird offen auf den Abwurfstoß daneben gelegt.*
The player on the dealer's left starts the game.	*Der Spieler links vom Geber beginnt das Spiel.*
Players look at their hands for the beginnings of any of the above groups or sequences of cards.	*Die Spieler sehen anhand ihres Blatts, ob sie eine der oben genannten Sätze oder Sequenzen bilden können.*

HOW TO PLAY RUMMY cont.

DER SPIELABLAUF VON ROMMÉ Forts.

If you are lucky enough to have any group or sequence you can lay it on the table in front of you.	*Wenn man das Glück hat, eine der Sätze oder Sequenzen auf der Hand zu haben, kann man sie vor sich auf den Tisch auslegen.*
If not, you can either pick up the turned-up waste card or take one from the stock pile.	*Wenn dies nicht der Fall sein sollte, kann man entweder eine abgeworfene Karte oder die oberste vom Abhebestoß aufnehmen.*
You have to throw one card away - either the one you have just picked up or one from your existing hand.	*Man muß eine Karte abwerfen- entweder eine, die man gerade aufgenommen hat oder eine von Hand.*
Players can also add cards to any other player's cards already laid on the table.	*Die Spieler können auch Karten an Kombinationen anlegen, die bereits auf den Tisch liegen.*
You win when you are the first person to get rid of all your cards.	*Man gewinnt, wenn man als erster Spieler alle Karten losgeworden ist.*

SCORING

ERZIELTE PUNKTEZAHL

When someone has won the game, all other players add up the points they still hold in their hand as follows:- • Aces count low as one. • Number cards count their number value. • Jacks, Queens and Kings count ten each.	*Wenn jemand das Spiel gewonnen hat, zählen alle anderen Spieler wie folgt ihre Punkte zusammen:* • *Asse zählen als eins* • *Die Zahlen-Karten zählen soviel wie ihr aufgedruckter Punktewert.* • *Bube, Dame, König zählen jeweils zehn.*

RUMMY - SCORING cont.

RUMMY - ERZIELTE PUNKTEZAHL Forts.

The winner is awarded the total number of points held by all other players.

If the winner was able to put all his cards straight down on the table on his first go the he is said to have "gone rummy" and gets awarded double the other players' total points.

The overall winner can be the first one to reach five hundred points or some other pre-determined score.

Dem Gewinner wird die Gesamtpunktzahl von allen anderen Spielern gutgeschrieben.

Ist es dem Sieger gelungen, auf einen Schlag seine sämtlichen Karten als Erstmeldung auf den Tisch zu legen, dann hat er "Rommé" gemacht und wird damit belohnt, daß er doppelt so viele Punkte bekommt wie die Gesamtpunktzahl aller anderen Spieler.

Der Gesamtsieger kann derjenige sein, dem es als erstem gelungen ist, fünfhundert Punkte zu erreichen oder eine andere vorher festgelegte Punktezahl.

PONTOON

SIEBZEHN-UND-VIER

You need:
A fifty two card pack

Dead matchsticks or counters for laying bets.
Someone to be banker / dealer.

Man braucht:
Ein Spiel mit zweiundfünfzig Karten

Gebrauchte Streichhölzer oder Spielchips um Einsätze zu legen.
Jemand der Bankhalter / Geber ist.

Scoring
- Kings, Queens & Jacks count as ten each.
- Aces count 'low' as one or 'high' as eleven - whichever is convenient at the time.
- All the number cards have their ordinary value.

Punktezahl
- *Könige, Damen & Buben zählen zehn Punkte.*
- *Asse zählen als ein oder elf Punkte- wie es gerade am günstigsten ist.*
- *Alle anderen Karten zählen soviel wie ihr aufgedruckter Punktewert.*

PONTOON cont.

SIEBZEHN-UND-VIER Forts.

How to Play

- Choose someone to be dealer who in the game of Pontoon is called the banker.
- Players can take turns to be banker.
- The banker plays against the other players.
- Any reasonable number of people can play.
- All suits are ignored.
- The banker shuffles the cards (which are not shuffled again until a new banker takes over).

Spielablauf

- *Wähle einen Geber aus, den man bei Siebzehn-Und-Vier Bankhalter nennt.*
- *Die Spieler können sich als Bankhalter abwechseln.*
- *Der Bankhalter spielt gegen die anderen Spieler.*
- *Jede angemessene Zahl an Spielern kann mitspielen.*
- *Farben spielen keine Rolle.*
- *Der Bankhalter mischt die Karten (diese werden nicht mehr gemischt, bis ein neuer Bankhalter übernimmt.*

THE RULES OF PONTOON

DIE SPIELREGELN VON SIEBZEHN-UND-VIER

- The banker deals one card face down to each player, including himself.

- The other players look at their own card, keeping it secret, but the banker cannot look at his own card yet.

- Each player then makes a bet with counters or matchsticks, putting a lot on if they think their card is good and only one counter if not. Each has to bet something.

- *Der Bankhalter teilt eine Karte verdeckt an jeden Spieler aus, er selber eingeschlossen.*

- *Ohne sie zu zeigen, schauen sich die anderen Spieler ihre Karten an. Der Bankhalter kann sich seine Karte noch nicht anschauen.*

- *Einen hohen, wenn er glaubt eine gute Karte zu haben und einen niedrigen, wenn er glaubt eine schlechte Karte zu haben. Jeder muß einen Einsatz legen.*

THE RULES OF PONTOON cont.

DIE SPIELREGELN VON SIEBZEHN-UND-VIER Forts.

- The banker then deals a second card to each player.

- The aim of the game is to score twenty one exactly, or as close to twenty one as possible.

- Players add up their score.

- The banker then asks each player in turn if they want to "stick" (i.e. not take any more cards) or if they want to "twist" (i.e. be dealt another card but this time face up).

- Players can twist up to three times (making a maximum total of five cards).

- If the total score in a player's hand exceeds twenty one then that player is "bust" and puts his cards down on the table.

- When all players have decided either to stick or are bust, the banker turns his cards over for everyone to see and proceeds to stick or twist like everyone else.

- *Dann teilt der Bankhalter an jeden Spieler eine zweite Karte aus.*

- *Das Ziel des Spiels ist es entweder genau einundzwanzig Punkte zu erreichen oder so nah wie möglich an einundzwanzig Punkte heranzukommen.*

- *Die Spieler zählen ihre Punkte zusammen.*

- *Danach fragt der Bankhalter die Spieler reihum, ob sie "halten" wollen (d.h. keine Karte mehr wollen) oder ob sie "noch eine Karte" wollen (welche dann aber offen ausgeteilt wird).*

- *Spieler können drei Mal eine neue Karte bekommen (das macht insgesamt maximal fünf Karten).*

- *Wenn ein Spieler mehr als einundzwanzig Punkte hat, ist er "kaputt" und muß seine Karten auf den Tisch legen.*

- *Wenn alle Spieler sich entschlossen haben zu Halten oder "kaputt" sind, dreht der Bankhalter seine Karten für jeden sichtbar um und entscheidet sich nun selber, ob er "halten" oder noch eine Karte nehmen soll.*

THE RULES OF PONTOON cont.

DIE SPIELREGELN VON SIEBZEHN-UND-VIER Forts.

- The banker takes all the counters bet by players who either went bust or scored lower than himself or the same as himself.

- He has to pay players who scored higher than he did himself the same number of counters as they bet.

- If the banker scores twenty one made with an Ace together with any King, Queen or Jack he calls "Pontoon" and receives double stakes from each player, **unless** one of the players has a five card trick (which beats Pontoon) or a "Royal Pontoon" which consists of three sevens and beats everything.

- A player with a Royal Pontoon receives treble stakes. If the banker has a Royal Pontoon it only counts as an ordinary Pontoon.

- *Der Bankhalter bekommt den Einsatz von Spielern die entweder "kaputt" gegangen sind oder die weniger oder die gleiche Punktezahl haben wie er selber.*

- *Der Bankhalter muß an Spieler die eine höhere Punktezahl erreicht haben als er selber, die gleiche Anzahl an Spielchips ausbezahlen, wie die Spieler eingesetzt haben.*

- *Wenn der Bankhalter mit einem As und einem König oder einer Dame oder einem Buben einundzwanzig Punkte erreicht, sagt er einen "Black Jack" an und erhält den doppelten Einsatz von jedem Spieler. Dies ist nicht der Fall, **wenn** ein Spieler "Fünf Karten" (die einen Black Jack überbieten) oder einen "Großen Black Jack" bekommt, der aus drei Siebenern besteht und alles überbietet.*

- *Ein Spieler mit einem Großen Black Jack erhält den dreifachen Einsatz zurück. Wenn der Bankhalter einen Großen Black Jack bekommt, zählt er nur als ein normaler Black Jack.*

BRIDGE

Counting the points in your hand

ALLOW:

- four points for an Ace
- three points for a King
- two points for a Queen
- one point for a Jack

PLUS

Either:

- one point for each trump over four trumps

- one point for each card over three in each side suit

Or:

- one point for each suit with two cards in it
- two points for each singleton

- three points for each void suit

Who is bidding?

Who's turn is it to bid first?

It's my / your / his / her / our / their bid.

Are you ready to bid?

Are you going to bid?

to open the bidding

BRIDGE

Die Punkte in Deiner Hand zählen

ZÄHLE:

- *vier Punkte für ein As.*
- *drei Punkte für einen König*
- *zwei Punkte für eine Dame*
- *einen Punkt für einen Buben*

ZUSÄTZLICH

Entweder:

- *einen Punkt für jeden Trumpfkarte bei mehr als vier Trümpfen.*

- *einen Punkt für jede Karte über Drei in jede nicht Hauptfarbe.*

Oder:

- *einen Punkt für jede Farbe mit mehr als zwei karten*
- *zwei Punkte für jede Farbe mit nur eine Karte*

- *drei Punkte für jede nicht bestehende Farbe*

Wer Sagt zuerst an?

Wer soll zueist ansagen

Ich , Du, Er, Sie, Wir, Sie soll(en) ansagen.

Bist Du zum ansagen bereit?

Wirst Du ansagen?

der Erste der Ansagt.

BRIDGE cont.   *BRIDGE Forts.*

What are you bidding?	*Was sagst du an?*
No bid.	*Keine Ansage*
One club/diamond/heart/spade.	*Ein Kreuz / Karo / Herz / Pik.*
One no-trump.	*Einen nicht-Trumpf.*
Two clubs/diamonds/hearts/spades	*Zwei Kreuz / Karo / Herz / Pik.*
An opening bid of two of a suit.	*Eine Ansage über zwei von einer Farbe.*
He / she did not bid.	*Er / Sie hat nicht angesagt.*
I did not bid.	*Ich habe nicht angesagt.*
My partner did not bid.	*Mein Partner hat nicht angesagt.*

The type of bid	*Verschiedene Ansagen*
a weak bid.	*eine weiche Ansage.*
a strong bid.	*eine starke Ansage.*
a no-trump bid.	*eine nicht-Trumpf Ansage.*
a re-bid.	*nochmals Ansagen.*

The responses	*Antwort*
Pass / No bid.	*Nichts machen.*
to re-bid	*nochmals Ansagen*
..in your partner's suit	*..in der Farbe ihres Partners.*
..in your own suit.	*..in Ihre Farbe.*
to jump	*sehr Stark Ansagen*
to keep on bidding	*weiter Ansagen*
to force to game	*ein Teil das Spiels zu Ende bringen*

BRIDGE cont.

BRIDGE Forts.

Scoring	*Aufzählen*
Who is going to keep the score?	*Wer soll aufzählen?*
I'll score.	*Ich werde aufzählen.*
Will you score?	*Willst du aufzählen?*
What's the score at the moment?	*Wie steht es im Moment?*

Necessary numbers	*Zahlen die man braucht*
ten / twenty / thirty / forty / fifty	*zehn / zwanzig / dreißig / vierzig / fünfzig*
sixty / seventy / eighty / ninety	*sechzig / siebzig / achtzig / neunzig*
one hundred	*einhundert*
one hundred and ten / twenty etc.	*einhundertundzehn / zwanzig usw..*
two hundred / three hundred etc	*zweihundert / dreihundert usw.*
one thousand	*eintausend*
one thousand, five hundred and fifty	*eintausenfünfhundertundfünfzig*

The tricks	*Die Stiche*
to take a trick	*einen Stich machen*
the first trick	*der este Stich*
subsequent tricks	*weitere Stiche*
an undertrick / an overtrick	*einen Unterstich / einen Überstich*

Doubling	*Verdoppeln*
doubled / undoubled	*verdoppelt / un-verdoppelt*
redoubled	*nochmals verdoppelt*

Vulnerable	*Ungeschütztheit*
not vulnerable	*nicht ungeschützt*

Above the line	*Über den Strich*
below the line	*unter den Strich*

BRIDGE cont.	BRIDGE Forts.

Slams	*Schlemm (m)*
a small slam	*Kleinschlemm*
a grand slam	*Großschlemm*

Honours	*Bonus Punkte*
four trump honours	*As, König, Dame, und Bube in Trumpf Farbe*
five trump honours	*As, König, Dame, Bube und Zehn in Trumpf Farbe*
four aces in one hand	*Vier Asse in einer Hand*

Rubbers	*Rubber / Robber (m)*
a two / three game rubber	*eine Zwei / Drei Spiel Robber*
an unfinished rubber	*eine unfertige Robber*

Games	*Spiele*
for one game	*für einen Spiel*

CHESS   *SCHACH*

The Chessboard	*Die Schachbrett*
portable	*tragbar*
electronic	*elektronisch*
a black square	*ein schwarzes Feld*
the white squares	*die weißen Felder*
the right / left corner	*die rechte / linke Ecke*
opposite	*gegenüber*
diagonal	*diagonal*

CHESS cont.

SCHACH Forts.

The pieces	Die Figuren
The King	*Der König*
The Queen	*Die Dame*
The Bishop	*Der Läufer*
The Knight	*Der Springer*
The Rook	*Der Turm*
The Pawns	*Die Bauern*

Common words (abc)	Allgemeine Ausdrücke
back	*zurück*
behind	*hinter*
black	*schwarz*
to capture	*schlagen*
to castle	*eine Rochade ausführen*
"check"	*"Schach"*
to check	*Schach bieten*
checkmate	*schachmatt*
a draw	*remis*
defensive	*defensiv*
forward	*nach vorne*
in front of	*vor*
lined up	*aufgestellt*
mate	*matt, schachmatt*
a move	*ein Zug*
my / your move	*mein / Dein Zug*
to move	*ziehen*
occupied	*besetzt*
opposite	*gegenüber*
powerful	*wirksam*
protected	*gedeckt*
to remove	*wegrücken*
safe	*sicher*

| CHESS cont. | **SCHACH Forts.** |
| COMMON WORDS (ABC) | **ALLGEMEINE AUSDRÜCKE** |

to take	*nehmen*
shielded	*geschützt*
taken	*genommen*
threatened	*bedroht*
unoccupied	*unbesetzt*
unprotected	*ungeschützt*
white	*weiß*

DRAUGHTS   *DAME*

The Pieces	***Die Spielsteine***
black	*schwarz*
white	*weiß*
red	*rot*

Rules for Draughts	***Die Spielregeln für Dame***
• A game for two players	• *Ein Spiel für zwei Spieler.*
• Each player has twelve pieces.	• *Jeder Spieler hat zwölf Steine.*
• One player has all white pieces.	• *Ein Spieler hat alle weißen Steine.*
• The other player has all black pieces.	• *Der andere Spieler hat alle schwarzen Steine.*
• Both players move only on the black squares.	• *Beide Spieler bewegen ihre Steine nur auf den schwarzen Feldern.*
• Black always starts.	• *Schwarz fängt immer an.*

RULES FOR DRAUGHTS cont.

DIE SPIELREGELN FÜR DAME Forts.

- The pieces move forwards diagonally one square at a time.

- A player can take his opponent's pieces by jumping over them provided there is an empty square to land on.

- A player can capture more than one of his opponent's pieces at once.

- When a piece reaches the opposite side of the board it is made into a king (by placing a second piece on top of the first).

- A king can move backwards as well as forwards one square at a time.

- The winner is the one who takes all his/her opponent's pieces or who immobilizes his/her opponent's pieces.

- *Die Steine werden diagonal um ein Feld vorwärts bewegt.*

- *Ein Spieler kann die Steine des Gegners wegnehmen, indem er über sie springt (voraus gesetzt es ist ein leeres Feld vorhanden, auf dem er landen kann).*

- *Ein Spieler kann seinem Gegner mehrere Steine auf einmal wegnehmen.*

- *Wenn man mit einem Stein die oberste Reihe des gegnerischen Feldes erreicht, so erhält man eine Dame (indem man einen Stein auf diesen Stein setzt).*

- *Eine Dame kann um ein Feld zurück- oder vorrücken.*

- *Ein Spieler der alle Spielsteine seines Gegners genommen hat oder die Steine des Gegners so einschließt, daß der nicht mehr ziehen kann, hat das Spiel gewonnen.*

DOMINOES   *DOMINO*

The Pieces	*Die Spielsteine*
a blank	*ein Nullstein*
a double blank	*ein doppelter Nullstein*
a spot / a pip	*Ein Auge / ein Punkt*
one/two/three spots	*eins / zwei / drei Augen*
four/five/six spots	*vier / fünf / sechs Augen*
a piece with a six and a five	*ein Stein mit einer Sechs und einer Fünf*
a double six	*eine Doppel-Sechs*
face up / face down	*offen / verdeckt*
One end is a..	*In einem Halbfeld ist eine...*
The other end is a..	*Im anderen Halbfeld ist eine...*

Playing dominoes	*Domino spielen*
• Shall we play dominoes?	• *Sollen wir Domino spielen?*
• Have you got a set of dominoes?	• *Hast du ein Dominospiel?*
• Is it a full set of twenty eight?	• *Besteht das Spiel aus achtundzwanzig Steinen?*
• Turn the pieces face downwards.	• *Drehe die Steine verdeckt um.*
• Mix the pieces up.	• *Mische die Steine durcheinander.*
• Any number of people can play.	• *Jede beliebige Zahl an Spielern kann mitspielen.*
• Draw a piece to see who starts.	• *Ziehe einen Stein, um herauszufinden, wer anfängt.*
• The player who draws the highest domino is the first to play.	• *Der Spieler mit dem höchsten Stein beginnt das Spiel.*
• Each player then takes it in turn to select one domino until all the dominoes are used up.	• *Dann nimmt sich jeder Spieler reihum einen Stein, bis keiner mehr übrig ist.*

PLAYING DOMINOES cont. *DOMINO SPIELEN Forts.*

- Each player sets his dominoes on edge so that his opponent cannot see his dominoes.

- The first player places a domino face up on the table.

- The second player then has to add one of his dominoes to form a match - i.e. if the first domino played was one with three spots at one end and four spots at the other, the second player must put down a domino with either three or four spots on one side.

- The dominoes are laid short end to short end unless a double is played. Doubles are placed crosswise at right angles to the line of dominoes.

- If a player has no domino that matches either end of the line he has to miss his go.

- The game ends when one player manages to play all his dominoes.

- *Jeder Spieler stellt seine Steine hochkant, so daß seine Gegenspieler sie nicht sehen können.*

- *Der erste Spieler legt einen Stein offen auf den Tisch.*

- *Dann muß der zweite Spieler einen seiner Steine anlegen, um ein Paar zu bilden - z.B. wenn auf dem Halbfeld des zuerst heraus-gespielten Steins drei Augen sind und auf dem anderen Halbfeld vier Augen, muß der zweite Spieler entweder einen Stein mit drei oder vier Augen an eines der Halbfelder anlegen.*

- *Man legt die Enden der Steine aneinander. Doppelsteine darf man im rechten Winkel an die Domino-Reihe anlegen.*

- *Wenn ein Spieler keinen Stein mehr hat, der an eines der Enden der Domino-Reihe paßt, muß er eine Runde aussetzen.*

- *Wenn ein Spieler es schafft, alle seine Steine anzulegen, ist das Spiel beendet.*

PLAYING DOMINOES cont. *DOMINO SPIELEN Forts.*

- If at any stage no player can play a domino, everyone counts up the number of spots on their remaining dominoes and the winner is the player with the fewest spots.

- If there is a draw between two players with the same number of spots, the winner is the person with the fewest dominoes.

- *Wenn es während des Spiels dazu kommen sollte , daß kein Spieler einen Stein mehr anlegen kann, zählt jeder die Augen auf seinen übriggebliebenen Steinen zusammen. Der mit den wenigsten Augen hat das Spiel gewonnen.*

- *Wenn zwei Spieler die gleiche Anzahl an Augen haben, gewinnt derjenige mit den wenigsten Dominosteinen.*

JIGSAW PUZZLES *EIN PUZZLE*

Types of jigsaws	*Puzzlearten*
a one hundred piece puzzle	*ein Puzzle mit hundert Teilen*
a five hundred piece puzzle	*ein Puzzle mit fünfhundert Teilen*
a one thousand piece puzzle	*ein Puzzle mit eintausend Teilen*
an easy one	*ein leichtes*
a difficult one	*ein schweres*
a pretty one	*ein schönes*

JIGSAW PUZZLES cont.   *EIN PUZZLE Forts.*

Choosing and starting a jigsaw	*Ein Puzzle aussuchen und anfangen*
Would you like to do a jigsaw?	*Möchtest Du ein Puzzle machen?*
Shall we do a jigsaw together?	*Sollen wir ein Puzzle zusammen machen?*
Which one would you like to do?	*Welches möchtest Du gerne machen?*
Where shall we do it?	*Wo sollen wir es machen?*
Have you got a tray to do it on?	*Haben Sie einen Tablett zum draufbauen?*
Can we use this table?	*Können wir diesen Tisch benutzen?*
Turn over all the pieces.	*Drehe alle Teile um.*
face up / face down	*offen / verdeckt*
Shall we sort out all the edge pieces first?	*Sollen wir als erstes alle Eckteile aussortieren?*
Have we got the four corner pieces?	*Haben wir die vier Eckteile gefunden?*
Here is..	*Hier ist...*
..one corner piece	*...ein Eckteil.*
Here is another corner piece.	*Hier ist ein anderes Eckteil.*
Here's the last corner piece.	*Hier ist das letzte Eckteil.*
Shall we sort the pieces out into colour groups?	*Sollen wir die Teile nach Farben sortieren?*
There is one piece missing.	*Ein Teil fehlt.*

Finding particular pieces	*Bestimmte Teile finden*
Have you seen the piece that goes here?	*Weißt Du wo das Teil ist, das hier einpaßt?*
It has two tabs and one indent.	*Es hat zwei Streifen und eine Einkerbung.*
It has one straight edge.	*Es hat einen geraden Rand.*
Have you seen a sky piece?	*Hast Du eins gesehen mit einem Stück Himmel?*
Have you seen a piece with yellow flowers on?	*Hast Du eins gesehen mit gelben Blumen?*

JIGSAW PUZZLES cont.	*EIN PUZZLE Forts.*
FINDING PARTICULAR PIECES cont.	*BESTIMMTE TEILE FINDEN Forts.*

I'm looking for a mainly green piece with a bit of red on it.	*Ich suche ein fast grünes Teil mit etwas Rot.*
Try this one.	*Versuch dieses hier.*
This might fit.	*Das könnte passen.*
It fits.	*Es paßt.*
It doesn't fit.	*Es paßt nicht.*

Useful verbs (abc)	*Nützliche Ausdrücke*
to break it up	*es auseinandernehmen*
to carry on	*weitermachen*
to collect together	*gemeinsam die Teile sammeln*
to find	*finden*
to finish	*beenden*
to get it out	*es rausholen*
to leave it	*es sein lassen*
to look at the picture	*sich das Bild anschauen*
to look for	*schauen nach*
to put it away	*es weglegen*
to put a piece on one side	*ein Teil zur Seite legen.*
to search for	*suchen nach*
to sort	*sortieren*
to start	*anfangen*
to stop	*aufhören*
to try	*versuchen*
to turn over	*umdrehen*

SHORTER GAMES   *TISCHSPIELE*

SNAP   *SCHNIPP-SCHNAPP*

You need:	*Man braucht:*
A pack of fifty two cards for two to five players. Two packs of cards for more than five players.	*Ein Spiel mit zweiundfünfzig Karten für zwei bis fünf Spieler.* *Zwei Kartenspiele für mehr als fünf Spieler.*

The Object of the Game	*Das Ziel des Spiels*
To win all the cards.	*Alle Karten gewinnen.*

How to Play	*Der Spielablauf*
• Deal out all the cards face down equally between all players.	• *Teile alle Karten verdeckt an jeden Spieler gleichmäßig aus.*
• Players must not look at their cards but should keep them in a pile face down in front of them.	• *Die Spieler dürfen sich ihre Karten nicht anschauen und müssen sie verdeckt in einem Haufen vor sich hinlegen.*
• The first player turns over the top card of his pile and places this face up in the middle of the table.	• *Der erste Spieler dreht die oberste Karte seines Haufens um und legt sie offen in die Mitte des Tisches.*
• The next player does the same.	• *Der nächste Spieler macht das Gleiche.*
• If any of the players notice that the second card is of the same rank as the one underneath they can shout "Snap!".	• *Wenn einer der Spieler bemerkt, daß die zweite Karte den gleichen Wert hat wie die untere, kann er "Schnapp!" rufen.*

SNAP - HOW TO PLAY cont.	*SCHNIPP-SCHNAPP - DER SPIELABLAUF Forts.*

- The first person to shout "Snap!" picks up the central pile of cards and adds them, face down, to the bottom of his pile. He then turns over his top card and the game proceeds as before.

- If you lose all your cards you are out of the game.

- *Die erste Person, die "Schnapp" ruft, nimmt den Haufen von der Mitte des Tisches auf und legt ihn verdeckt unter seinen eigenen Haufen. Er dreht dann seine erste Karte um und das Spiel geht weiter wie vorher.*

- *Wer alle seine Karten verliert, ist ausgeschieden.*

BEETLE / *KÄFER*

You need:
Paper and pencils.
A dice and a shaker.
Any number of people can play.

Man braucht:
Papier und Bleistifte.
Ein Würfel und ein Würfelbecher.
Eine beliebige Anzahl von Spielern kann mitspielen.

How to Play / *Die Spielregeln*

- The object of the game is to draw a complete beetle.

- The players take it in turns to throw one dice.

- Each person has to throw a six to start because a six means that you can draw the beetle's body.

- Throwing a five means that you can add a head to the body.

- *Das Ziel des Spiels ist es, einen vollständigen Käfer zu zeichnen.*

- *Die Spieler wechseln sich mit dem Würfeln ab.*

- *Jeder Spieler muß zunächst eine Sechs würfeln. Erst dann darf er damit anfangen, den Körper des Käfers zu zeichnen.*

- *Um den Kopf des Körpers zu zeichnen, muß man eine Fünf würfeln.*

BEETLE cont.　　　　　　*KÄFER Forts.*

HOW TO PLAY cont.　　　*DIE SPIELREGELN Forts.*

- Throwing a four gives your beetle a leg (a complete beetle needs six legs).

- Throwing a three gives your beetle an eye (two eyes needed).

- Throwing a two gives your beetle an antenna (two needed).

- Throwing a one gives your beetle a tail.

- Eyes and antennae cannot be drawn without first getting a five for a head.

- The first person to complete their beetle wins the game.

- *Um die Beine des Käfers zu zeichnen, muß man eine Vier würfeln (ein vollständiger Käfer braucht sechs Beine).*

- *Um das Auge des Käfers zu zeichnen, muß man eine Drei würfeln (man braucht zwei Augen).*

- *Um die Fühler des Käfers zu zeichnen, muß man eine Zwei würfeln (man braucht zwei).*

- *Um den Schwanz des Käfers zu zeichnen, muß man eine Eins würfeln.*

- *Um Augen und Fühler zeichnen zu dürfen. muß man zuerst eine Fünf für den Kopf gewürfelt haben.*

- *Wer als erster seinen Käfer vollständig gezeichnet hat, gewinnt das Spiel.*

I SPY

ICH SEHE WAS, WAS DU NICHT SIEHST

How to Play	*Spielregeln*
• Any number can play.	• *Jede beliebige Anzahl von Spielern kann mitspielen.*
• The first person says:	• *Der erste Spieler sagt:*
"I spy with my little eye something beginning with…."	***"Ich sehe was, was Du nicht siehst, das mit einem…anfängt."***
• He/she then adds the first letter of an object they can see.	• *Er fügt dann den ersten Buchstaben eines Gegenstandes hinzu ,den all sehen können.*
• The other people have to guess what the word is by asking: "Is it a…..?"	• *Die anderen Spieler versuchen dann zu erraten, welches Wort gemeint ist. Sie fragen: "Ist es ein.."*
• and then adding a word beginning with the chosen letter.	• *und fügen dann ein Wort hinzu, das mit dem ausgewählten Buchstaben anfängt.*
• The person who guesses the object correctly takes over and becomes the next person to spy a new object.	• *Die Person, die den Gegenstand richtig errät, darf sich nun einen Gegenstand aussuchen, der zu erraten ist.*

NOUGHTS AND CROSSES

TIC, TAC TOE

You need	*Man braucht*
Paper and two pencils.	*Papier und zwei Bleistifte*
Two people to play.	*Zwei Spieler*

Useful expressions	*Nützliche Ausdrücke*
Draw a noughts and crosses frame.	*Zeichne ein Tic, Tac Toe-Feld*
Are you going to be noughts?	*Willst Du die Nuller sein?*
I'll be noughts.	*Ich bin die Nuller.*
You can be crosses.	*Du bist die Kreuze.*
You start.	*Du fängst an.*
It's my turn to start.	*Jetzt fange ich an.*
You have to get three noughts or three crosses in a row.	*Du mußt drei Nuller oder drei Kreuze in einer Reihe kriegen.*
The rows can be horizontal, vertical or diagonal.	*Die Reihen dürfen waagerecht, senkrecht oder diagonal sein.*
I've won / You've won.	*Ich habe gewonnen / Du hast gewonnen.*
to win	*gewinnen*
to lose	*verlieren*
Shall we play again?	*Sollen wir nochmal spielen?*
Shall we play the best of three?	*Sollen wir spielen: wer die meisten von drei Spielen gewinnt?*

OUTDOOR GAMES

SPIELE IM FREIEN

SKIPPING	***SEILSPRINGEN***
to skip	*springen*
a skipping rope	*ein Springseil*

HOP SCOTCH	***HICKELN***
to hop	*hüpfen*
to turn around	*sich umdrehen*

HIDE AND SEEK	***VERSTECKEN***
Cover your eyes.	*Verdecke Deine Augen.*
Don't peep.	*Nicht gucken*
Count to a hundred.	*Zähle bis hundert.*
Coming ready or not.	*Kommen oder nicht kommen.*
To hide / to look for / to find	*verstecken / suchen / finden*

A TREASURE HUNT	***EINE SCHATZSUCHE***
Divide into teams.	*Teile in Gruppen auf.*
Will you be on my team?	*Willst du in meiner Gruppe sein?*
Do it in pairs.	*Spielt in Paaren.*
Here is a clue.	*Hier ist eine Spur.*
Read the clue.	*Die Spur lesen.*
What does it say?	*Was steht drauf?*
What does that mean, do you think?	*Was meinst Du, was das bedeutet?*
to look for	*danach suchen*
to find	*finden*
to be unable to find	*es nicht finden können*
to win	*gewinnen*
to get the prize	*den Preis bekommen*

OUTDOOR GAMES cont.   *SPIELE IM FREIEN Forts.*

ROLLER SKATING	*ROLLSCHUHLAUFEN*
a pair of roller skates	*ein Paar Roller-Skates*
roller boots	*Rollschuhe*
roller blades	*Roller-Blades*
Have you got any roller skates?	*Hast Du ein paar Roller-Skates?*
May I borrow your roller skates?	*Kann ich mir ein Paar Roller-Skates ausleihen?*
to put on	*anziehen*
to lace up	*Schnürbändel binden*
to adjust	*einstellen*
to balance	*die Balance halten*
to hold on to something	*sich an etwas festhalten*
to fall over	*umfallen*
to take off	*ausziehen*

FLYING A KITE	*DRACHEN STEIGEN*
a kite	*ein Drache*
a string	*eine Schnur*
to hold on to	*festhalten*
to rise up	*aufsteigen*
to fall	*fallen*
to swoop	*herabstürzen*
the wind	*der Wind*
There isn't enough wind.	*Es ist nicht genügend Wind.*
It's too windy.	*Es ist zu windig.*

OTHER ACTIVITES	*ANDERE AKTIVITÄTEN*
to do cartwheels	*Radschlagen*
to do handstands	*Handstand machen*
to climb trees	*auf Bäume klettern*

PUTTING A TENT UP	*EIN ZELT AUFBAUEN*
Have you got a tent?	*Hast du ein Zelt?*
Shall we try to put it up?	*Sollen wir versuchen es aufzubauen?*
Can you remember how to do it?	*Weißt Du noch wie es geht?*
Would your mother / father help?	*Würde Deine Mutter / Dein Vater helfen?*
to put up the tent pole	*die Zeltstange aufstellen*
to put the frame together	*das Gestell zusammenstecken*
to throw over the canvas	*die Zeltplane überwerfen*
to hammer in the pegs	*die Heringe reinhämmern*
to tighten the guy ropes	*die Zeltschnüre spannen*
to put down a ground sheet	*einen Zeltboden auslegen*
to do up the zip	*den Reißverschluß zuziehen*
to unzip the door flap	*die Zelttür aufziehen*
to spend a night in the tent	*eine Nacht im Zelt verbringen*
a torch	*eine Taschenlampe*
to switch on / switch off	*an-/ ausschalten*
to get cold	*kalt werden*
to go inside	*reingehen*

GARDEN PLAY EQUIPMENT

GARTENSPIELE-AUSRÜSTUNG

SWINGING	*SCHAUKELN*
a swing	*eine Schaukel*
to swing	*schaukeln*
to give someone a push	*jemanden anschubsen*
Will you push me, please?	*Kannst Du mich bitte anschubsen?*
Do you want a push?	*Soll ich dich anschubsen?*
to stand up	*sich aufstellen*
to sit down	*sich setzen*
to go very high	*sehr hoch schwingen*
to jump off	*runterspringen*

GARDEN PLAY EQUIPMENT
cont.

GARTENSPIELE-
AUSRÜSTUNG Forts.

A SEE-SAW	*EINE WIPPE*
to see-saw	*wippen*
to go up and down	*auf und ab gehen*
to balance	*Balance halten*
to bump	*anstoßen*

A SLIDE	*EINE RUTSCHE*
to climb the ladder	*die Leiter hochsteigen*
to sit down	*sich setzen*
to slide down	*runterrutschen*
feet first / head first	*zuerst die Füße/ zuerst der Kopf*
to have another go	*es nochmal machen*

A CLIMBING FRAME	*EIN KLETTERGERÜST*
a ladder	*eine Leiter*
to climb	*klettern*
a monkey bar	*eine Affenstange*
to hang from	*dranhängen*
to hang upside down	*mit dem Kopf nach unten hängen*

COMPUTERS
COMPUTER

TYPES OF COMPUTER	*COMPUTERARTEN*
a personal computer	*ein Personal-Computer*
a desktop computer	*ein Desktop-Computer*
a laptop computer	*ein Laptop-Computer*
a network computer	*ein Netzwerk-Computer*

HARDWARE	*DIE HARDWARE*
the monitor	*der Monitor*
the screen	*der Bildschirm*
the keyboard (see 133-136)	*das Keyboard*

THE MOUSE	*DIE MAUS*
to click	*klicken*
to double-click	*doppel-klicken*
to right click / to left click	*rechts klicken / links klicken*
a mouse mat	*ein Maus-Pad*
a joystick	*ein Joystick*

A TOWER	*EIN TOWER*
the CD-ROM drive	*Das CD-ROM-Laufwerk*
the floppy disk drive	*Das Disketten-Laufwerk*
the tape drive	*das Kasetten-Laufwerk*

A MODEM	*EIN MODEM*
a fax	*ein Fax*
e mail	*E-Mail*
an e mail address	*eine E-Mail- Adresse*
to send	*schicken*
to receive	*erhalten*

COMPUTERS cont.   *COMPUTER*

THE SPEAKERS	*DIE LAUTSPRECHER*
multi-media	*Multi-Media*
to turn up / down	*lauter/leiser stellen*

THE PRINTER	*DER DRUCKER*
a colour printer	*ein Farbdrucker*
a black and white printer	*ein Schwarzweißdrucker*
a print preview	*eine Druckvorschau*
to zoom in / out	*vergrößern / verkleinern*
to print out	*ausdrucken*
all pages	*alle Seiten*
odd / even pages	*ungerade / gerade Seiten*
the current page	*die jetzige Seite*
selected pages	*ausgesuchte Seiten*
three copies	*drei Kopien*

THE MEMORY	*DER SPEICHER*
ROM	*ROM*
RAM	*RAM*
How much memory does your computer have?	*Wie groß ist die Speicherkapazität Deines Computers*
My computer doesn't have enough memory.	*Die Speicherkapazität meines Computers ist nicht groß genug.*

THE SOFTWARE	*DIE SOFTWARE*
system software	*Die System Software*
application software	*Anwendungsprogramme*
a floppy disk	*eine Diskette*
a CD-ROM	*eine CD-ROM*
a programme	*ein Programm*

COMPUTERS - THE SOFTWARE cont.	*COMPUTER - DIE SOFTWARE Forts.*
a computer game (See page 139-144)	*ein Computerspiel*
educational software	*Lernprogramme*
word processing software	*Textverarbeitungsprogramme*
database software	*Datenbankprogramme*
desktop publishing software	*Graphik, Layout und Bildverarbeitungsprogramme*
draw / paint software	*Zeichnen / Malprogramme*
a typing course	*ein Tipp-Kurs*
an encyclopaedia	*ein Lexikon*
art gallery software	*eine Software zur Kunstausstellung*

THE KEYBOARD   *DAS KEYBOARD*

TYPING	*EINGEBEN*
to touchtype	*Blindschreiben*
speed	*Schnelligkeit*
to be slow	*langsam sein*
to be quick	*schnell sein*
accuracy	*Genauigkeit (f)*
to make mistakes	*Fehler machen*
to be very accurate	*sehr genau sein*
to type with two fingers	*mit zwei Fingern tippen*

THE KEYS   *DIE TASTATUR*

The Alphabet	*Das Alphabet*
capital letters	*Großbuchstaben*
lower case letters	*Kleinbuchstaben*
caps lock	*eine Feststelltaste*

THE KEYBOARD   *DAS KEYBOARD*

Punctuation	*Zeichensetzung*
a full stop	*ein Punkt*
a comma	*ein Komma*
a semi-colon	*ein Semikolon*
a colon	*ein Doppelpunkt*
an exclamation mark	*ein Ausrufezeichen*
a question mark	*ein Fragezeichen*
inverted commas	*ein Anführungszeichen*
an apostrophe	*ein Apostroph*
brackets	*Klammern*

Numeric keys	*Die Zahlentasten*
addition	*Addition*
subtraction	*Subtraktion*
multiplication	*Multiplikation*
division	*Division*
brackets	*Klammern*
a decimal point	*Komma vor der ersten Dezimalstelle*
the equals sign	*das Gleichheitszeichen*
the ampersand	*das Und-Zeichen*

The function keys	*Die Funktionstasten*
the enter key	*die Eingabetaste*
the return key	*die Return-Taste*
the tab key	*die Tabulaturtaste*
the shift key	*die Umschalttaste*
the caps lock key	*die Feststelltaste*
the number lock key	*die Nummernfeststeltaste*
control	*Kontrolltaste*
alt	*Wahltaste*
escape	*die Escape-Taste*

THE KEYBOARD cont.   *DAS KEYBOARD Forts.*

The edit keys	*Die Edit-Tasten*
scroll up / down	*hoch/runter fahren*
scroll left / right	*links / rechts fahren*
delete	*die Löschtaste*
insert	*eingeben*
home	*Hometaste*
end	*beendigen*
page up / down	*Seite hoch / runter*
print screen	*Bildschirmansicht drucken*

WORD PROCESSING   *TEXTVERARBEITUNG*

Entering text	*Einen Text eingeben*
a cursor	*eine Einfügetaste*
to type	*tippen*
to enter	*eingeben*
to insert	*einfügen*
to overwrite	*überschreiben*

Editing	*Bearbeitung*
to edit	*überarbeiten*
to cut	*schneiden*
to paste	*kleben*
to copy	*kopieren*
to delete	*streichen*
to spell-check	*Die Rechtschreibung überprüfen*
to indent	*einrücken*
word-wrap	*Zeilenumbruch*
to sort text alphabetically	*den Text alphabetisch ordnen*

WORD PROCESSING cont.   *TEXTVERARBEITUNG* Forts.

Formatting	***Formatierung***
to format	*formatieren*
the font	*der Schriftsatz*
font style / font size	*Schriftstil / Schriftgrösse*
colour	*Farbe*
italics	*kursiv*
bold	*deutlich*
underlined	*unterstrichen*
highlighted	*hervorgehoben*

The page set-up	***Das Papierformat***
a page break	*ein Seitenumbruch*
page layout view	*die Seitenansicht*
to set the margins	*die Ränder*
headers and footers	*Überschriften und Fußnoten*

Paragraphs	***Die Absätze***
single / double line spacing	*einfacher / doppelter Abstand*
left / right indents	*links / rechts einrücken*
to align	*ausrichten*
the tabs	*die Tabulatortasten*

Justification	***Ausrichtung***
right / left justification	*rechts / links ausrichten*
to justify both sides	*beide Seiten ausrichten*
justification on / off	*Ausrichtung an / aus*
to centre	*zentrieren*

The tools	***Die Werkzeuge***
a tool bar	*ein Werzeugmenü*
to word count	*eine Seitenangabe*
a dictionary	*ein Wörterbuch*
the spell-checker	*das Rechtsschreibeprogramm*
a thesaurus	*Thesaurus*

WORD PROCESSING cont.

TEXTVERARBEITUNG Forts.

File management	*Datei*
a file	*eine Datei*
to open	*öffnen*
to close	*schließen*
to save	*sichern*
to name	*benennen*
to re-name	*es neu benennen*

THE INTERNET

DAS INTERNET

The Superhighway	*Der Superhighway*
The World Wide Web	*Das World Wide Net*

Getting on to the Internet	*Ins Internet einwählen*
an access provider	*ein Provider*
an online service provider	*eine Online Service Provider*
an e mail address	*eine E-Mail-Adresse*
a joining fee	*eine Abonnementgebühr*
to pay a subscription	*eine Abonnementgebühr zahlen*
a subscriber	*ein Abonnement*
to register	*registrieren*

Browsing	*Stöbern / "Browsing"*
to log in	*einloggen*
to use your password	*ein Paßwort benutzen*
to browse	*stöbern / "browsen"*
a web browser	*ein "Webbrowser"*
to surf	*surfen*
an interest group	*eine Interessensgruppe*
a newsgroup	*eine Newsgroup*
an information source	*eine Informationsquelle*

THE INTERNET

DAS INTERNET

Browsing cont.	***Stöbern / "Browsing" Forts.***
hypertext	*Hypertext*
to click on	*anklicken*
to return to the home page	*zurück zur Homepage*
to download information	*Informationen auf Rechner herunterladen*
to join a mailing list	*eine Newsgroup abonnieren*
to prepare a message	*eine Nachricht vorbereiten*
on-line	*im Netz*
off-line	*nicht im Netz*

Internet jargon	***Internet Jargon***
Gopher	*"Gopher" (ein bestimmtes Übertragungsprotokoll)*
Archie	*"Archie" (ein bestimmter Dienst in der Datei)*
a lurker	*ein "Lurker"*
netiquette	*eine Netiquette*
to flame someone	*jemanden zurechtweisen*
virtual reality	*Virtual Reality*
a Cyber café	*ein Cyber Café*
a Cyber pub	*eine Cyber Kneipe*
Cyberspace	*Cyberspace*
Sig (Signature file)	*Signature File*
Usenet	*"Usenet"*
Winsock	*"Winsock"*

Smileys	***Smileys***
a smiley / an emoticon	*ein Smiley / ein Emoticon*
☺ happy	*glücklich*
;-) winking	*ein Witz gemacht*
:-p tongue in cheek	*ironisch gemeint*

COMPUTER GAMES
COMPUTERSPIELE

GENERAL EXPRESSIONS	*ALLGEMEINE AUSDRUCKSWEISEN*
Would you like to play on the computer?	*Möchtest Du am Computer spielen?*
Do you have any good computer games?	*Hast du gute Computerspiele?*
I have a Game Gear.	*Ich habe ein Game Gear.*
I have a Super Nintendo.	*Ich habe ein Super Nintendo.*
Does it run on batteries or mains?	*Funktioniert es mit Batterien oder mit Netzanschluß?*
Have you a mains adaptor?	*Hast Du ein Adaptor?*
May I have a turn now?	*Darf ich jetzt mal?*
You've had a long go.	*Du spielst schon so lange.*
How many can play at once?	*Wieviele können zur gleichen Zeit spielen?*
This game is for one / two players only.	*Man kann das Spiel nur alleine / zu zweit spielen.*
I'd like to get it - was it expensive?	*Ich möchte es mir gerne holen - war es teuer?*

STARTING A GAME	*EIN SPIEL BEGINNEN*
Where is the on / off button?	*Wo ist die An / Aus Taste?*
How do you load the game?	*Wie lädt man das Spiel auf?*
You type in the word…	*Du tippst das Wort…ein.*
Then you press this..	*Dann drückst Du das..*
What's the password?	*Was ist das Kennwort?*
The password is..	*Das Kennwort ist…*
What's the aim of the game?	*Was ist das Ziel des Spiels?*
Explain to me what happens.	*Erkläre mir was passiert.*
Are there any secret passageways or hidden rooms?	*Gibt es Geheimgänge oder versteckte Räume?*

COMPUTER GAMES cont.   *COMPUTERSPIELE Forts.*

THE CONTROLS	DIE BEDIENUNGSELEMENTE
Do you use a joystick or a mouse or special keys?	*Benutzt Du einen Joystick oder eine Maus oder spezielle Tasten?*
You right click / left click the joystick / the mouse.	*Den Joystick / die Maus rechts klicken / links klicken*
You shoot with the joystick.	*Du schießt mit dem Joystick.*
Which keys do you use?	*Welche Tasten benutzt man?*
What do the different keys do?	*Was kann man mit den verschiedenen Tasten machen?*
These keys make you go up / down.	*Mit diesen Tasten kann man hoch / runter gehen.*
These keys make you go right / left.	*Mit diesen Tasten kann rechts / links gehen.*
What does the space bar do?	*Was kann man mit der Zwichentaste machen?*
The space bar makes you jump.	*Mit der Zwichentaste kann man springen.*
Can you pause this game?	*Kann man das Spiel unterbrechen?*
You pause it like this..	*Man unterbricht es so...*

The Volume	Die Lautstärke
How do you turn the volume up / down?	*Wie stellt man die Lautstärke lauter / leiser?*
You increase / decrease the volume like this.	*Man stellt die Lautstärke so lauter und leiser.*
It's a bit loud.	*Es ist ein wenig zu laut.*
It's disturbing people.	*Es stört die Leute.*
It's too quiet.	*Es ist zu leise.*
I can't hear it properly.	*Ich kann es nicht richtig hören.*

COMPUTER GAMES cont.   *COMPUTERSPIELE Forts.*

SCORING   *TREFFER MACHEN*

Lives and bonus points	*Extra-Leben und Bonuspunkte*
How many lives do you have to start with?	*Mit wie vielen Leben fängt man an?*
I've just lost a life.	*Ich habe eben ein Leben verloren.*
I've got three lives left.	*Ich habe noch drei Leben übrig.*
How do you get bonuses?	*Wie bekommt man die Extra-Leben / Bonuse?*
You have to pick up these things to score extra.	*Man muß diese Dinger aufsammeln, um nochmal zu treffen.*

Time limits	*Zeit-Limit*
Is there a time limit?	*Gibt es ein Zeit-Limit?*
No, there's no need to hurry.	*Nein, Du mußt Dich nicht beeilen.*
Yes, the time limit is five minutes.	*Ja, das Zeit-Limit ist fünf Minuten lang.*

Level of difficulty	*Schwierigkeitslevel*
Have you ever managed to finish this game?	*Hast Du es schon einmal geschafft, bis zum Ende des Spiels zu kommen?*
No, it's very difficult.	*Nein, das ist sehr schwierig.*
Yes, but it takes a lot of practice.	*Ja, aber man muß sehr viel üben.*
What level have you got to?	*Bis zu welchem Level bist Du gekommen?*
I've got to the first / second / third level.	*Ich bin bis zum ersten / zweiten / dritten Level gekommen.*
I've got to the last / next to the last level.	*Ich bin bis zum letzten / vorletzten Level gekommen.*

COMPUTER GAMES cont.	*COMPUTERSPIELE Forts.*

Level of Difficulty cont.	*Schwierigkeitslevel Forts.*
Does it speed up at each level?	*Wird es von Level zu Level schneller?*
It gets much quicker at the next level.	*Es wird viel schneller beim nächsten Level.*
You get a bonus life at each level.	*Bei jedem Level bekommt man ein Extra-Leben.*

What's your score?	*Was ist dein Ergebnis?*
What's your total now?	*Was hast Du jetzt für ein Gesamtergebnis?*
What did you score last time?	*Was für ein Ergebnis hattest Du beim letzten Mal?*
What's the best you've ever scored?	*Was ist das beste Ergebnis das Du jemals hattest?*

USEFUL VERBS (abc)	*NÜTZLICHE WÖRTER*
to accelerate	*beschleunigen*
to attack	*angreifen*
to avoid	*vermeiden*
to chase	*verfolgen*
to click	*klicken*
to climb	*klettern*
to collect	*sammeln*
to concentrate	*sich konzentrieren*
to decrease	*abnehmen*
to defend	*verteidigen*
to die	*sterben*
to duck	*sich ducken*
to enter	*eintreten*
to exit	*herausgehen*
to fly	*fliegen*
to follow	*verfolgen*
to get a bonus	*einen Bonus bekommen*

COMPUTER GAMES cont. *COMPUTERSPIELE Forts.*

USEFUL VERBS (abc) *NÜTZLICHE WÖRTER*

to hide	*sich verstecken*
to increase	*zunehmen*
to insert	*einsetzen*
to jump	*springen*
to kill	*töten*
to leave	*verlassen*
to live	*leben*
to load	*laden*
to lose	*verlieren*
to lose concentration	*die Konzentration verlieren*
to pause	*unterbrechen*
to press	*drücken*
to print	*drucken*
to remember	*sich merken*
to score	*treffen*
to shoot	*schießen*
to slow down	*langsamer werden*
to speed up	*schneller werden*
to surprise	*überraschen*
to switch on / off	*An- / ausschalten*
to take	*nehmen*
to throw	*werfen*
to turn around	*sich umdrehen*
to type	*tippen*
to win	*gewinnen*

DIRECTION WORDS *RICHTUNGSWÖRTER*

in / on	*in / auf*
over / under	*über / unter*
round / through	*herum / durch*
up / down	*hoch / runter*
before / after	*vorher / nachher*
left / right	*links / rechts*
near / far away	*nahe / weit weg*

COMPUTER GAMES cont. *COMPUTERSPIELE Forts.*

DESCRIPTIVE WORDS (abc)	*BESCHREIBENDE WÖRTER*
clumsy	*ungeschickt*
complicated	*kompliziert*
correct	*korrektt*
dangerous	*gefährlich*
difficult	*schwierig*
easy	*leicht*
exposed	*offen*
false	*falsch*
flashing	*blinkend*
hidden	*versteckt*
highest	*am höchsten*
long	*lang*
lowest	*am tiefsten*
quick	*schnell*
round	*rund*
safe	*sicher*
secret	*geheim*
short	*kurz*
skilful	*geschickt*
slow	*langsam*
tense	*gespannt*
vulnerable	*verwundbar*

TELEVISION, VIDEO & RADIO
FERNSEHER, VIDEO & RADIO

BASIC VOCABULARY	*GRUNDVOKABULAR*
a television	*ein Fernseher*
the remote control	*die Fernbedienung*
to point	*richten*
a video player	*ein Videorekorder*
a video cassette	*eine Videokassette*
a video game	*ein Videospiel*
a radio	*ein Radio*

WATCHING TELEVISION	*FERNSEHEN SCHAUEN*
Would you like to watch T.V.?	*Möchtest Du gerne fernsehen?*
What's on the television at the moment?	*Was läuft gerade im Fernseher?*
Is there anything good on the television?	*Gibt es etwas gutes im Fernseher?*
What's on the other channels?	*Was läuft in den anderen Programmen?*
Shall we turn over?	*Sollen wir umschalten?*
We have this programme in my country.	*Diese Sendung gibt es auch in meinem Land*
Do you like..?	*Gefällt Dir...?*
Shall we stop watching television?	*Sollen wir aufhören fernsehen zu schauen?*
My family want to watch something else now.	*Meine Familie möchte jetzt etwas anderes schauen.*
Shall we do something else instead?	*Sollen wir etwas anderes machen?*

TELEVISION cont.   *FERNSEHER Forts.*

THE CONTROLS FOR T.V., VIDEO AND RADIO (abc)	*DIE BEDIENUNGSELEMENTE FÜR FERNSEHER, VIDEO UND RADIO*
the aerial point	*die Antennenbuchse*
a channel	*ein Kanal*
a counter	*ein Zählwerk*
counter reset	*Zurückstellung des Zählwerks*
eject / to eject	*eject / herausholen*
fast forward / to fast forward	*Vorlauftaste / vorspulen*
indicator light / to flash	*Hinweislicht / blinken*
on / off	*an / aus*
pause / to pause	*Pause / unterbrechen*
play / to play	*Wiedergabe / spielen*
to press a button	*einen Knopf drücken*
programme / to programme	*Programm / programmieren*
record / to record	*Aufnahme / aufnehmen*
to repeat	*wiederholen*
to reset	*neu einstellen*
rewind / to rewind	*Rücklauftaste / zurückspulen*
search	*suchen*
slow	*langsam*
speed	*Geschwindigkeit*
a switch / to flick a switch	*ein Schalter / einen Schalter umschalten*
the timer	*Der Timer*
to tune	*einstellen*
to use the remote control	*die Fernbedienung benutzen*
video / to insert	*Video / einschalten*
video in / video out	*Video eingeschaltet / Video ausgeschaltet*

TELEVISION etc. cont.	*FERNSEHER usw. Forts.*
USEFUL EXPRESSIONS	*NÜTZLICHE AUSDRÜCKE*

Turning it on and off	*An- ausschalten*
How do you turn it on / off?	*Wie schaltest Du ihn an / aus?*
You turn it on / off here.	*Man schaltet ihn hier an / aus.*

Volume control	*Lautstärke Kontrolle*
It's a bit too loud.	*Es ist etwas zu laut.*
How do you turn it up / down?	*Wie stellt man ihn lauter / leiser?*
I can't hear it properly.	*Ich kann nicht richtig hören.*

Playing a video	*Einen Video abspielen*
How do you insert the video?	*Wie tut man den Video rein?*
The video needs rewinding.	*Man muß den Video erst zurückspulen.*
How do you rewind it ?	*Wie spult man zurück?*
How do you fast forward it?	*Wie spult man vor?*
Can you pause it for a moment, please?	*Kannst Du bitte kurz mal unterbrechen?*
How do you pause / eject it?	*Wo unterbricht man? / Wie holt man sie heraus?*

Recording	*Aufnehmen*
How do you record something?	*Wie nimmt man etwas auf?*
Is it recording properly?	*Nimmt es richtig auf?*
Are you sure you are recording the right programme?	*Bist Du sicher, daß Du die richtige Sendung aufnimmst?*
Can you programme the video to record while we are out?	*Kannst Du den Videorekorder zum Aufnehmen programmieren, während wir weg sind?*
Shall we record it and watch it some other tine?	*Sollen wir es aufnehmen und ein anderes Mal anschauen?*
Would you like to watch that programme we recorded?	*Möchtest Du Dir die Sendung die wir aufgenommen haben, anschauen?*

RECORDING ON VIDEOS cont.

PROGRAMME AUFNEHMEN

How does the remote control work?	*Wie funktioniert die Fernbedienung?*
Do you have Video Plus programming?	*Hast du eine Video-Plus Programmierung?*
The tape has come to an end.	*Die Kassette ist zu Ende.*
Have you got another tape?	*Hast du noch eine Kassette?*

TUNING THE RADIO

DAS RADIO EINSTELLEN

How do you tune the radio?	*Wie stellt man das Radio ein?*
Can you find me the local radio station?	*Kannst du mir die lokale Radiostation suchen?*
Which is the best pop music programme?	*Welcher Sender ist am besten für Pop-Musik?*
What wavelength do you tune it to?	*Auf welcher Frequenz empfängt man ihn?*

DIFFERENT TYPES OF T.V. PROGRAMMES

VERSCHIEDENE ARTEN VON FERNSEHSENDUNGEN

an advertisement	*eine Werbung*
a cartoon	*ein Zeichentrickfilm*
a chat show	*eine Talk-Show*
a discussion programme	*eine Diskussion*
a documentary	*ein Dokumentarfilm*
an education programme	*eine Lehrsendung*
a film	*ein Film*
a party political broadcast	*eine parteipolitische Sendung*
a quiz	*eine Quiz-Sendung*
a report	*eine Reportage*
a situation comedy	*eine Komödie*
a sports programme	*eine Sport-Sendung*
a thriller	*einen Thriller*

DIFFERENT TYPES OF T.V. PROGRAMMES
VERSCHIEDENE ARTEN VON FERNSEHSENDUNGEN

Soap operas	***Fernsehspiele / Soap Operas***
Which soaps do you have in your country?	*Welche Fernsehserien gibt es in Eurem Land?*
We watch this at home.	*Zuhause schauen wir uns das an.*
We are further behind / ahead of you.	*Wir sind hinter / vor euch.*

The news	***Die Nachrichten***
the news headlines	*Die Schlagzeilen*
I'd like to watch the headlines, please.	*Ich möchte bitte die Schlagzeilen sehen.*
Did you see the news?	*Hast du die Nachrichten gesehen?*
What was on the news?	*Was war in den Nachrichten?*
Was there any news about..?	*Gab es Nachrichten über...?*
I didn't hear the news today.	*Ich habe heute noch keine Nachrichten gehört.*
The news was boring / depressing / appalling.	*Die Nachrichten waren langweilig / deprimierend / schrecklich.*
What has happened?	*Was ist passiert?*
Was there anything interesting on the news?	*Gab es etwas Interessantes in den Nachrichten?*

DIFFERENT TYPES OF T.V. PROGRAMMES

VERSCHIEDENE ARTEN VON FERNSEHSENDUNGEN

The weather forecast	***Die Wettervorhersage***
Did you hear the weather forecast?	*Hast du die Wettervorhersage gehört?*
It's going to be....(abc)	*Es wird...*

breezy	*frisch*	rainy	*regnerisch*
cloudy	*bewölkt*	showery	*schauerartig*
cold	*kalt*	snowy	*schneien*
freezing	*gefrieren*	sunny	*sonnig*
hot	*heiß*	thundery	*gewitterig*
icy	*eisig*	windy	*windig*
minus five	*minus fünf Grad*		

When?	***Wann?***		
later	*später*	overnight	*übernacht*
this morning	*heute morgen*	tomorrow	*morgen*
this afternoon	*heute nachmittag*	the day after	*übermorgen*
this evening	*heute abend*	next week	*nächste Woche*
tonight	*heute nacht*	soon	*bald*

THE VIDEO HIRE SHOP
DER VIDEO-LADEN

USEFUL EXPRESSIONS	*NÜTZLICHE AUSDRÜCKE*
Shall we go and get a video out?	*Sollen wir uns einen Video ausleihen?*
Have you got your ticket?	*Hast Du Deine Ausweiskarte?*
You have to show your ticket.	*Du mußt Deinen Ausweis zeigen.*
Can you get any film out on your ticket?	*Kannst Du Dir jeden Film mit Deinem Ausweis ausleihen?*
Are there some films you can't get out on your ticket?	*Gibt es Filme, die Du Dir mit Deinem Ausweis nicht ausleihen kannst?*
How much does it cost to hire this video?	*Wieviel kostet es, sich diesen Video auszuleihen?*
When does it have to be back by?	*Wann muß man ihn zurückbringen?*
How many videos can we get out?	*Wieviele Videos dürfen wir uns ausleihen?*
What do you want to watch?	*Was möchtest Du Dir gerne anschauen?*
I'd like to see this one.	*Ich möchte gerne diesen sehen.*
Is this one good?	*Ist der gut?*
Is it very frightening?	*Ist er sehr schrecklich?*
Where is the comedy / thriller / cartoon / horror section?	*Wo ist die Comedy- / Thriller- / Zeichentrick- / Horror-Abteilung?*
Where are the new releases?	*Wo sind die Neuerscheinungen?*
Is it out on video yet?	*Ist est schon auf Video erhältlich?*
When is it going to be out on video?	*Wann gibt es ihn auf Video?*
I've got that one on video at home.	*Den habe ich zuhause auf Video.*

MUSIC
MUSIK

LISTENING TO MUSIC *MUSIK HÖREN*

HI FI STEREO SYSTEM *HI FI STEREO ANLAGE*

A Compact Disc (C.D.) player	*Ein Compact Disc (C.D.) Spieler*
to play	*spielen*

A tape deck	*Ein Tape Deck*
a cassette tape	*eine Kassette*
to record on	*aufnehmen*
to record over	*überspielen*
to erase	*löschen*
to rewind	*zurückspulen*
to fast forward	*vorspulen*
to pause	*unterbrechen*

A record turntable	*Ein Plattenspieler*
a record	*eine Platte*
a short playing record	*eine Kurzspielplatte*
a single	*eine Single*
a long playing record (an L.P.)	*eine Langspielplatte (eine L.P.)*
a track	*eine Spur*
a stylus	*eine Plattennadel*
a scratch	*ein Kratzer*
an old seventy eight	*eine alte achundsiebziger*

LISTENING TO MUSIC CONT. *MUSIK HÖREN Forts.*

SOUND REPRODUCTION	*TONWIEDERGABE*
the amplifier	*der Verstärker*
the speakers	*die Lautsprecher*
the headphones	*die Kopfhörer*
the sound quality	*die Tonqualität*
to adjust	*einstellen*
the volume	*die Lautstärke*
the bass / the treble	*der Baß / die Höhen*
the balance	*die Balance*
poor	*schlecht*
good	*gut*
excellent	*ausgezeichnet*
true	*wahrheitsgetreu*
stereophonic	*stereophonisch*
quadrophonic	*quadrophonisch*

AM / FM RADIO	*MW / UKW RADIO*
the tuner	*Der Empfänger*
to tune in	*einstellen*
to be out of tune	*nicht richtig eingestellt sein*
to retune	*neu einstellen*
to crackle	*knacken*
the band	*Der Empfangsbereich*
the wavelength	*Wellenlänge*

LISTENING TO MUSIC CONT. *MUSIK HÖREN Forts.*

USEFUL VERBS AND COMMANDS (abc)	*NÜTZLICHE WÖRTER UND BEDIENUNGSBEFEHLE*
to adjust the controls	*die Bedienungselemente einstellen*
to decrease	*abnehmen*
to erase	*löschen*
to fast forward	*vorspulen*
to increase	*zunehmen*
to listen	*hören*
to pause	*unterbrechen*
to play	*spielen*
to programme	*programmieren*
to record	*aufnehmen*
to record on	*aufnehmen auf*
to record over	*überspielen*
to repeat	*wiederholen*
to replay	*wieder spielen*
to retune	*neu einstellen*
to rewind	*zurückspulen*
to skip a track	*ein Stück auslassen*
to switch off	*ausschalten*
to tune in	*einstellen*
to turn down	*runter drehen*
to turn on	*anstellen*
to turn up	*hoch drehen*

LISTENING TO MUSIC	*MUSIK HÖREN*
Would you like to listen to some music?	*Möchtest du gerne etwas Musik hören?*
Shall we go and listen in my room?	*Sollen wir in mein Zimmer gehen und Musik hören?*
What sort of music do you like?	*Was für Musik magst Du?*

LISTENING TO MUSIC cont. *MUSIK HÖREN Forts.*

What would you like to listen to?	*Was möchtest Du gerne hören?*
What's your favourite group?	*Wer ist Deine Lieblingsband?*
Who's your favourite singer?	*Wer ist Dein Lieblingssänger / Deine Lieblingssängerin?*
What's number one in your country at the moment?	*Was ist in Eurem Land momentan Nummer eins?*
Did this stereo system cost a lot?	*Hat die Stereo-Anlage viel gekostet?*
It's very good reproduction.	*Sie hat eine sehr gute Wiedergabe.*
The quality of this recording isn't all that good.	*Die Qualität dieser Aufnahme ist nicht sehr gut.*
It was recorded live.	*Es war eine Live-Aufnahme.*
Is this group popular in your country?	*Ist diese Gruppe sehr beliebt in deinem Land?*
I've never heard of them before.	*Ich kenne sie nicht.*
I play in a group.	*Ich spiele in einer Band*
I'm the lead singer / guitarist / drummer.	*Ich bin der Sänger / die Sängerin / der Gittarist / die Gittaristin / der Schlagzeuger / die Schlagzeugerin.*
We formed a group a year ago.	*Wir haben vor einem Jahr eine Gruppe gegründet.*

I LIKE..		ICH MAG...	
classical	*Klassik*	pop	*Pop*
folk	*Folk*	rap	*Rap*
inde	*Inde*	reggae	*Reggae*
jazz	*Jazz*	soul	*Soul*
New Age	*New Age*		

MUSIC LESSONS AND PRACTICE
MUSIKUNTERRICHT UND ÜBEN

MUSIC LESSONS	*MUSIKUNTERRICHT*
a music teacher	*ein Musiklehrer*
a piano lesson	*eine Klavierstunde*
How long have you had piano lessons?	*Seit wann nimmst Du Klavierunterricht?*
I am only a beginner.	*Ich bin nur ein Anfänger.*
I've been learning for three years.	*Ich nehme seit drei Jahren Unterricht.*

THE PIANO	*DAS KLAVIER*
an upright piano	*Ein Klavier*
a grand piano	*ein Flügel*
Would it be O.K. if I played your piano?	*Ist es O.K., wenn ich auf Deinem Klavier spiele?*
Am I disturbing anyone?	*Störe ich jemanden?*
to put on the practice pedal	*die Übungspedale anbringen*
the loud pedal	*das laute Pedal*
the soft pedal	*das sanfte Pedal*
the piano stool	*der Klavierhocker*
Is the stool the right height?	*Hat der Hocker die richtige Höhe?*
How do you make it a little higher / lower?	*Wie macht man ihn ein wenig höher / tiefer?*
to raise	*höherdrehen*
to lower	*tieferdrehen*
to adjust	*einstellen*
a metronome	*ein Taktmesser / ein Metronom*

MUSIC LESSONS AND PRACTICE cont.	*MUSIKUNTERRICHT UND ÜBEN Forts.*

THE VIOLIN	*EINE GEIGE*
a violin case	*ein Geigenkasten*
a bow	*ein Bogen*
a string	*eine Saite*
to tune the violin	*die Geige stimmen*
It sounds a bit out of tune.	*Sie hört sich etwas verstimmt an.*
Can you help me to tune it properly?	*Kannst Du mir helfen, sie richtig zu stimmen?*
to break a string	*eine Saite reißen*
a music stand	*ein Notenständer*
a music case	*ein Musikkasten*

MUSIC PRACTICE	*MUSIK ÜBEN*
to practise	*üben*
to practise the piano	*Klavierspielen üben*
to practise one's pieces	*Stücke üben*
to practise one's scales	*Tonleitern üben*
Do you mind if I do my piano practice now?	*Macht es Dir etwas aus, wenn ich jetzt Klavierspielen übe?*
I haven't done enough practice.	*Ich habe nicht genügend geübt.*
I am supposed to do half an hour a day.	*Eigentlich sollte ich jeden Tag eine halbe Stunde üben.*

EXAMINATIONS	*PRÜFUNGEN*
Do you take music exams?	*Machst Du Musikprüfungen?*
What grade are you up to now?	*Welche Stufe hast Du bisher erreicht?*
Which grade are you taking next?	*In welcher Stufe läßt Du Dich beim nächsten Mal prüfen?*
I failed my last exam.	*Ich bin durch meine letzte Prüfung gefallen.*
I got a pass / merit / distinction.	*Ich bin durchgekommen / Ich habe gute Noten / Ich bin aufgestiegen*

READING
LESEN

BOOKS   ***BÜCHER***

TYPES OF BOOKS	***BÜCHERARTEN***
a hardback	*ein gebundenes Buch*
a paperback	*ein Taschenbuch*
a best seller	*ein Bestseller*
a prize winner	*ein preisgekröntes*
a novel	*ein Roman*
a book of poetry	*ein Gedichtband*
a play	*ein Stück*

FICTION	***ROMANE***
a thriller	*ein Thriller*
a romance	*ein Liebesgeschichte*
a mystery	*ein Krimi*
science fiction	*Science fiction*
a horror story	*Horrorgeschichten*
a series	*eine Serie*
a sequel	*ein Fortsetzungsroman*

NON-FICTION	***SACHBÜCHER***
biography	*eine Biographie*
autobiography	*eine Autobiographie*
historical	*ein Geschichtsbuch*
faction (mixture of fact and fiction)	*Faktion (eine Mischung aus Fakten und Fiktion)*

READING cont.   *LESEN Forts.*

REFERENCE BOOKS	*NACHSCHLAGEWERKE*
a dictionary	*ein Wörterbuch*
to look a word up	*nach einem Wort suchen*
alphabetical order	*alphabetische Reihenfolge*
an atlas	*ein Atlas*
an encyclopaedia	*ein Lexikon*

CHILDREN'S BOOKS	*KINDERBÜCHER*
a fairy tale	*ein Märchen*
a picture book	*ein Bilderbuch*
a cartoon	*ein Comic*

THE WRITERS OF BOOKS	*DIE SCHRIFTSTELLER*
an author	*ein Autor*
a biographer	*ein Biograph*
a poet	*ein Poet*
a playwright	*ein Stückeschreiber*

READING	*LESEN*
to read	*lesen*
Do you mind if I read for a while?	*Macht es Dir etwas aus, wenn ich für eine Weile lese?*
I am in the middle of a really good book at the moment.	*Ich lese momentan ein sehr gutes Buch.*
Do you feel like reading for a bit?	*Möchtest du gerne ein wenig lesen?*
Would you like to see what books I have?	*Möchtest Du gerne meine Bücher sehen?*
What is this book like?	*Wie ist dieses Buch?*
This book is excellent.	*Dieses Buch ist ausgezeichnet.*
Where are you up to?	*Wo bist Du gerade?*
What has just happened?	*Was ist gerade passiert?*

READING cont.	*LESEN Forts.*

My sister / brother has some books you might like to read.	*Meine Schwester / mein Bruder hat ein paar Bücher, die Du vielleicht lesen möchtest.*
I love reading.	*Ich mag Lesen.*
I like to read in bed before I go to sleep.	*Ich lese gerne noch etwas im Bett, bevor ich einschlafe.*
I don't read much.	*Ich lese nicht viel.*
She is a real bookworm.	*Sie ist ein echter Bücherwurm.*
to use a bookmark	*ein Lesezeichen benutzen*

NEWSPAPERS — *ZEITUNGEN*

TYPES OF NEWSPAPERS	*ZEITUNGSARTEN*
a daily newspaper	*eine Tageszeitung*
a weekly newspaper	*eine Wochenzeitung*
a national newspaper	*eine Nationalzeitung*
a local newspaper	*eine lokale Zeitung*
the gossip columns	*die Klatschspalte*
the gutter press	*die Regenbogenpresse*

SECTIONS OF A NEWSPAPER	*DIE ABSCHNITTE EINER ZEITUNG*
the headlines	*die Schlagzeilen*
a leading article	*der Leitartikel*
a report	*ein Bericht*
a letter	*ein Kommentar*
the sports pages	*die Sportseiten*
the fashion pages	*die Modeseiten*
the weather forecast	*die Wettervorhersage*
Births, Marriages and Deaths	*Geburten, Hochzeiten und Todesfälle*
a crossword	*ein Kreuzworträtsel*
the horoscope (See 165-166)	*ein Horoskop*

NEWSPAPERS cont.   *ZEITUNGEN Forts.*

PRODUCERS OF NEWSPAPERS	*DIE HERSTELLER EINER ZEITUNG*
the editor	*der Chefredakteur*
the sub-editor	*der Redakteur*
the journalists	*die Journalisten*
the foreign correspondent	*der Auslandskorresondent*
a freelance journalist	*ein freischaffender Journalist*
the photographer	*der Fotograf*
the press	*die Druckerei*
the paparazzi	*der Skandalreporter*

MAGAZINES   *ZEITSCHRIFTEN*

TYPES OF MAGAZINES	*ZEITSCHRIFTENARTEN*
a glossy magazine	*eine Hochglanz-Zeitschrift*
a monthly	*ein Monatlichesheft*
a weekly	*eine Wochenzeitschrift*
an expensive magazine	*eine teure Zeitschrift*
a fashion magazine	*eine Modezeitschrift*
a music magazine	*eine Musikzeitschrift*
a specialist magazine	*eine Fachzeitschrift*
children's magazines	*eine Kinderzeitschrift*
comics	*Comics*

LENDING AND BORROWING BOOKS   *BÜCHER AUSLEIHEN UND BORGEN*

to lend	*ausleihen*
to borrow	*ausborgen*
This book is a good one.	*Dies ist ein gutes Buch*
I can lend it to you if you like.	*Wenn Du möchtest, kann ich es Dir ausleihen.*
Would you like to borrow a book?	*Möchtest Du Dir gerne ein Buch ausborgen?*

LENDING AND BORROWING BOOKS cont.

BÜCHER AUSLEIHEN UND BORGEN Forts.

Don't forget to return it, will you?	*Vergiß bitte nicht, es zurückzubringen.*
I'll write my name in it.	*Ich schreibe meinen Namen rein.*
You can take it back home with you if you want and post it back to me.	*Wenn Du möchtest, kannst Du es mit nach Hause nehmen und mir zurückschicken.*

THE LIBRARY	*DIE BÜCHEREI*
a public library	*eine Stadtbücherei*
the librarian	*der Bibliothekar/ die Bibliothekarin*
a library ticket	*ein Büchereiausweis*
to take out a book	*sich ein Buch ausleihen*
Would you like to take out a book on my ticket?	*Möchtest Du Dir ein Buch mit meinem Ausweis ausleihen?*
How many books may I borrow at once?	*Wieviele Bücher kann ich insgesamt ausleihen?*
It has to be back by 3rd November.	*Bis zum dritten November muß es zurück sein.*
My library books are due back today.	*Meine Bücher aus der Bücherei müssen heute zurückgebracht werden.*
My books are overdue.	*Meine Bücher sind überfällig.*
How much is the fine?	*Wie hoch ist die Strafe?*
Can you also borrow films / cassettes?	*Kann man sich auch Filme / Kassetten ausleihen?*

READING cont.   *LESEN Forts.*

BUYING BOOKS AND MAGAZINES	*BÜCHER UND ZEITSCHRIFTEN KAUFEN*
a book shop	*eine Buchhandlung*
a second-hand book shop	*ein Second-Hand Buchhandel*
a bookstall	*ein Bücherstand*
a news stand	*ein Zeitungsstand*
Where can I buy English books and newspapers?	*Wo kann ich englische Bücher und Zeitungen kaufen?*
I have got a book token.	*Ich habe einen Büchergutschein.*
Can I use this token here?	*Kann ich den Gutschein hier benutzen?*
May I pay (partly) with this book token, please?	*Kann ich bitte dieses Buch mit dem Gutschein anzahlen?*
How much extra do I owe?	*Wieviel muß ich drauf bezahlen?*

DESCRIBING BOOKS	*DIE BÜCHER BESCHREIBEN*
The plot is…	*Die Handlung ist...*
This book is about…	*Dieses Buch handelt von...*
The characterisation is..	*Das Besondere daran ist....*
The language / setting is...	*Die Sprache / der Schauplatz ist...*

boring	*langweilig*	poetic	*poetisch*
clever	*geistreich*	predictable	*voraussehbar*
concise	*präzise*	pretentious	*anspruchsvoll*
contrived	*erfunden*	romantic	*romantisch*
different	*anders*	sad	*traurig*
difficult	*schwierig*	sarcastic	*sarkastisch*
easy to read	*leicht zu lesen*	slow	*langsam*
exciting	*spannend*	surprising	*überraschend*
fast	*temporeich*	tense	*festgefahren*
funny	*witzig*	typical	*typisch*
gripping	*fesselnd*	unexpected	*unerwartet*
hysterical	*hysterisch*	untypical	*untypisch*
long-winded	*weitausholend*	unusual	*ungewöhnlich*

HOROSCOPES
HOROSKOPE

THE SIGNS OF THE ZODIAC	***DIE TIERKREISZEICHEN***
• Aries (The Ram)	• *Widder*
• Taurus (The Bull)	• *Stier*
• Gemini (The Twins)	• *Zwillinge*
• Cancer (The Crab)	• *Krebs*
• Leo (The Lion)	• *Löwe*
• Virgo (The Virgin)	• *Jungfrau*
• Libra (The Balance)	• *Waage*
• Scorpio (The Scorpion)	• *Skorpion*
• Sagittarius (The Archer)	• *Schütze*
• Capricorn (The Goat)	• *Steinbock*
• Aquarius (The Water Bearer)	• *Wasserman*
• Pisces (The Fishes)	• *Fisch*

THE HEAVENLY BODIES	***DIE HIMMELSKÖRPER***
the Sun	*die Sonne*
the Moon	*der Mond*
the Planets	*die Planeten*
• Mercury	• *Merkur*
• Venus	• *Venus*
• Mars	• *Mars*
• Jupiter	• *Jupiter*
• Saturn	• *Saturn*

HOROSCOPES cont.   *HOROSKOPE Forts.*

USEFUL EXPRESSIONS	*NÜTZLICHE AUSDRÜCKE*
What does your horoscope say?	*Was steht in Deinem Horoskop?*
My horoscope sounds interesting.	*Mein Horoskop hört sich interessant an.*
My horoscope sounds terrible.	*Mein Horoskop klingt schrecklich.*
Listen to what my horoscope says.	*Hör´ zu, was in meinem Horoskop steht.*
Read me my horoscope.	*Lies mir mein Horoskop vor.*
What sign are you?	*Was für ein Sternzeichen bist Du?*
I am a Gemini.	*Ich bin Zwilling.*
I was born under the star sign of Aries.	*Ich wurde geboren im Sternzeichen des Widders.*
What time of day were you born?	*Um wieviel Uhr wurdest du geboren?*
Where were you born?	*Wo wurdest Du geboren?*
in conjunction with....	*In Verbindung mit...*
under the influence of…	*unter dem Einfluß von...*
on the cusp	*auf dem Halbmond*
position	*Position*
house	*Haus*
Do you believe in horoscopes?	*Glaubst Du an Horoskope?*
I think they're rubbish.	*Ich glaube, das ist Quatsch.*
I think they are very accurate.	*Ich glaube, sie treffen sehr genau zu.*
Let me guess what star sign you are.	*Laß mich raten, was für ein Sternzeichen Du bist.*
Are you a Capricorn?	*Bist Du ein Steinbock?*

FOOD
ESSEN

MEALS , COURSES & SNACKS	*MAHLZEITEN, GERICHTE & IMBIß´*
early morning tea	*Morgentee*
breakfast	*Frühstück*
elevenses	*Elf Uhr Morgen- Imbiß*
lunch	*Mittagessen*
afternoon tea	*Nachmittagstee*
dinner	*Hauptmahlzeit*
supper	*Abendessen*
a snack	*ein Snack*
the first course / a starter	*erster Gang / Vorspeise*
the fish course	*das Fischgericht*
the main course	*das Hauptgericht*
the dessert	*der Nachtisch*
cheese and biscuits	*Käse und Gebäck*
coffee and mints	*Kaffee und Süßigkeiten*

SEATING ARRANGEMENTS	*SITZORDUNG*
Would you like to sit here?	*Möchtest Du gerne hier sitzen?*
Sit next to me.	*Setz´ Dich neben mich.*
Sit opposite me.	*Setz´ Dich mir gegenüber.*
Sit anywhere.	*Setz´ wo Du willst.*

FOOD PREFERENCES   *VORZÜGE BEIM ESSEN*

LIKES	*VORLIEBEN*
I thought that was..	*Das war...*
gorgeous / delicious / really good	*großartig / köstlich / sehr gut.*
How did you make it?	*Wie hast Du das gemacht?*
Would you give me the recipe?	*Kannst Du mir das Rezept geben?*
Is it difficult to cook?	*Ist es schwierig zu kochen?*

FOOD PREFERENCES cont.   *VORZÜGE BEIM ESSEN*

LIKES cont.   *VORLIEBEN Forts.*

Shall we cook a meal for you tomorrow?	*Sollen wir morgen für Dich kochen?*
I love cooking.	*Ich mag Kochen.*
Would you like some more?	*Möchtest Du noch mehr?*
Would you like a second helping?	*Möchtest Du noch eine Portion?*
Only if no-one else wants it.	*Nur, wenn niemand anderes noch was möchte.*

DISLIKES   *ABNEIGUNGEN*

Is there anything you don't like eating?	*Gibt es etwas, was Du nicht gerne ißt?*
Just say if you don't like it.	*Sag' es nur, wenn Du etwas nicht magst.*
I am just not very hungry.	*Ich habe nur keinen Hunger.*
I'm afraid I don't eat…	*Ich esse kein / keine…..*
I'm sorry but….disagrees with me.	*Es tut mir leid, aber….bekommt mir schlecht.*
I can get you something else.	*Ich kann dir etwas anderes bringen.*
What do you feel like eating?	*Was möchtest du gerne essen?*
Have you any…?	*Habt ihr / haben Sie….?*

EXPERIMENTING WITH FOOD   *ESSEN AUSPROBIEREN*

This is typically English / German	*Das ist typisch Englisch / Deutsch.*
Have you ever tried this before?	*Hast Du das schon mal versucht?*
Can I try just a little bit, please?	*Kann ich bitte nur ein bißchen probieren?*
What do you think of it?	*Wie findest Du es?*
How do you cook this?	*Wie kocht man das?*
How do you prepare this?	*Wie bereitet man das zu?*

FOOD cont.   *ESSEN Forts.*

EATING	*ESSEN*
to eat	*essen*
to drink	*trinken*
to bite	*beißen*
to chew	*kauen*
to taste	*probieren*
to swallow	*schlucken*
to digest	*verdauen*
to choke	*würgen*
to burn your mouth	*seinen Mund verbrennen*

DIFFERENT DIETS	*VERSCHIEDENE DIÄTEN UND ERNÄHRUNGSWEISEN*
I am vegetarian.	*Ich bin Vegetarier.*
I am a vegan.	*Ich bin ein Vegan.*
I am diabetic.	*Ich bin Diabetiker.*
I like junk food.	*Ich mag Junk Food.*
I am allergic to…	*Ich reagiere allergisch auf…*
I am trying to lose weight.	*Ich versuche abzunehmen.*
I am trying to gain weight.	*Ich versuche zuzunehmen.*
I am trying to count my calories.	*Ich versuche meine Kalorien zu zählen.*
How many calories does this have?	*Wieviele Kalorien hat das?*
I don't eat starch with protein.	*Ich nehme keine Stärke zusammen mit Eiweiß zu mir.*
I prefer my vegetables raw.	*Ich esse mein Gemüse lieber roh.*
I am on a low fat diet.	*Ich mache eine fettarme Diät.*
I can't eat fried food.	*Ich vertrage nichts Gebratenes.*

TYPICALLY BRITISH FOOD

TYPISCHES ENGLISCHES ESSEN

Bangers and mash - sausages and mashed potatoes.
Shepherd's pie - minced beef and onion, topped with mashed potato.

Cornish pasty - an individual pie containing potatoes, vegetables and minced meat, typical of Cornwall.

A full English breakfast - fried eggs, bacon, sausage, grilled tomato, mushrooms, fried bread and sometimes black pudding.

Porridge - oats or oatmeal simmered with water and/or milk which the Scots eat with salt not sugar.
Yorkshire pudding - made from batter and traditionally eaten with roast beef for Sunday lunch.

Fish and chips - fish deep fried in batter with chips.

Bangers and mash (Würste und Brei - Würste und Kartoffelbrei.
Shepherd's pie (Schäfer's Pastete)-Rinderhackfleich und Zwiebeln, bedeckt mit Kartoffelbrei.
Cornish pasty (Kornische Pastete)- eine Pastete gefüllt mit Kartoffeln, Gemüse und Hackfleisch, ein typisches Gericht aus Cornwall.
A full English Breakfast (ein komplettes englisches Frühstück)- Spiegeleier, Speck, Wurst, gegrillte Tomaten, Champignons, Toastbrot und manchmal Blutwurst.
Porridge (Haferbrei)-Hafer oder Hafermehl gekocht mit Wasser und / oder Milch . Die Schotten essen es mit Salz, nicht mit Zucker.
Yorkshire pudding (Yorkshire Pudding)-aus Eierteig zubereitet, wird traditionell mit Rinderbraten sonntags zum Mittagessen gegessen.
Fisch and chips (Fisch und Pommes frites)-In Eierteig gebratener Fisch mit Pommes frites.

TYPICALLY BRITISH FOOD cont.

TYPISCHES ENGLISCHES ESSEN Forts.

A hot cross bun - a small bread like bun with currants in and a cross marked on top eaten on Good Friday.

A hot cross bun (ein Korinthenbrötchen)-ein kleines Korinthenbrötchen, oben markiert mit einem Kreuz. Wird am Karfreitag gegessen.

Cheddar - a common British cheese often known as 'mousetrap'.

Cheddar (Cheddarkäse)- ein alltäglicher britischer Käse, vielen bekannt als "Mausefalle".

Lardy cake - a bread made with lard and dried fruit topped with a sticky sugary mixture.

Lardy cake (Schweineschmalzkuchen)- ein Brot hergestellt aus Schweineschmalz und getrockneten Früchten, bedeckt mit einer klebrigen Zuckermischung.

Bakewell tart - a tart filled with almond paste and jam created in Bakewell in Derbyshire.

Bakewell tart (Bakewell Torte)- eine Torte gefüllt mit Mandelmus und Marmelade hergestellt in Bakewell in Derbyshire.

Christmas pudding - a rich pudding made with a variety of dried fruit which can be kept for over a year.

Christmas Pudding (Weihnachtspudding)-ein kräftiger Rührkuchen, hergestellt aus verschiedenen getrockneten Früchten, den man über ein Jahr aufbewahren kann.

TYPICALLY GERMAN FOOD

TYPISCHES DEUTSCHES ESSEN

Eel soup - boiled eel in a soup.	***Hamburger Aalsuppe** - gekochter Aal in der Suppe.*
Kale with pork sausage - cooked together - from North Germany.	***Grünkol mit Pinkel** - gekochter Grünkol mit heißer Mettwurst aus Norddeutschland.*
Trotter with sauerkraut - from Berlin.	***Eisbein mit Kraut** - Schweinefleisch mit Knochen und Sauerkraut aus Berlin.*
Hotchpotch from Leipzig - all sorts of vegetables cooked together.	***Leipziger Allerlei** - Gemüse aus Spargel, Karotten, Erbsen, Blumenkohl, Bohnen, Kohlrabi aus Leipzig.*
Green sauce - a thick sauce made with seven herbs - from Frankfurt.	***Frankfurter Grüne Soße** - dickflüssige Soße aus sieben Frühlingskräutern.*
Frankfurters cooked with mashed potatoes, pork ribs and sauerkraut.	***Frankfurter Würstchen** - feine Würste, die mit Kartoffelbrei, Rippchen und Sauerkraut gekocht werden.*
Noodles from Swabia - small noodles homemade from batter.	***Schwäbische Spätzle** - kleine Nudeln aus Mehl-Eierteig, handgemacht.*
Dumplings from Bavaria - made of breadcrumbs or mashed potatoes, served with roast pork.	***Bayerische Semmel** - und Teigknödel - Klöße aus Brot - oder Kartoffelteig, wird zu Schweinebraten gegessen.*

COOKING   *KOCHEN*

Cookery books	*Kochbücher*
a recipe	*ein Rezept*
to look up	*nachschauen*
to follow	*sich daran halten*
instructions	*Anweisungen*
method	*Verfahren*
ingredients	*Zutaten*
cooking time	*Kochzeit*
Serves three to four people.	*Ausreichend für drei bis vier Personen*
an illustration	*eine Abbildung*

COOKERY TERMS (abc)		**KOCHBEGRIFFE**	
to add	*hinzufügen*	to grate	*reiben*
to arrange	*anordnen*	to grill	*grillen*
to bake	*backen*	to grind	*mahlen*
to blend	*vermischen*	to heat up	*erhitzen*
to boil	*kochen*	to incorporate	*integrieren*
to casserole	*schmoren*	to knead	*kneten*
to chop	*hacken*	to liquidize	*pürieren / flüssig machen*
to combine	*verbinden*	to mash	*zerdrücken*
to cool	*kühlen*	to measure	*wiegen*
to cover	*bedecken*	to melt	*schmelzen*
to crimp	*schlitzen*	to mince	*hacken*
to cut into cubes	*in Würfel schneiden*	to peel	*schälen*
to divide	*trennen*	to pour	*gießen*
to drain	*trocknen*	to press	*drücken*
to flip over	*umdrehen*	to rise	*aufgehen*
to fold	*falten*	to roast	*rösten*
to fold in	*falten*	to roll out	*ausrollen*
to fry	*braten*	to season	*durchsieben*
to garnish	*garnieren*	to sift	*sieben*

COOKERY TERMS (abc) cont.

KOCHBEGRIFFE Forts.

to simmer	*auf kleiner Flamme kochen*	to test	*probieren*
to skewer	*aufspießen*	to time	*Zeit messen*
to slice	*schneiden*	to toss	*anmachen / wenden*
to sprinkle	*streuen*	to turn down	*runterdrehen*
to steam	*dünsten*	to turn out	*stürzen*
to stir	*rühren*	to turn up	*ausdrehen*
to strain	*filtrieren*	to whisk	*schlagen*
to taste	*schmecken*		

COOKING MEASURES

MAßEINHEITEN ZUM KOCHEN

a teaspoonful	*ein Teelöffelvoll*
a quarter / half a teaspoonful	*ein viertel / halber Teelöffelvoll*
three quarters of a teaspoonful	*Dreiviertel eines Teelöffels*
a dessertspoonful	*ein Dessertlöffelvoll*
a tablespoonful	*ein Eßlöffelvoll*
a cupful / half a cupful	*eine Tassevoll / halbe Tassevoll*
a pinch of	*ein Quentchen*

COOKING INGREDIENTS (AND HOW TO PREPARE THEM)

KOCHZUTATEN (UND WIE MAN SIE ZUBEREITET)

DAIRY PRODUCTS

MOLKEREIPRODUKTE

Milk	*Milch*
whole milk	*Vollmilch*
semi-skimmed / skimmed milk	*fettarme Milch / Magermilch*
long life milk / powdered milk	*H-Milch / Trockenmilch*
a milk bottle / a carton	*eine Milchflasche / ein Karton*
a milk jug / to pour	*ein Milchkrug / gießen*
a drink of milk	*ein Milchgetränk*

COOKING INGREDIENTS cont.
KOCHZUTATEN Forts.

DAIRY PRODUCTS cont.
MOLKEREIPRODUKTE Forts.

Cream	*Sahne*
double cream	*3,5 Fett Sahne*
single cream	*1,5 Fett Sahne*
clotted cream	*geronnene Sahne*
whipped cream	*Schlagsahne*
soured cream	*saure Sahne*
a jug of cream	*ein Sahnekrug*
to whisk / to whip	*schaumig schlagen / steif schlagen*

Butter, margarine etc.	*Butter, Margarine usw.*
salted / unsalted butter	*gesalzene Butter / ungesalzene Butter*
margarine	*Margarine*
soft / hard	*weich / hart*
suet / lard / dripping	*Nierenfett / Schmalz / Bratfett*
a butter dish	*eine Butterdose*
a butter knife	*ein Buttermesser*
to spread	*streichen*
to butter	*mit Butter streichen*

Yoghurt	*Joghurt*
set yoghurt	*Sahneyoghurt*
natural yoghurt	*Naturjoghurt*
low fat yoghurt	*fettarmer Joghurt*
fruit yoghurt	*Fruchtjoghurt*
a pot of yoghurt	*ein Joghurtbecher*

COOKING INGREDIENTS cont.

KOCHZUTATEN Forts.

DAIRY PRODUCTS cont.

MOLKEREIPRODUKTE Forts.

Cheese	*Käse*
hard / soft cheese	*harter / weicher Käse*
cream cheese	*Rahmkäse*
cottage cheese	*Hüttenkäse*
goat's cheese	*Ziegenkäse*
Parmesan cheese	*Parmesankäse*
cheese biscuits	*Käsegebäck*
a cheese board / a cheese knife	*ein Käseteller / ein Käsemesser*
to cut	*schneiden*
a cheese grater	*eine Käsereibe*
to grate	*reiben*

EGGS	*EIER*
a hen's egg	*ein Hühnerei*
a quail's egg	*ein Wachtel*
brown / white	*braun / weiß*
fresh / old	*frisch / alt*
large / medium / small	*groß / mittel / klein*
size one / two / three etc.	*Gewichtsklasse eins / zwei / drei usw.*
free range eggs	*Eier aus Freilandhaltung*
farmyard	*Bauernhof*
battery	*Legebatterie*
a dozen / half a dozen	*ein Dutzend / halbes Dutzend*
an egg box	*ein Eierkarton*
the shell	*die Schale*
to crack / to break	*einen Sprung haben / brechen*
the yolk / the white	*das Eigelb / das Eiweiß*

COOKING INGREDIENTS cont.
KOCHZUTATEN Forts.

Cooking eggs	*Eier kochen*
a boiled egg	*ein gekochtes Ei*
hard boiled / soft boiled	*hart gekocht / weich gekocht*
cooked for four / five / six minutes	*vier / fünf / sechs Minuten gekocht*
an egg cup	*ein Eierbecher*
soldiers	*In Ei getunkte Brotstreifen*
to take the top off the egg	*Ei aufschneiden*
scrambled egg	*Rührei*
poached egg - no German equivalent	*Eine Englische Spezialität*

Preparing eggs	*Eier zubereiten*
to separate the whites from the yolks	*das Eiweiß vom Eigelb trennen*
to whisk the whites	*das Weiße aufschlagen*
an egg whisk	*ein Eierbesen*
an electric beater	*ein elektrischer Schneebesen*
stiffly beaten	*Steif schlagen*
soft peaks	*Sahnehäubchen*

BREAD	*BROT*
wholemeal / organic	*Vollkornmehl / Bio-Brot*
brown / white	*dunkel / weiß*
large / small	*groß / klein*
round / oblong	*rund / länglich*
unsliced / sliced	*ungeschnitten / geschnitten*
thick / medium / thin sliced	*dick / mittel / dünn geschnitten*
a bread bin	*ein Brotkasten*
a bread board / a bread knife	*ein Brotbrett / ein Brotmesser*
to cut / to slice / a slice	*schneiden / es in Scheiben*
	schneiden / eine Scheibe
to make breadcrumbs	*Paniermehl machen*

COOKING INGREDIENTS cont.

KOCHZUTATEN Forts.

OTHER TYPES OF BREAD AND BAKED GOODS	*ANDERE BROT- UND GEBÄCKSORTEN*
a French stick	*ein Baguette*
a roll	*ein Brötchen*
Ciabatta	*ein Ciabatta (indisches Brot)*
pitta bread	*ein Pitta-Brot*
crumpets	*Matzen*
muffins	*Weiche Kuchen*
tea cakes	*Teekuchen*

COFFEE, TEA AND OTHER DRINKS	*KAFFEE, TEE UND ANDERE GETRÄNKE*
Coffee	*Kaffe*
Do you like black or white coffee?	*Magst Du Deinen Kaffee schwarz oder mit Milch?*
instant coffee	*Instant-Kaffee*
decaffeinated coffee	*Koffeinfreier Kaffee*
real coffee / coffee beans	*richtiger Kaffee / Kaffeebohnen*
full / medium / light roast	*schwarz / mittel / leicht geröstet*
to grind	*mahlen*
a coffee grinder	*eine Kaffeemühle*
fine / medium / coarse ground	*fein / mittel / grob gemahlen*

Tea	*Tee*
a tea pot	*eine Teekanne*
to warm the pot	*die Teekanne erwärmen*
to let it brew	*ziehen lassen*
to pour / to strain	*gießen / filtern*
tea bags / tea leaves	*Teebeutel / Teeblätter*
an infuser / a tea strainer	*ein TeeEi / ein Teesieb*
Do you like your tea with milk and sugar?	*Magst Du Deinen Tee mit Milch und Zucker?*
Milk and no sugar, please.	*Mit Milch ohne Zucker, bitte.*
No milk and one sugar, please.	*Ohne Milch und Zucher, Bitte.*

COOKING INGREDIENTS cont.

KOCHZUTATEN Forts.

OTHER DRINKS	*ANDERE GETRÄNKE*
tonic water	*Tonic Water*
soda water	*Soda Wasser*
ginger ale	*Ginger Ale*
lemonade	*Limonade*
coca cola	*Coca Cola*
water	*Wasser*
squash / to dilute	*Sirup / verdünnen*
strong / weak / average	*stark / schwach / normal*

Fruit juice / freshly squeezed		*Fruchtsäfte / frisch ausgepreßt*	
orange	*Orange*	tomato	*Tomate*
grapefruit	*Pampelmuse*	vegetable	*Gemüse*
pineapple	*Ananas*	tropical juice	*Tropenfrüchte*
Additions to drinks		*Getränkezugaben*	
ice cubes		*Eiswürfel*	
a slice of lemon		*eine Zitronenscheibe*	
a cherry		*eine Kirsche*	

ALCOHOLIC DRINKS		*ALKOHOLISCHE GETRÄNKE*	
cider	*Apfelwein*	rosé	*Rosé*
beer	*Bier*	sparkling	*Sekt*
lager	*Lagerbier*	Champagne	*Champagner*
bottled	*in Flaschen*	**Spirits**	***Spirituosen***
draught	*gezapft*	gin	*Gin*
canned	*in Dosen*	whisky	*Whisky*
Wine	***Wein***	brandy	*Kognak*
a glass of	*ein Glas*	vodka	*Wodka*
half a bottle of	*eine halbe Flasche*	rum	*Rum*
red	*Rot*	a single	*einen Einfachen*
white	*Weiß*	a double	*einen Doppelten*

COOKING INGREDIENTS cont.

KOCHZUTATEN Forts.

MEAT

FLEISCH

How do you like your meat cooked?	*Wie willst Du Dein Fleisch gebraten haben?*
rare / medium rare	*leicht durch / halb*
well done / crispy	*ganz durch / knusprig*

TYPES OF MEAT

FLEISCHSORTEN

beef	***Rind***	Parma ham	*Parma Schinken*
a steak	*ein Steak*	**veal**	***Kalb***
pork	***Schwein***	**lamb**	***Lamm***
bacon	*Speck*	**offal**	***Innereien***
smoked	*geräuchert*	liver	*Leber*
unsmoked	*ungeräuchtert*	kidney	*Nieren*
streaky	*durchwachsen*	sweetbreads	*Hirn*
ham	*Schinken*	**sausages**	***Würste***

POULTRY AND GAME

GEFLÜGEL UND WILD

a chicken	*eine Huhn*	a guinea fowl	*ein Perlhuhn*
a duck	*eine Ente*	a pheasant	*eine Fasan*
a goose	*eine Gans*	a hare	*ein Hase*
a turkey	*ein Truthahn*	a rabbit	*ein Kaninchen*
venison	*Wildbret*		

COMMON FRUITS

ALLTÄGLICHES OBST

apple	*Apfel*	orange	*Orange*
apricot	*Aprikose*	peach	*Pfirsich*
banana	*Banane*	pear	*Birne*
grapefruit	*Pampelmuse*	pineapple	*Ananas*
grapes	*Trauben*	plum	*Pflaume*
lemon	*Zitrone*	raspberry	*Himbeere*
lime	*Limone*	satsuma	*Satsuma*
melon	*Melone*	strawberry	*Erdbeere*

COOKING INGREDIENTS cont.   *KOCHZUTATEN Forts.*

PREPARING FRUIT   *OBST ZUBEREITEN*

to peel	*schälen*
the peel	*die Schale*
the pith	*das Weiße*
to quarter	*vierteln*
to remove the pips	*die Kerne entfernen*
to take out the stone	*den Kern entfernen*

VEGETABLES & SALAD   *GEMÜSE & SALAT*

aubergine	Aubergine	mushroom	*Champignons*
avocado	Avokado	onion	*Zwiebeln*
broad beans	Saubohne	Spring onion	Frühlings-zwiebel
French beans	grüne Bohne	parsnip	*Petersilienworzel*
green beans	grüne Bohne	peas	*Erbsen*
runner beans	*Stangenbohne*	red pepper	*rote Paprika*
beetroot	*Rotebeete*	green pepper	*grüne Paprika*
broccoli	*Broccoli*	potato	*Kartoffel*
Brussels sprouts	*Rosenkohl*	jacket potato	*gebackene Kartoffel*
cabbage	*Kohl*	boiled	*gekocht*
carrot	*Karotte*	mashed	*puree*
cauliflower	*Blumenkohl*	roasted	*braten*
celeriac	*Sellerieknolle*	chips	*Pommes frites*
celery	*Sellerie*	spinach	*Spinat*
courgette	*Zuchinis*	swede	*Steckrübe*
cress	*Kresse*	sweetcorn	*Mais*
cucumber	*Gurke*	radish	*Rettich*
garlic	*Knoblauch*	tomato	*Tomate*
leek	*Lauch*	turnip	*Rübe*
lettuce	*Salatkopf*	watercress	*Wasserkresse*

COOKING INGREDIENTS cont.

KOCHZUTATEN Forts.

SUGAR, HONEY, JAM etc.	*ZUCKER, HONIG, MARMELADEN usw.*
white sugar / granulated sugar	*weißer Zucker / Kristallzucker*
castor sugar / icing sugar	*Streuzucker / Puderzucker*
lump sugar / to sweeten	*Zuckerstücke / süßen*
brown sugar	*brauner Zucker*
syrup / golden syrup	*Zuckersaft / Kunsthonig*
black treacle / molasses	*Rübenkraut / Zuckersirup*
honey / runny honey	*Honig / flüssiger honig*
honeycomb	*Honigwabe*
jam	*marmelade*
orange / ginger marmelade	*Orange / Ingwermarmelade*

FLOUR etc.	*MEHL usw.*
plain flour	*einfaches Mehl*
self-raising flour	*Mehlback-pulvergemisch*
white flour / wholemeal flour	*Weißes Mehl / Vollkornmehl*
buckwheat flour	*Buchenweizen-mehl*
cornflour / baking powder	*Maismehl / Backpulver*
bicarbonate of soda	*Natron*
arrowroot	*Pfeilwurzstärke*
gelatine / yeast	*Gelatine / Hefe*

PREPARING NUTS	*NÜSSE ZUBEREITEN*
to crack the shell	*knacken die Schale*
nutcrackers	*Nußknacker*
whole nuts / chopped nuts	*Ganze Nüsse / zerkleinert Nüsse*
ground nuts	*Erdnüsse*
salted / unsalted nuts	*gesalzene / ungesalzene Nüsse*
roasted nuts	*geröstete Nüsse*

COOKING INGREDIENTS cont.　*KOCHZUTATEN Forts.*

SALT AND PEPPER etc.　*SALZ UND PFEFFER usw.*

table salt	*Tischsalz*
sea salt	*Meersalz*
crystal rock salt	*Kristallsalz*
celery salt	*Selleriesalz*
a salt mill	*eine Salzmühle*
to grind	*mahlen*
to season	*würzen*
to sprinkle	*streuen*
a pinch of salt	*eine Brise Salz*
peppercorns	*Pfefferkörner*
black / white / green	*Schwarz / weiß / grün*
a pepper mill	*eine Pfeffermühle*
to grind	*füllen*
to fill	*Tomaten-Ketchup*

BARBECUES
GRILLPARTIES

SHOULD WE HAVE A BARBECUE?	*SOLLEN WIR EINE GRILLPARTY MACHEN?*
Should we eat outside?	*Sollen wir draußen essen?*

LIGHTING THE BARBECUE   *DEN GRILL ANZÜNDEN*

Have we got..?	*Haben wir...?*
• aluminium foil	• *Aluminiumfolie?*
• charcoal	• *Holzkohle?*
• lighter fluid	• *Zündflüssigkeit*
to squirt	*spritzen*
to pour over	*übergießen*
to soak	*eintränken*
to light	*zünden*
a match	*ein Streichholz*
to stand back	*Abstand halten*
to get going well	*es gut hinbekommen*
to go out	*ausgehen*

COOKING ON A BARBECUE   *DEN GRILL BENUTZEN*

to be ready to cook	*fertig zum Grillen*
to barbecue	*grillen*
to grill	*grillen*
tongs	*Zangen*
skewers	*Fleischspieße*
to turn over	*umdrehen*

BARBECUES cont.

GRILLPARTIES Forts.

FOOD

ESSEN

sausages	*Würste*	spare ribs	*Rippchen*
bacon	*Schinken*	marinade	*Marinade*
steaks	*Steaks*	sauce	*Soße*
chops	*Koteletts*	to brush over	*einpinseln*
kebabs	*Kebabs*	marshmallows	*Marshmallows*
chicken drumsticks	*Hühnerschenkel*		

COMMON EXPRESSIONS FOR BARBECUES

ALLGEMEINE AUSDRUCKWEISEN BEIM GRILLEN

Is it ready yet?	*Ist es soweit?*
Are they ready yet?	*Sind sie soweit?*
They won't be long now.	*Sie sind bald soweit.*
Another few minutes.	*Noch ein paar Minuten.*
This isn't cooked properly.	*Es ist nicht richtig durch:*
I'm afraid this is a bit burnt.	*Ich glaube, es ist ein wenig verbrannt.*

M^CDONALDS

M^CDONALD'S

HAMBURGER ROYAL
A wheatroll, 100% beef, cheese spread, onions, slices of gherkins, ketchup and mustard sauce.

HAMBURGER ROYAL
Weizenbrötchen mit Sesam, 100% Rindfleisch, Chester-Schmelzkäsezubereitung, frische Zwiebeln, Gurkenscheiben, Ketchup und Senfsauce.

BIG MAC
A wheatroll, 100% beef, onions, slices of gherkins, iceberg lettuce, cheese spread and Big Mac-sauce.

BIG MÄC
Weizenbrötchen, 100% Rindfleisch, Zwiebeln, Gurkenscheiben, Eisbergsalat, Chester-Schmelzkäsezubereitung und Big Mäc-Sauce.

M^CRIB
A wheatroll, pork, fresh onions, slices of gherkins and M^CRib-Sauce.

M^CRIB
Weizenbrötchen, Schweinefleisch, frische Zwiebeln, Gurkenscheiben und M^CRib-Sauce.

FISHMAC
A wheatroll, a battered fillet of fish, FishMac Sauce with a relish of dill gherkins, onions and cheese spread.

FISCHMÄC
Weizenbrötchen, Seefischfilet paniert, FischMäc-Sauce mit Dillgurken-Relish und Zwiebeln, sowie Chester-Schmelzkäsezubereitung.

CHICKEN M^CNUGGETS
Chicken in breadcrumbs. Variety of sauces:-
- mustard sauce
- sweet and sour sauce
- barbecue sauce
- curry sauce

M^CCHICKEN
Hähnchen paniert. Verschiedene Saucen:-
- *Senfsauce*
- *süßsaure Sauce*
- *Barbecue Sauce*
- *Currysauce*

M^CDONALDS cont.

M^CDONALDS forts.

CHEF'S SALAD
A variety of salad leaves, carrot,
Edam cheese, slices of ham, boiled
egg with a choice of dressings:-

- Housedressing
- Light Housedressing
- Herbal dressing
- Italian dressing

CHEFSALAT
Verschiedene Blattsalate,
Karotten, Edamer Käse,
Schinkenstreifen, geckochtes Ei.
Wahlweise mit:-

- *Hausdressing*
- *Hausdressing leicht*
- *Kraüterdressing*
- *Italienische Dressing*

CHIPS
with Ketchup or Mayonnaise

POMMES FRITES
mit Ketchup oder Mayonnaise

DOUGHNUTS

APPLE & CHERRY PIE

DONUTS

APFEL & KIRSCHTASHE

CINEMA, THEATRE, CLUBS AND PARTIES.

KINO, THEATER, DISCOS UND PARTIES

THE CINEMA

DAS KINO

USEFUL EXPRESSIONS

NÜTZLICHE AUSDRUCKWEISEN

Would you like to go to the cinema..?	*Möchtest Du gerne....ins Kino gehen?*
• this afternoon?	*-heute nachmittag*
• this evening?	*-heute abend*
• tomorrow?	*-morgen*
• one day?	*-irgendwann*
• while you are here?	*-solange Du hier bist*
There's a very good film on at the moment.	*Es läuft gerade ein sehr guter Film.*
It starts at…	*Er fängt um....an.*
It ends at…	*Er hört um...auf.*
Is there a supporting film first?	*Gibt es einen Vorfilm?*
Is there an interval?	*Gibt es eine Pause?*
Who's in the film?	*Wer spielt in dem Film mit.*
The star of the film is..	*Die Hauptrolle des Films ist...*
It's starring…	*Die Hauptrolle ist...*
It's that man who was in..	*Das ist der Mann, der in ....mitgespielt hat.*
Wasn't she in..?	*Hat sie nicht in....mitgespielt?*
Who is the director?	*Wer ist der Regisseur?*

THE CINEMA cont.　　　　*DAS KINO Forts.*

BUYING TICKETS AND　　*DIE KARTEN KAUFEN UND*
GOING IN　　　　　　　*REINGEHEN*

Could we have two tickets, please?	*Wir möchten bitte zwei Karten.*
Can you reserve seats?	*Kann man Plätze reservieren?*
Do you give a reduction to students?	*Gibt es bei ihnen eine Schülerermäßigung?*
We are .....years old.	*Wir sind...Jahre alt.*
Would you like some pop corn?	*Möchtest Du Pop Corn haben?*
Would you like an ice cream or a drink?	*Möchtest Du gerne ein Eis oder etwas zu trinken?*
Do you want to go to the loo first?	*Mußt du vorher nochmal auf's Klo?*
Where are the toilets?	*Wo sind die Toiletten?*
We'd better hurry - the film's just starting.	*Wir müssen uns beeilender Film fängt an.*
Where would you like to sit?	*Wo möchtest Du Dich hinsetzen?*
Do you like to be near the front or not?	*Möchtest Du lieber nah oder weit von der Leinwand sitzen?*
Can you see O.K.?	*Kannst Du gut sehen?*
I can't see because of the person in front of me.	*Wegen der Person vor mir, kann ich nichts sehen.*
Can we try to sit somewhere else?	*Können wir uns woanders hinsetzen?*

FOLLOWING THE PLOT　　*DER HANDLUNG FOLGEN*

Does it have subtitles?	*Hat er Untertitel?*
It has subtitles?	*Er hat Untertitel.*
It's dubbed.	*Er ist synchronisiert.*
Can you understand what's going on?	*Verstehst Du, um was es geht?*
I don't understand it.	*Ich verstehe es nicht.*
What just happened?	*Was ist gerade passiert?*
What did he say?	*Was hat er gesagt?*

THE THEATRE   *DAS THEATER*

BOOKING SEATS   *KARTEN BESTELLEN*

the booking office	*die Vorverkaufsstelle*
to reserve seats	*Plätze reservieren*
Which performance?	*Welche Vorstellung?*
the matinée	*die Matineé-Vorstellung*
the evening performance	*die Abend-Vorstellung*
Where do you want to sit?	*Wo möchtest Du sitzen?*
in the stalls	*im Parkett*
in the circle	*auf den Rängen*
What seats are available?	*Welche Plätze sind noch erhältlich?*
How much are the seats?	*Wieviel kosten die Plätze?*

BUYING A PROGRAMME   *EIN PROGRAMM KAUFEN*

to buy a programme	*sich ein Programm kaufen*
to look at the programme	*sich das Programm anschauen*
to see who is in the play	*herausfinden, wer in dem Stück mitspielt*
to study the plot	*die Handlung lesen*
to read about the actors' backgrounds	*über die Hintergründe der Schauspieler lesen*

HAVING SOMETHING TO EAT OR DRINK   *ETWAS ESSEN ODER TRINKEN*

the bar	*die Bar*
the restaurant	*das Restaurant*
to have a drink	*etwas trinken*
before the performance	*vor der Aufführung*
in the interval	*in der Pause*
to book a table	*einen Tisch bestellen*

THE THEATRE cont.   *DAS THEATER Forts.*

THE AUDITORIUM   *DER ZUSCHAUERRAUM*

an aisle	*ein Gang*
a box	*eine Loge*
the toilets	*die Toiletten*
a fire exit	*ein Notausgang*
the acoustics	*die Akustik*

THE SEATING   *DIE PLÄTZE*

to show your ticket	*seine Karte zeigen*
row A, B etc.	*Reihe A, B usw.*
an usher	*ein Platzanweiser*
to be shown to your seat	*zu seinem Platz geführt werden*
the stalls	*das Parkett*
the circle	*die Ränge*

BEFORE THE PERFORMANCE   *VOR DER AUFFÜHRUNG*

to read the programme	*das Programm lesen*
to have a chocolate	*eine Schokolade essen*
to let someone past	*jemanden vorbei lassen*
to stand up	*aufstehen*
to sit down	*sich setzen*
to take your coat off	*sich seinen Mantel ausziehen*
to get a good view	*eine gute Sicht haben*
to be able to see	*es sehen können*
to use the opera glasses	*das Opernglas benutzen*
to insert a coin	*eine Münze einwerfen*
to borrow	*leihen*

THE THEATRE cont.   *DAS THEATER Forts.*

THE STAGE   *DIE BÜHNE*

a theatre in the round	*ein Rundtheater*
a raised stage	*eine erhöhte Bühne*
the wings	*die Seitenbühne*
the scenery	*das Bühnenbild*
a scene-change	*ein Szenenwechsel*
the props	*die Requisiten*
to make an entrance	*seinen Auftritt haben*
to come on stage	*auf der Bühne erscheinen*
to exit	*einen Abgang machen*
to leave	*verlassen*

THE LIGHTING   *DIE BELEUCHTUNG*

spotlights	*Punktscheinwerfer*
floodlights	*Scheinwerfer*
coloured	*farbig*
to dim	*abblenden*
to go down	*runtergehen*
to go off	*ausgehen*
to come back on	*nochmal angehen*
the lighting effects	*die Lichteffekte*

THE CURTAIN   *DER VORHANG*

to open	*öffnen*
to shut	*schließen*
to raise	*aufgehen*
to fall	*fallen*
a safety curtain	*ein Sicherheitsvorhang*

THE THEATRE cont.   *DAS THEATER Forts.*

THE PERFORMERS   *DIE VORSTELLUNG*

the cast	die Besetzung
the lead	die Hauptrolle
the star	der Star
the hero / the heroine	der Held / die Heldin
the villain	der Schurke
the actors	die Schauspieler
the actresses	die Schauspielerinnen
the understudy	der Ersatzschauspieler

THE WRITERS   *DIE AUTOREN*

the playwright	der Bühnenschriftsteller
the composer	der Komponist
the librettist	der Textbuchschreiber
the choreographer	der Choreograph
the musical director	der musikalische Leiter

THE TECHNICAL STAFF   *DIE TECHNISCHEN ANGESTELLTEN*

the stage manager	der Bühnendirektor
the technical director	der technische Direktor
the lighting technicians	die Beleuchtungs- Techniker

THE PLAY   *DAS STÜCK*

a Shakespeare play	ein Shakespeare-Stück
a play by Pinter	ein Stück von Pinter
a comedy / a farce	eine Komödie / eine Posse
slapstick	ein Klamauk
a tragedy	eine Tragödie
a history	ein Geschichtsstück
a thriller / a whodunnit	ein Thriller / ein Krimi
a romance	eine Romanze
a pantomime	eine Pantomime
the plot	die Handlung

THE THEATRE cont.	**DAS THEATER Forts.**

REHEARSALS / *PROBEN*

REHEARSALS	*PROBEN*
to rehearse	*proben*
to have a dress rehearsal	*eine Kostümprobe haben*
a final rehearsal	*die Generalprobe*

THE SET DESIGN / *DIE BÜHNENAUSSTATTUNG*

abstract	*abstrakt*	functional	*funktional*
artistic	*künstlerisch*	eccentric	*exzentrisch*
realistic	*realistisch*	unusual	*ungewöhnlich*

THE COSTUME DESIGN / *DIE KOSTÜMIERUNG*

historical	*historisch*
period costume	*zeitgebundene Kostüme*
contemporary	*zeitgemäß*
imaginative	*phantasievoll*
masked	*maskiert*
bold / extravagant	*gewagt / extravagant*

THE MAKEUP / *DIE MASKE*

to be made up / to exaggerate	*geschminkt werden / übertreiben*
to conceal	*verdecken*
to distort	*entstellen*
to emphasize	*betonen*
to remove greasepaint	*entfernen Fettschminke*

THE SPECIAL EFFECTS / *DIE SPEZIALEFFEKTE*

sound effects / lighting effects	*Toneffekte / Lichteffekte*
music	*Musik*
thunder	*Donner*
battle noises / smoke	*Schlacht-Geräusche / Rauch*

THE THEATRE cont.

DAS THEATER Forts.

THE PARTS OF THE PLAY

DIE ABSCHNITTE DES STÜCKES

a scene / the first scene	*Eine Szene / die erste Szene*
second / third	*zweite / dritte*
a change of scene	*ein Szenenwechsel*
an act / the last act	*ein Akt / der letzte Akt*
a speech / a soliloquy	*eine Rede / ein Monolog*
an aside	*beiseite gesprochene Worte*

THE INTERVAL

DIE PAUSE

a brief interval	*eine kurze Pause*
a long interval	*eine lange Pause*
to go to the bar	*zur Bar gehen*
a long queue	*eine lange Schlange*
to go to the toilet	*auf die Toilette gehen*
to ring the bell	*die Glocke klingeln*
to return to your seat	*auf seine Plätze zurückgehen*

THE END OF THE PLAY

DAS ENDE DES STÜCKES

to applaud	*applaudieren*
the applause	*der Applaus*
to clap	*klatschen*
a standing ovation	*eine stehende Ovation*
to give a curtain call	*die Schauspieler vor den Vorhang rufen*
to bow / to curtsy	*sich verbeugen / knicksen*
to be given a bouquet	*einen Blumenstrauß bekommen*

AFTER THE PLAY

NACH DEM STÜCK

to go to the stage door	*zum Bühnenausgang gehen*
to try to get an autograph	*versuchen, ein Autogramm zu bekommen*
a signature	*eine Unterschrift*
to sign an autograph book	*ein Autogrammheft signieren*

THE THEATRE cont.   *DAS THEATER Forts.*

DISCUSSING THE   *ÜBER DIE AUFFÜHRUNG*
PERFORMANCE (abc)   *REDEN*

amateur	*amateurhaft*	realistic	*realistisch*
convincing	*überzeugend*	sad	*traurig*
excellent	*ausgezeichnet*	sensitive	*einfühlsam*
funny	*witzig*	spectacular	*spektakulär*
hysterical	*hysterisch*	tense	*spannend*
imaginative	*einfallsreich*	terse	*knapp*
impressive	*eindrucksvoll*	theatrical	*theatralisch*
ironic	*ironisch*	tragic	*tragisch*
moving	*bewegend*	true to life	*wahrheitsgetreu*
professional	*professionell*	unconvincing	*nicht überzeugend*
psychological	*psychologisch*		

OPERA   *OPER*

TYPES OF OPERA   *OPERNARTEN*

an opera / an operetta	*eine Oper / eine Operette*
a comic opera	*eine komische Oper*
a rock opera	*eine Rock-Oper*

TYPES OF SONG   *GESANG*

a solo / a duet	*ein Solo / ein Duett*
a chorus	*ein Chor*
an aria	*eine Arie*
a recitative	*ein Sprechgesang*
a part-song	*ein mehrstimmiger Gesang*

OPERA cont.   *OPER Forts.*

THE SINGERS   *DIE SÄNGER*

soprano	*Sopran*	falsetto	*Falsett*
contralto	*Mezzosopran*	baritone	*Bariton*
alto	*Alt*	bass	*Baß*
tenor	*Tenor*	a prima donna	*eine Primadonna*

THE MUSIC   *DIE MUSIK*

the score	*Die Partitur*	the overture	*die Ouvertüre*
the libretto	*das Libretto*		

THE BALLET   *DAS BALLETT*

THE DANCERS etc.   *DIE TÄNZER usw.*

a ballerina	*eine Ballerina*
a prima ballerina	*eine Primaballerina*
the corps de ballet	*die Ballettgruppe*
the choreographer	*der Choreograph*
the composer	*der Komponist*

GETTING READY TO DANCE   *FERTIG MACHEN ZUM TANZEN*

to do exercises at the barre	*Übungen an der Stange machen*
to warm up	*sich aufwärmen*
to limber	*sich lockern*
to stretch the muscles	*die Muskeln dehnen*
to loosen the joints	*die Gelenke lockern*

THE BALLET cont.

DAS BALLETT Forts.

THE POSITIONS

DIE STELLUNGEN

the position of..	*die Stellung*	third position	*dritte Stellung*
the head	*des Kopfes*	fourth position	*vierte Stellung*
the arms	*der Arme*	fifth position	*fünfte Stellung*
the body	*des Körpers*	turned out	*weggedreht*
the legs	*der Beine*	in line	*in einer Linie*
the feet	*der Füße*	in the air	*in der Luft*
first position	*erste Stellung*	pointed	*gerichtet*
second position	*zweite Stellung*		

THE MOVEMENTS

DIE BEWEGUNGEN

to jump	*hüpfen*
to leap	*springen*
to turn	*drehen*
to beat the feet	*die Füße zusammenschlagen*
to change the leg position	*die Beinstellung verändern*
to do pointe work	*Spitzentanz*
to mime	*mimen*
to gesture	*sich gebärden*
an arabesque	*eine Arabeske*
a pirouette	*eine Pirouette*
a fouetté	*ein Fouetté*
an entrechat	*ein Entrechat*
a jeté	*ein Jeté*
a pas de deux	*ein Pas de Deux*
to partner somebody	*jemandes Partner sein*
a partner	*ein Partner*

THE BALLET cont.	*DAS BALLETT Forts.*

BALLET CLOTHES etc.	*BALLETTKLEIDUNG usw.*

ballet shoes	*Ballettschuhe*
blocked shoes	*Spitzenschuhe*
to darn	*stopfen*
tights	*Tänzerstrumpfhose*
a tutu	*ein Tutu*
a hair net	*ein Haarnetz*
to put one's hair up	*sich die Haare hochstecken*
to tie one's hair back	*sich die Haare nach hinten binden.*
to plait one's hair	*sich einen Zopf binden*

THE BALLET ITSELF	*DIE BALLETVORSTELLUNG*

the music	*die Musik*	the plot	*die Handlung*
the composer	*der Komponist*	the libretto	*das Libretto*
the steps	*die Schritte*	the scenario	*das Szenario*
the choreographer	*der Choreograph*	the orchestra	*das Orchester*
the conductor	*der Dirigent*	the pit	*das Parkett*

PARTIES & CLUBS
PARTIES & DISCOS

GETTING IN   *REINKOMMEN*

a nightclub	*eine Disco*
a bouncer	*ein Türsteher*
How old do you have to be to get in?	*Wie alt muß man sein, um rein zu kommen?*
Have you got an identity card?	*Hast du einen Personalausweis?*
Have you got anything that proves your age?	*Hast Du irgend etwas, das Dein Alter angibt?*
How much does it cost to get in?	*Wieviel kostet es reinzugehen?*

PARTIES   *PARTIES*

Have you got an invitation?	*Hast Du eine Einladung?*
I am / am not invited.	*Ich bin / bin nicht eingeladen.*
a gatecrasher	*ein ungeladener Gast*
to give a party	*eine Party machen*
to draw up a list of people to invite	*eine Liste mit Leuten schreiben, die man einladen will.*
to take a bottle	*eine Flasche nehmen*

THE MUSIC   *DIE MUSIK*

What's the music like?	*Wie ist die Musik?*
It's just a disco.	*Es ist nur eine Disco.*
There's live music.	*Es spielt eine Live-Band.*
The group is good.	*Die Gruppe ist gut:*
What sort of music do you like?	*Welche Musik magst Du?*
This music isn't my sort of thing.	*Diese Musik ist nicht gerade mein Ding.*
I prefer…	*Ich finde… besser.*
Which groups do you like?	*Welche Gruppen magst Du?*
Should we ask them to play..?	*Sollen wir fragen, ob sie….spielen?*

PARTIES & CLUBS cont.

INTRODUCTIONS

PARTIES & DISCOS Forts.

KENNENLERNEN UND VORSTELLEN

What nationality are you?	*Aus welchem Land kommst Du?*
Are you English / French / German / Spanish?	*Bist Du Engländer / Franzose / Deutscher / Spanier?*
Can you speak English?	*Kannst Du Englisch sprechen?*
What are you called? I'm called..	*Wie heißt Du? Ich heiße...*
What's your name? My name is..	*Was ist Dein Name? Mein Name ist...*
This is my friend….	*Das ist mein Freund...*
Where do you live?	*Wo wohnst Du?*
Where are you staying?	*Wo bist Du hier unter gekommen? oder Wo wohnst Du hier?*
How old are you?	*Wie alt bist Du?*
I'm sixteen.	*Ich bin sechzehn.*
Have you been here before?	*Bist Du schon mal hier gewesen?*
Are you at school / college / working?	*Gehst Du in die Schule / Studierst Du / Arbeitest Du?*
Which school / college do you go to?	*Auf welcher Schule / Universität bist Du?*
Where do you work?	*Wo arbeitest Du?*
What do you do?	*Was machst Du?*
Do you know those people over there?	*Kennst Du die Leute da drüben?*
How old are they?	*Wie alt sind die?*
What's he / she like?	*Wie ist er / sie so?*
Shall we go and talk to …?	*Sollen wir rübergehen und mit.....sprechen?*
Do you like dancing?	*Tanzt Du gerne?*
She's a really good dancer.	*Sie tanzt sehr gut.*
The music is so loud.	*Die Musik ist zu laut.*
I can't hear what you're saying.	*Ich verstehe nicht was Du sagst.*

PARTIES & CLUBS cont.   *PARTIES & DISCOS Forts.*

DRINKS   *GETRÄNKE*

Shall we go to the bar?	*Sollen wir an die Bar gehen?*
Which bar shall we go to?	*An welche Bar sollen wir gehen?*
Would you like a drink?	*Möchtest Du etwas trinken?*
What would you like to drink?	*Was möchtest Du gerne trinken?*
I'd like a coke / a beer.	*Ich will eine Cola / ein Bier.*
I'll have what you're having.	*Ich nehme dasselbe wie Du.*
You have to be eighteen.	*Man muß achtzehn sein.*
The drinks are very expensive.	*Die Getränke sind sehr teuer.*

GETTING HOME AFTERWARDS   *NACHHAUSE KOMMEN*

What time do you have to leave?	*Wann mußt Du nach Hause?*
What time does the club shut?	*Um wieviel Uhr macht die Disco zu?*
What time does the party finish?	*Wann ist die Party zu Ende?*
Are you being picked up?	*Wirst Du abgeholt?*
Yes, I'm being picked up at one.	*Ja, ich werde um eins abgeholt.*
How are you getting home?	*Wie kommst Du nach Hause?*
Do you want a lift with us?	*Sollen wir Dich mitnehmen?*
Could I possibly have a lift in your car?	*Kannst Du mich in Deinem Auto mitnehmen?*
Should we share a taxi?	*Sollen wir uns ein Taxi teilen?*
Which bus / train are you getting?	*Welchen Bus / Zug mußt Du nehmen?*
Can I see you again sometime?	*Kann ich Dich mal wieder sehen?*
Should we go somewhere together tomorrow night?	*Sollen wir morgen abend zusammen ausgehen?*
Would you like to go to the cinema with us tomorrow?	*Möchtest Du mit uns morgen ins Kino gehen?*
Shall we go and get something to eat?	*Sollen wir uns etwas zu essen holen?*

FAIR, CIRCUS & ZOO
RUMMEL, ZIRCUS & ZOO

THE FAIR

DER RUMMEL - PLATZ

USEFUL EXPRESSIONS

NÜTZLICHE AUSDRUCKSWEISEN

There is a fair on - would you like to go?	*Es gibt einen Rummel- möchtest du gerne hingehen?*
What rides do you like?	*Welche Fahrten magst Du*
Which rides would you like to go on?	*Mit was möchtest Du gerne fahren?*
How much money have you got to spend?	*Wieviel Geld kannst Du ausgeben?*
How much is it to go on the dodgems?	*Wieviel kosten die Stoßautos?*
Should we have another go on that?	*Sollen wir das noch mal machen?*
What would you like to go on next?	*Wo möchtest Du das nächste Mal reingehen?*
What time do we have to be home by?	*Um wieviel Uhr müssen wir Zuhause sein?*
If we get separated, shall we meet by the big wheel?	*Falls wir uns verlieren, sollen wir uns dann am Riesenrad treffen?*

THE RIDES

DIE FAHRTEN

The Ferris Wheel	***das Riesenrad***
Shall we sit together?	*Sollen wir uns zusammensetzen?*

THE FAIR - RIDES cont.

DER RUMMELPLATZ -DIE FAHRTEN Forts

The Ghost Train	*Die Geisterbahn*
It's very dark!	*Es ist sehr dunkel!*
I can't see.	*Ich kann nichts sehen.*
I am frightened!	*Ich habe Angst!*
Hold my hand.	*Halt meine Hand.*
It will be over in a minute.	*Es ist gleich vorbei.*

The Dodgems	*Autoscooter*
to wait for them to stop	*warten bis sie anhalten*
to climb in	*einsteigen*
to put your seat belt on	*sich seinen Gurt anlegen*
to steer	*lenken*
to turn the wheel	*das Lenkrad drehen*
to the left / to the right	*nach links / nach rechts*
to go round in circles	*im Kreis fahren*
to go the other way	*den anderen Weg fahren*
to accelerate	*beschleunigen*
to chase	*verfolgen*
to get stuck	*stecken bleiben*
to hit / to bump	*gegenfahren / stoßen*
Let's try to bump them.	*Wir versuchen sie zu stoßen.*
Please don't bump us.	*Bitte, stoßt uns nicht.*

The Waltzers	*Die Krake*
Where do you want to sit?	*Wo möchtest Du sitzen?*
Can I sit in the middle, please?	*Kann ich bitte in der Mitte sitzen?*
You're squashing me.	*Du drückst mich zusammen.*
Please twirl us some more.	*Wirbel uns bitte noch mehr herum.*
Please don't do that.	*Mach´ das bitte nicht.*

THE FAIR - RIDES cont.

DER RUMMELPLATZ -DIE FAHRTEN Forts

The Merry-go-Round	*Das Kinderkarussell*
Which horse / animal would you like to go on?	*Auf welchem Pferd / Tier möchtest Du gerne sitzen?*
Do you like to be on the inside or the outside?	*Möchtest Du lieber auf der Innenbahn oder auf der Außenbahn sitzen?*

The Rollercoaster	*Die Achterbahn*
to scream	*schreien*
to feel sick	*übel sein*
to hate it / to love it	*es hassen / es lieben*
to loop the loop	*sich einmal im Looping überschlagen*
to be upside down	*verkehrt herum sein*

The Helter Skelter	*eine Rutschbahn*
to take a mat	*Sich eine Matte nehmen*
to climb to the top	*nach oben steigen*
to slide down	*runterrutschen*

A Centrifuge	*Enterprise*
the centrifugal force	*die Zentrifugal- Kraft*
to be pinned to the side	*an die Seite gedrückt werden*

A simulator	*Ein Simulator*
realistic	*realistisch*
not very realistic	*nicht sehr realistisch*

THE FAIR cont.   *DER RUMMELPLATZ Forts.*

Darts and the rifle range	*Pfeilwerfen und der Schießstand*
a dart	*ein Pfeil*
a dartboard	*eine Zielscheibe*
to throw	*werfen*
to aim	*zielen*
to score	*treffen*
a gun / a rifle	*eine Luftpistole / ein Luftgewehr*
to point	*zielen*
to shoot	*schießen*
the target	*das Ziel*
to hit / to miss	*treffen / daneben treffen*
to hit the bull's eye	*das Auge des Stiers treffen*
I need twenty more.	*Ich brauche noch zwanzig.*
I have to score one hundred.	*Ich muß einhundert erreichen.*

Hoopla	*Ringe werfen*
to throw the ring	*den Ring werfen*
to get the ring over	*den Ring drüber bekommen*
nearly	*fast*
to win	*gewinnen*

A Coconut Shy	*Büchsenwerfen*
to throw a ball	*einen Ball werfen*
to try to hit	*versuchen zu treffen*
to throw harder	*härter werfen*
to make it wobble	*es zum Wackeln kriegen*
to knock it down	*es runter schlagen*
to fall off	*runterfallen*
to win a coconut	*eine Cocosnuß gewinnen*

THE FAIR cont.	DER RUMMELPLATZ Forts.
WINNING PRIZES	**PREISE GEWINNEN**

Well done!	Gut gemacht!
What prize would you like?	Welchen Preis möchtest Du / möchten Sie?
I would like a..	Ich möchte...
• goldfish	-einen Goldfisch
• a teddybear	-einen Teddybär
• one of those	-eins von diesen
Have you won anything yet?	Hast Du schon etwas gewonnen?
Yes, I've won this.	Ja, ich habe das gewonnen.
No, I never win anything.	Nein, ich gewinne nie etwas.

THE GAMES ARCADE **DIE SPIELHALLE**

I haven't any change.	Ich habe kein Kleingeld.
Where do you get change from?	Wo kann man sich Kleingeld besorgen?
There is a change machine over there.	Da vorne steht eine Wechselmaschine.
What coins does this game take?	Welche Münzen braucht man für dieses Spiel?
a fruit machine	ein einarmiger Bandit
a pinball machine	ein Flipper
Where do you put the money in?	Wo steckt man das Geld rein?
How do you play?	Wie spielt man es?
You have to…	Man muß...
to roll a coin	eine Münze rollen
to make it land on..	es auf..... landen zu lassen.
to pull this handle	diesen Griff ziehen
to press this button	diesen Knopf drücken

THE FAIR cont.   *DER RUMMELPLATZ Forts.*

FOOD   *ESSEN*

Candy Floss	*Zuckerwatte*
on a stick	*an einem Stab.*
in a bag	*in einer Tüte*
pink	*rosa*
yellow	*gelb*

Hot Dogs	*Hot Dogs*
Do you want your hot dog with..?	*Möchtest Du Deinen Hot Dog....... haben?*
• mustard	• *mit Senf*
• tomato ketchup	• *mit Tomaten Ketchup*
• fried onions	• *mit Zwiebeln*
• plain	• *ohne alles*
• a lot of	• *mit viel....*
• just a little	• *mit wenig....*
• no onions, thanks.	• *ohne Zwiebeln, danke.*

Popcorn	*Popcorn*
a bag of	*eine Tüte Popcorn*
a carton of	*ein Karton Popcorn*
large / medium / small	*groß / mittel / klein*
sweet	*süß*
salted	*salzig*
Would you like some of my popcorn?	*Möchtest Du etwas von meinem Popcorn?*

THE FAIR cont.
DER RUMMELPLATZ Forts.

PROBLEMS
PROBLEME

a pickpocket	*ein Taschendieb*
My money has been stolen.	*Man hat mir mein Geld gestohlen.*
Take care of your money.	*Paß auf Dein Geld auf.*
My purse / wallet has disappeared.	*Mein Portemonnaie / meine Brieftasche ist verschwunden.*
I feel dizzy / a bit sick.	*Mir ist schwindlig / mir ist schlecht.*
It's rather noisy.	*Es ist etwas laut.*
Can we go home soon?	*Können wir bald nach Hause gehen?*

USEFUL ADJECTIVES
NÜTZLICHE ADJEKTIVE

awful	*fürchterlich*	fun	*ein Spaß*
dizzy	*schwindlig*	funny	*lustig*
excellent	*ausgezeichnet*	horrible	*schrecklich*
fantastic	*phantastisch*	terrible	*furchtbar*
frightening	*beängstigend*	terrifying	*furchterregend*

THE CIRCUS
DER ZIRKUS

THE BIG TOP
DAS GROSSE ZIRKUSZELT

the ring	*die Manege*
sawdust	*Sägemehl*
the seats	*die Plätze*

THE PEOPLE
DIE LEUTE

The Ring Master	***Der Zirkusdirektor***
a top hat	*ein Zylinder*
a whip	*eine Peitsche*
to crack the whip	*die Peitsche knallen*

THE CIRCUS - THE PEOPLE cont.	*DER ZIRKUS - DIE LEUTE Forts.*

The Clown	*Der Clown*
a big nose	*eine große Nase*
big feet	*große Füße*
to walk on stilts	*auf Stelzen laufen*
to ride a monocycle	*ein Einrad fahren*
to trip up	*stürzen*
to fall down	*runterfallen*
to squirt water	*Wasser spritzen*
to make people laugh	*Leute zum Lachen bringen*

The Acrobats	*Die Akrobaten*
a trapeze artist	*ein Trapezkünstler*
the high wire	*das Hochseil*
a safety net	*ein Sicherheitsnetz*
a ladder	*eine Leiter*
a swing / to swing	*eine Schaukel / schaukeln*
to balance	*balancieren*
to wobble	*wackeln*
to fall	*fallen*

Other Circus Performers	*Andere Zirkusdarsteller*
a bareback rider	*ein Reiter ohne Sattel*
a lion tamer	*ein Löwenbändiger*

CIRCUS ANIMALS	*ZIRKUSTIERE*
a horse	*ein Pferd*
a lion	*ein Löwe*
an elephant	*ein Elefant*

THE ZOO   *DER ZOO*

PARTS OF THE ZOO   *ANLAGEN DES ZOOS*

the elephant house	*das Elefantenhaus*
the aquarium	*das Aquarium*
a tank	*ein Aquarium*
the cages / the monkeys' cage	*die Käfige / der Affenkäfig*
the reptile house	*Reptilien-Haus*
the model train	*die Kleinbahn*
Would you like a ride on the model train?	*Möchtest Du gerne mit der Kleinbahn fahren*
Do you want to go to the adventure playground?	*Möchtest Du auf den Abenteuerspielplatz gehen?*
a lake / an island	*ein See / eine Insel*
the cafeteria / the toilets	*die Cafeteria / die Toiletten*

THE ANIMALS (abc)   *DIE TIERE*

a bat	*eine Fledermaus*	a monkey	*ein Affe*
a bear	*ein Bär*	an ostrich	*ein Straußenvogel*
a crocodile	*ein Krokodil*	a panda	*ein Panda*
a dolphin	*ein Delphin*	a pelican	*ein Pelikan*
an elephant	*ein Elefant*	a penguin	*ein Pinguin*
an emu	*ein Emu*	a rhinoceros	*ein Rhinozeros*
a fish	*ein Fisch*	a seal	*ein Seehund*
a pink flamingo	*ein rosa Flamingo*	a snake	*eine Schlange*
a giraffe	*eine Giraffe*	a tarantula	*eine Tarantel*
a hippopotamus	*ein Nilpferd*	a tiger	*ein Tiger*
a kangaroo	*ein Känguruh*	a tortoise	*eine Schildkröte*
a leopard	*ein Leopard*	a turtle	*eine Meeresschildkröte*
a lion	*ein Löwe*	a zebra	*ein Zebra*

SIGHTSEEING
SEHENSWÜRDIGKEITEN

STATELY HOMES & CASTLES
LANDSITZE & BURGEN

OPENING HOURS	ÖFFNUNGSZEITEN
What are your opening hours?	*Wann sind Ihre Öffnungszeiten?*
Are you open every day of the week?	*Haben Sie jeden Tag geöffnet?*
How much is it to go round?	*Wieviel kostet es reinzugehen?*
Is there a guided tour?	*Gibt es eine Führung?*
What time is the tour?	*Wann beginnt die Führung?*
Is there a commentary one can listen to?	*Gibt es Erläuterungen, die man sich auf Tonband anhören kann.*
Do you have the commentary in English / French / Spanish / German?	*Haben Sie den Kommentar auf Englisch / Französisch / Spanisch / Deutsch?*
How do the headphones work?	*Wie funktionieren die Kopfhörer?*
Could I have a guide book, please?	*Könnte ich bitte einen Führer haben?*

COULD I HAVE A TICKET FOR...?	KANN ICH EINE EINTRITTSKARTE FÜR....HABEN?
• the house only	• *das Haus*
• the gardens only	• *die Gärten*
• one adult	• *einen Erwachsenen*
• one student	• *einen Studenten*
Is there a reduction for students / groups?	*Gibt es eine Ermäßigung für Schüler- / Gruppen?*

STATELY HOMES & CASTLES cont.

LANDSITZE & BURGEN Forts.

ARCHITECTURAL STYLES		*ARCHITEKTONISCHE STILRICHTUNGEN*	
Who was the architect?		*Wer war der Architekt?*	
What style was this built in?		*Nach welcher Stilrichtung wurde dies gebaut?*	
Norman	*frühmittelalterlich (Normannisch)*	Classical	*klassizistisch (Klassisch)*
medieval	*mittelalterlich*	Georgian	*klassizistisch (Georgianisch)*
gothic	*gotisch*		
Tudor	*spätgotisch*	Regency	*klassizistisch*
Renaissance	*Renaissance*	Victorian	*wilhelminisch-Gründerzeit*
Baroque	*Barock*		

TYPES OF BUILDINGS	*GEBÄUDEARTEN*
(in approximately descending size)	*(in abnehmender Größe)*
a palace / a castle	*ein Schloß / eine Burg*
a mansion	*ein herrschaftliches Haus*
the manor house	*ein Herrenhaus*
the court	*der fürstliche Hof*
a priory / the chapel	*ein Kloster / eine Kapelle*
the lodge / the gatehouse	*die Jagdhütte / das Pfortnerhäuschen*
a folly	*eine künstliche Ruine*
a conservatory	*ein Wintergarten*
a coach house / a coach	*ein Kutscherhaus / eine Kutsche*
a royal coach	*eine königliche Kutsche*
a thatched cottage	*eine strohbedecktes Bauernhaus*
a stable	*ein Stall*
a greenhouse	*ein Gewächshaus*

STATELY HOMES &
CASTLES cont.

LANDSITZE & BURGEN
Forts.

EXTERNAL DETAILS	ÄUSSERLICHE DETAILS
(top downwards)	*(von oben nach unten)*
a turret / battlements	*ein Türmchen / die Zinnen*
the parapet / a facade	*die Brüstung / eine Fassade*
a balcony	*ein Balkon*
the windows / French windows	*die Fenster / Französische Fenster*
the porch / the door	*das Portal / die Eingangstür*
a flight of steps	*ein Treppenhaus*
a portcullis / a drawbridge	*ein Fallgatter / eine Zugbrücke*
a moat / a rampart	*ein Burggraben / ein Schutzwall*
the gateway / floodlighting	*das Tor / die Beleuchtung*

THE PARK AND GARDENS	DER PARK UND DIE GÄRTEN
the park	*der Park*
the garden	*der Garten*
a formal garden	*ein gestalteter Garten*
a rose garden	*ein Rosengarten*
a knot garden	*ein Blütengarten*
a path	*ein Weg*
a terrace	*eine Terrasse*
an informal garden	*ein ungestalteter Garten*
a wild flower garden	*ein Wildblumen-garten*
a ha-ha	*eine Gartenlaube*

A MAZE	EIN IRRGARTEN
to go in	*reingehen*
to get lost	*verloren gehen*
to turn back	*zurückgehen*
to try to get out	*versuchen rauszukommen*
to find your way out	*seinen Weg nach draußen finden*
to be gone ages	*seit Ewigkeiten gelaufen sein*

**STATELY HOMES &
CASTLES cont.**

*LANDSITZE & BURGEN
Forts.*

GARDEN BUILDINGS AND ORNAMENTS	*GARTENGEBÄUDE UND VERZIERUNGEN*
a conservatory	*ein Wintergarten*
an orangery	*eine Orangerie*
a greenhouse	*ein Gewächshaus*
a dovecote / a dove	*ein Taubenschlag / eine Taube*
a statue	*eine Statue*
an urn	*eine Urne*
a pedestal	*ein Sockel*

WATER FEATURES	*WASSERMERKMALE*
a lake / an island	*ein See / eine Insel*
a river	*ein Fluß*
a fountain	*ein Springbrunnen*
a waterfall	*ein Wasserfall*
an ornamental pond	*ein Zierteich*
water lilies / goldfish	*Seerosen / Goldfische*
a water garden	*ein Wassergarten*
When are the fountains turned on?	*Wann sind die Springbrunnen angestellt?*

HIRING BOATS	*BOOTE AUSLEIHEN*
a boat / a motorboat	*ein Boot / ein Motorboot*
to go for a trip	*eine Fahrt machen*
to start the engine	*den Motor anwerfen*
a canoe / to go canoeing	*ein Kanu / Kanu fahren*
a paddle / to paddle	*ein Paddel / paddeln*
on the right / left	*rechts / links*
to steer	*lenken*
to row	*rudern*
to moor	*vertäuen*
to collide with someone	*mit jemanden zusammenstoßen*
to try to avoid someone	*jemandem ausweichen*

STATELY HOMES & CASTLES cont.	*LANDSITZE & BURGEN Forts.*

THE TEA ROOM	*DIE TEESTUBE*
Where is the tea room?	*Wo ist die Teestube?*
Shall we have a cup of tea?	*Sollen wir Tee trinken?*
Shall we take it into the garden?	*Sollen wir ihn in den Garten mitnehmen?*
Shall we stay inside?	*Sollen wir drinnen bleiben?*

THE GIFT SHOP	*DER SOUVENIR-LADEN*
Do you want to look round the gift shop?	*Möchtest Du Dich im Souvernir-Laden umschauen?*
Do you want to buy something for your family?	*Möchtest Du etwas für Deine Familie kaufen?*
Would you like to buy some postcards?	*Möchtest Du ein paar Postkarten kaufen?*

INTERNAL DETAILS	*INNENRÄUME*
THE MAIN ROOMS (in descending importance)	*DIE HAUPTRÄUME (in abnehmender Wichtigkeit)*

THE MAIN HALL	*DIE EINGANGSHALLE*
a suit of armour	*eine Rüstung*
chain mail	*ein Kettenpanzer*
heraldry / a coat of arms	*Wappenschilder / ein Wappen*
weapons / guns / pistols	*Waffen / Gewehre / Pistolen*
swords	*Schwerter*
shields	*Schutzschilder*

**STATELY HOMES &
CASTLES** cont.

*LANDSITZE & BURGEN
Forts.*

THE STATEROOM | | *DAS STAATSZIMMER* |
|---|---|---|---|
the mirrors | *die Spiegel* | the plasterwork | *der Stuck*
a portrait | *ein Porträt* | a mural | *die Wandgemälde*
the paintings | *die Gemälde* | a fresco | *ein Fresko*
a bust | *eine Büste* | the carpet | *der Teppich*
the fireplace | *der Kamin* | the curtains | *die Vorhänge*
the ceiling | *die Decke* | the furniture | *die Möbel*

THE BALLROOM	*DER BALLSAAL*
the chandelier	*der Kronleuchter*
the mirrors	*die Spiegel*

THE BANQUETING HALL | | *DER BANKETTSAAL* |
|---|---|---|---|
the dining table | *der Eßtisch* | the silver | *das Silber*
the chairs | *die Stühle* | the tureens | *die Terrinen*
a dinner service | *das Tafelgeschirr* | a banquet | *ein Bankett*

THE DRAWING ROOM | | *DER SALON* |
|---|---|---|---|
the panelling | *die Täfelung* | the armchairs | *die Sessel*
a grandfather clock | *eine Standuhr* | a tapestry | *ein Wandteppich*
the sofas | *eine Standuhr* | porcelain | *Porzellan (n)*

THE LIBRARY	*DIE BIBLIOTHEK*
the bookcases	*die Bücherschränke*
valuable books	*wertvolle Bücher*
antique books	*antike Bücher*
a family tree	*ein Familienstamm-baum*

**STATELY HOMES &
CASTLES cont.**

*LANDSITZE & BURGEN
Forts.*

THE MUSIC ROOM		*DAS MUSIKZIMMER*	
a harpsichord	*ein Cembalo*	a harp	*eine Harfe*

THE STAIRCASE & GALLERY	*DER TREPPENAUFGANG UND DIE GALERIE*
a spiral staircase	*eine Wendeltreppe*
a back staircase	*eine Hintertreppe*
a minstrels' gallery	*die Chorgalerie*
a servants' staircase	*die Dienstbot-entreppe*
a secret staircase	*eine Geheimtreppe*
to look down on	*hinunterschauen*

THE NURSERY	*DAS KINDERZIMMER*
a cradle / a cot	*eine Wiege / ein Kinderbettchen*
a dolls' house	*ein Puppenhaus*
toys	*Spielsachen*
a desk	*ein Schreibpult*
a rocking horse	*ein Schaukelpferd*

THE KITCHEN	*DIE KÜCHE*
a fireplace / an inglenook	*eine Feuerstelle / eine Kaminecke*
a hook / a rotisserie	*ein Haken / ein Drehspieß*
a spit / to turn	*ein Bratspieß / umdrehen*
to cook / to smoke	*kochen / rauchen*
the range	*der Herd*
a kitchen table	*ein Küchentisch*
pots and pans	*Töpfe und Pfannen*
the utensils	*die Küchengeräte*
copper / pewter	*Kupfer (n) / Zinn (n)*
the sink	*das Spülbecken*
the cold store	*die Vorratskammer*
a dumb waiter	*ein Teewagen*
the cook	*der Koch*

**STATELY HOMES &
CASTLES cont.**

*LANDSITZE & BURGEN
Forts.*

OTHER ROOMS — *ANDERE RÄUME*

Servants' accommodation — *Dienstbotenunterkunft*
the servants' rooms — *die Dienstbotenzimmer*
the attic — *das Dachgeschoß*

The cellar — *Der Keller*
a wine cellar — *ein Weinkeller*

The dungeons — *Der Kerker*
the torture chamber — *die Folterkammer*
a chamber of horrors — *eine Schreckenskammer*

THE ROYAL FAMILY — *DIE KÖNIGLICHE FAMILIE*

a King	*ein König*	a Prince	*ein Prinz*
a Queen	*eine Königen*	a Princess	*eine Prinzessin*
the Queen Mother	*die Königenmutter*	a Duke / Duchess	*ein Herzog / eine Herzogin*

THE SERVANTS — *DIE DIENERSCHAFT*

the butler	*der Butler*	the footmen	*der Bedienstete*
the chef	*der Küchenchef*	a maidservant	*ein Dienstmädchen*
the cook	*der Koch*	a manservant	*ein Diener*

STATELY HOMES & CASTLES cont.

LANDSITZE & BURGEN Forts.

USEFUL DESCRIPTIVE WORDS (abc)		*NÜTZLICHE BESCHREIBUNGEN*	
added on	*hinzugefügt*	dilapidated	*zerfallen*
ancient	*altertümlich*	dusty	*eingestaubt*
attractive	*reizvoll*	elegant	*elegant*
austere	*karg*	expensive	*teuer*
authentic	*authentisch*	faded	*verblaßt*
baroque	*barock*	gold	*Gold*
beautiful	*schön*	gothic	*gotisch*
built by	*gebaut von*	imposing	*imposant*
burnt down	*niedergebrannt*	in ruins	*in Ruinen*
century	***Jahrhundert***	luxurious	*luxuriös*
eleventh	*elftes*	modern	*modern*
twelfth	*zwölftes*	modernised	*modernisiert*
thirteenth	*dreizehntes*	old	*alt*
fourteenth	*vierzehntes*	ornate	*überladen*
fifteenth	*fünfzehntes*	over-restored	*restauriert*
sixteenth	*sechzehntes*	rare	*selten*
seventeenth	*siebzehntes*	rebuilt	*wiederauf-gebaut*
eighteenth	*achtzehntes*	reclaimed	*zurückgeführt*
nineteenth	*neunzehntes*	restored by	*wiederher-gestellt von*
twentieth	*zwanzigstes*	ruined	*verfallen*
twenty first	*einund-zwanzigstes*	splendid	*prächtig*
charming	*bezaubernd*	sumptuous	*kostbar*
commonplace	*alltäglich*	valuable	*wertvoll*
designed by	*entworfen von*	wonderful	*wundervoll*

CHURCHES *KIRCHEN*

ARCHITECTURAL CLASSIFICATIONS	*ARCHITEKTONISCHE EINTEILUNG*
Romanesque	*Romanisch*
Saxon	*Saxon*
Norman	*frühmittel-alterlich (Normannisch)*
Gothic	*Gotisch*
Early English	*Früh Englisch*
Decorated	*Spätgotik (Dekorativ)*
Perpendicular	*Spätgotik (Perpendicular)*
Tudor	*Spätgotik (Tudor)*
Flamboyant	*Spätgotisch (flamboyant)*
Jacobean	*Jakobean*
Renaissance	*Renaissance*
Baroque	*Barock*
Classical	*klassizistisch (Klassisch)*
Georgian	*klassizistisch (Georgianisch)*
Victorian	*wilhelminisch-Gründerzeit (Viktorianisch)*

EXTERNAL DETAILS	*ÄUSSERE DETAILS*
a buttress	*ein Strebepfeiler*
a flying buttress	*ein Schwibbogen*
a gargoyle	*ein Wasserspeier*
a pinnacle	*eine Fiale*
a spire / a tower	*eine Kirchturmspitze / ein Turm*
a weathercock	*ein Wetterhahn*
the churchyard / a grave	*der Kirchhof / ein Grab*
a tombstone	*ein Grabstein*
an inscription	*eine Inschrift*
to read	*lesen*
Roman numerals	*römische Zahlen*

CHURCHES cont.   *KIRCHEN Forts.*

INTERNAL DETAILS (abc)	*INNERE DETAILS*
alabaster	*Alabaster*
an arcade / an arch	*ein Säulengang / ein Bogen*
the aisle	*das Seitenschiff*
the altar / to kneel at / to pray	*der Altar / knien vor / beten*
the bell tower / a bell	*der Glockenturm / eine Glocke*
to ring the bells	*die Glocken läuten*
a candle / to buy / to light	*eine Kerze / kaufen / anzünden*
the chancel	*der Altarraum*
the choir / a choir stall	*der Chor / das Chorgestühl*
a column	*ein Pfeiler*
The Cross	*das Kreuz*
the crypt	*die Krypta*
the door / the porch	*die Tür / das Portal*
the font / a Baptism	*der Taufstein / eine Taufe*
a fresco / a mural	*ein Fresko / ein Wandgemälde*
the Lady Chapel	*die Marienkapelle*
the lectern	*das Chorpult*
marble	*Marmor*
the nave	*das Hauptschiff*
a niche	*eine Nische*
the organ / the organist	*die Orgel / der Organist*
to play the organ	*die Orgel spielen*
a pew	*ein Kirchenstuhl*
a pillar	*eine Säule*
the pulpit / to give a sermon	*die Kanzel / eine Predigt halten*
to preach	*predigen*
the roof / a beam	*das Dach / ein Balken*
a vault	*ein Gewölbe*
a statue	*eine Statue*
a tomb	*eine Grabstätte*
the transept	*das Querschiff*
a window / stained glass	*ein Fenster / bemaltes Fensterglas*

CHURCHES cont.   *KIRCHEN Forts.*

USEFUL DESCRIPTIVE WORDS (abc)		*NÜTZLICHE BESCHREIBUNGEN*	
cold	*kalt*	musty	*muffig*
dark	*dunkel*	open	*offen*
dilapidated	*zerfallen*	ornate	*kunstvoll*
elegant	*elegant*	peaceful	*friedlich*
humble	*bescheiden*	rich	*reich*
intricate	*kompliziert*	rural	*ländlich*
locked-up	*eingeschlossen*	sombre	*düster*

ART GALLERIES & EXHIBITIONS
KUNSTERGALERIEN UND AUSTELLUNGEN

ART GALLERIES	*KUNSTGALERIEN*
an art collection	*eine Kunstsammlung*
an artist	*ein Künstler*
a work of art	*ein Kunstwerk*
a painting	*ein Gemälde*
a private view	*Besichtigung durch geladene Gäste*
an invitation	*eine Einladung*

MUSEUMS	*MUSEEN*
an exhibition	*eine Ausstellung*
an exhibit	*ein Ausstellungsstück*

USEFUL EXPRESSIONS	*NÜTZLICHE AUSDRÜCKE*
There is an interesting exhibition on at the moment.	*Es läuft gerade eine interessante Ausstellung.*
Would you like to go to it?	*Möchtest Du sie gerne anschauen?*
Is there a catalogue?	*Gibt es einen Katalog?*
How much is an entrance ticket?	*Wieviel kostet die Eintrittskarte?*
Is there a reduction for students?	*Gibt es eine Ermäßigung für Schüler?*
Entrance is free.	*Der Eintritt ist frei*
How much do guide books cost?	*Wieviel kosten die Museumsführer?*
How much are these postcards?	*Wieviel kosten diese Postkarten?*
Do you have a guide book in English / French / German / Spanish?	*Haben sie einen Führer in Englisch / Französisch / Deutsch / Spanisch?*
Shall we split up and meet here in half an hour?	*Sollen wir uns trennen und uns in einer halben Stunde hier wiedertreffen?*

ART GALLERIES cont.

KUNSTGALERIEN Forts.

WHO / WHAT IS YOUR FAVOURITE..?		WER / WAS IST DEIN LIEBLINGS....?	
artist	*Künstler*	painting	*Bild (n)*
sculptor	*Bildhauer*	piece of sculpture	*Skulptur (f)*

WHAT TYPE OF ART DO YOU LIKE MOST? (abc)	WELCHE KUNSTRICHTUNG HAST DU AM LIEBSTEN?
abstract art	*Abstrakte Kunst (f)*
art deco	*Art-Deco (f)*
classical art	*Klassische Kunst (f)*
cubism	*Kubismus (m)*
engravings	*Stiche (m)*
etchings	*Radierungen (f)*
expressionism / impressionism	*Expressionismus/ Impressionismus*
landscapes	*Landschaften (f)*
life drawings	*Aktzeichnungen (f)*
miniatures / nudes	*Miniaturen (f) / Akt (m)*
oil paintings / water colours	*Ölgemälde (n) / Aquarell-malerei (f)*
pastels	*Pastellarbeiten (n)*
pop art	*Pop-Art*
portraits / self portraits	*Porträts (n) / Selbstportraits*
post-impressionism	*Post-Impressionismus (m)*
Pre-Raphaelite	*Präraffaeliten*
primitive art	*Primitive Kunst*
prints	*Drucke (m)*
realism	*Realismus (m)*
religious art	*Religiöse Kunst*
romantic art	*Romantische Kunst*
seascapes / townscapes	*Seestücke / Stadtlandschaften*
sporting works / still life	*Sportmalerei / Stilleben (n)*
surrealism / symbolism	*Surrealismus / Symbolismus*
wood cuttings	*Holzschnitte (m)*

ART GALLERIES cont. / *KUNSTGALERIEN Forts.*

WHAT IS YOUR FAVOURITE PERIOD? / *WELCHE PERIODE HAST DU AM LIEBSTEN?*

My favourite period is..	*Meine Lieblingsperiode ist...*
medieval	*das Mittelalter*
Renaissance	*die Renaissance*
High Renaissance	*die Hoch-Renaissance*
Baroque	*das Barocke*
eighteenth century	*das achtzehnte Jahrhundert*
nineteenth century	*das neunzehnte Jahrhundert*
twentieth century	*das zwanzigste Jahrhundert*

WHAT IS YOUR FAVOURITE MEDIUM? / *WELCHE TECHNIK HAST DU AM LIEBESTEN?*

I particularly like.. / *Am liebsten habe ich...*

acrylics	*Acrylfarben*	oil	*Öl*
chalk	*Kreide*	pastels	*Pastellfarbe*
charcoal	*Kohle*	tempera	*Tempera*
crayon	*Bleistift*	water colours	*Aquarellfarben*
gouache	*Bleistift*		

POSSIBLE POINTS FOR DISCUSSION (abc) / *MÖGLICHE DISKUSSIONSPUNKTE*

the allegorical meaning	*eine allegorische Bedeutung*
the background / the foreground	*der Hintergrund/ der Vordergrund*
the colour	*die Farbe*
the delicacy	*die Feinheit*
the effect on the viewer	*die Wirkung auf den Betrachter*
the emotion	*die Emotion*
the focus	*der Schwerpunkt*
the grouping	*die Anordnung*
the light and shade	*das Licht und der Schatten*
the meaning	*die Absicht*
the obscurity	*die Verborgenheit*

ART GALLERIES cont.
KUNSTGALERIEN Forts.

POSSIBLE POINTS FOR DISCUSSION (abc)
MÖGLICHE DISKUSSIONSPUNKTE

the poses	die Posen
the power	die Kraft
the structure	die Struktur
the subtlety	die Feinheiten
the suffering	das Mitfühlen
the symbolism	der Symbolismus
the technique	die Technik
the use of perspective	der Gebrauch der Perspektive
the vanishing point	der Fluchtpunkt

BASIC ART EQUIPMENT
DIE GRUNDAUSRÜSTUNG DES KÜNSTLERS

an easel	eine Staffelei
paper	Papier
canvas	Leinwand
paints / a paintbrush	Farben / ein Pinsel
a palette knife	ein Palettenmesser
a pencil	ein Bleistift
a rubber	ein Radiergummi
a water pot / white spirit	ein Wassergefäß / Terpentin

PAINTING METHODS
MALTECHNIKEN

to blend	vermengen	to mix	vermischen
to copy	kopieren	to paint over	übermalen
to dab	tupfen	to re-paint	neu malen
to dip	tunken	to sketch	skizzieren
to glaze	lasieren	to varnish	tünchen
to imitate	imitieren	to wash	mit Farbe überziehen

ART GALLERIES cont.   *KUNSTGALERIEN Forts.*

ART CLASSIFICATIONS	*KUNST-KLASSIFIZIERUNGEN*
Fine Art	*Malerei*
Applied Art	***Angewandte Kunst***
jewellery	*Goldschmiedekunst*
silversmithing	*Silberschmiedkunst*
porcelain making	*Porzellanherstellung*
metalwork	*Metallarbeiten*
pottery	*Töpfern*
Decorative Art	***Dekorative Kunst***
embroidery	*Stickerei*
tapestry	*Tapisserie*

VINEYARDS
WEINGÄRTEN

THE VINEYARD	*DER WEINBERG*
a chateau	*ein Schloß*

THE VINES	*DIE WEINREBEN*
a grapevine	*ein Weinstock*
a bunch of grapes	*Weintraube*
a grape	*eine Traube*
green / purple	*grün / rot*

VINEYARDS cont.   *WEINGÄRTEN Forts.*

PICKING THE GRAPES	*DIE WEINLESE*
ripe	*reif*
unripe	*unreif*
to harvest	*Ernten*
to pick	*pflücken*
to gather	*sammeln*
to press	*pressen*
the juice	*der Saft*

STORING THE WINE		*WEIN LAGERN*	
a barrel	*ein Faß*	to ferment	*gären*
wooden	*Hölzern*	fermentation	*Gärung*
oak	*Eiche*	to bottle	*abfüllen*
steel	*Stahl*	a bottle	*eine Flasche*
a vat	*ein Bottich*	to label	*beschriften*
a vatful	*ein Bottich voll*	a label	*ein Etikett*

CLASSIFYING WINE	*WEIN KLASSIFIZIEREN*
an officially classified wine	*ein offiziell eingestufter Wein*
alcoholic content	*alkoholisch Inhalt (m)*
vintage	*Jahrgang (m)*
a good year / a bad year	*ein gutes / ein schlechtes Jahr*
country of origin	*das Herstellungs-land*
region	*Region / Lage*
a table wine	*ein Tischwein*
red wine / white wine / rosé wine	*Rotwein / Weißwein / Rosé*
sweet wine / dry wine	*süßer Wein / trockener Wein*
sparkling wine	*Sekt*
champagne	*Champagner*
fortified wine	*angereicherter Wein*
an aperitif	*ein Aperitif*
sherry	*Sherry*
vermouth	*Wermut*

VINEYARDS cont.   *WEINGÄRTEN Forts.*

SERVING WINE	*WEIN AUSSCHENKEN*
to serve at the right temperature	*mit der richtigen Temperatur ausschenken*
to keep at room temperature	*bei Raumtemperatur lagern*
to chill	*kühlen*
to open a bottle	*eine Flasche öffnen*
to uncork	*entkorken*
a corkscrew	*ein Korkenzieher*
to decant	*umfüllen / dekantieren*
sediment	*Bodensatz*
to allow to breathe	*atmen lassen*
to pour	*gießen*

TASTING WINE	*WEIN PROBIEREN*
a wine tasting	*eine Weinprobe*
to savour	*kosten*
the bouquet	*das Bouquet*
the colour	*die Farbe*
to hold up to the light	*gegen das Licht halten*
to hold in the mouth	*schmecken*
to spit	*spucken*
a spittoon	*ein Spucknapf*
to sample	*prüfen*
to identify	*einschätzen*
to appreciate	*anerkennen*
to have a good palate	*einen guten Geschmack haben*

WALKS

WANDERUNGEN

A WALK	*EINE WANDERUNG / EIN SPAZIERGANG*
Would you like to go for a walk?	*Möchtest Du eine Wanderung machen / spazierengehen?*
How far do you feel like going?	*Wie weit möchtest Du gehen?*
Where would you like to go to?	*Wohin möchtest Du gehen?*
Do you like walking?	*Wanderst Du gerne / gehst Du gerne spazieren?*

TAKING THE DOG	*DEN HUND MITNEHMEN*
I'm taking the dog for a walk.	*Ich gehe den Hund ausführen.*
Would you like to come?	*Kommst Du mit?*
Where is its lead?	*Wo ist seine Hundeleine?*
How do you put on its lead?	*Wie befestigt man seine Leine?*
May I hold the lead?	*Kann ich die Leine halten?*
Don't let it off the lead here.	*Laß ihn hier nicht von der Leine.*
You can let it off the lead now.	*Du kannst ihn jetzt von der Leine lassen.*
Dogs must be kept on the lead.	*Hunde müssen an der Leine geführt werden.*

CLOTHES	*KLEIDUNG*
Footwear	***Das Schuhwerk***
socks / shoes / boots / wellingtons	*Strümpfe/ Schuhe/ Stiefel/ Regenstiefel*
Have you any walking shoes / boots / wellingtons with you?	*Hast Du Wanderschuhe / Stiefel / Regenstiefel dabei?*
Would you like to borrow a pair of wellingtons?	*Möchtest Du Dir ein Paar Regenstiefel borgen?*
We may have some that fit you.	*Vielleicht haben wir welche, die Dir passen.*
Try these. / Do they fit?	*Probier´ diese hier an./Passen sie?*
Are they comfortable?	*Sind sie bequem?*
They are too small / too big.	*Sie sind zu groß / zu klein.*

WALKS cont.   *WANDERUNGEN Forts.*

Clothes for bad weather	*Kleidung für schlechtes Wetter*
Bring...	*Bring....mit.*
a coat	*einen Mantel*
a jacket	*eine Jacke*
a mackintosh	*einen Regenmantel*
a pullover / a sweater	*einen Pullover / ein Sweatshirt*
trousers	*ein Paar Hosen*
a hat	*einen Hut*
a scarf	*einen Schal*
a pair of gloves	*ein Paar Handschuhe*
an umbrella	*einen Regenschirm*
spare clothes	*Ersatzkleider*

PICNICS   *EIN PICKNICK*

Shall we take a picnic?	*Sollen wir ein Picknick machen?*
Help me pack the picnic.	*Hilf mir den Picknickkorb zu packen.*
What would you like to eat and drink?	*Was möchtest Du gerne essen und trinken?*
Shall we stop for something to eat and drink now?	*Sollen wir jetzt anhalten, um etwas zu essen und zu trinken?*
Shall we take a rug?	*Sollen wir eine Decke ausbreiten?*
to sit down for a while	*sich eine Zeitlang hinsetzen*

PICNIC FOOD & DRINK   *ESSEN UND TRINKEN AUS DEM PICKNICKKORB*

a flask	*eine Thermoskanne*
to fill	*füllen*
to pour	*gießen*
a hot drink	*ein heißes Getränk*
a cold drink	*ein kaltes Getränk*
to be thirsty	*Durst haben*
to be hungry	*Hunger haben*

WALKS cont.	*WANDERUNGEN Forts.*
PICNIC FOOD & DRINK cont.	***ESSEN UND TRINKEN AUS DEM PICKNICKKORB Forts***

sandwiches	*belegte Brote*
What do you want on your sandwiches?	*Was möchtest Du auf deinem Brot haben?*
ham / chicken / salami / cheese / fish / salad / tomato / egg / mayonnaise	*Schinken / Huhn / Salami / Käse / Fisch / Salat / Tomaten / Ei / Mayonnaise*
a packet of crisps	*eine Packung Chips*
a piece of cake	*ein Stück Kuchen*
some fruit	*Obst*
an apple / a banana / an orange / some grapes	*ein Apfel / eine Banane / eine Orange / Trauben*
a bar of chocolate	*eine Tafel Schokolade*
Would you like a piece of chocolate?	*Möchtest Du ein Stück Schokolade haben?*

DISCUSSING THE ROUTE	***DIE STRECKE FESTLEGEN***
a plan / a sketch	*ein Plan / eine Wegbeschreibung*
a map / directions	*eine Karte / Richtungen*
Where are we?	*Wo sind wir?*
Show me where we are going to go.	*Zeig' mir wohin wir gehen.*
How far is that?	*Wie weit ist das?*
Are we lost?	*Haben wir uns verlaufen?*
Are we going in the right / wrong direction?	*Laufen wir in die richtige / falsche Richtung?*
Shall we ask someone?	*Sollen wir jemanden fragen?*
to use a compass	*einen Kompaß benutzen*
the needle / to point	*die Nadel / zeigen*
North / South / East / West	*Norden / Süden / Osten / Westen*
We need to go in this direction.	*Wir müssen in diese Richtung gehen.*

WALKS cont. *WANDERUNGEN Forts.*

PROBLEMS	*PROBLEME*
Is there a telephone box?	*Gibt es hier eine Telefonzelle?*
Could we possibly use your telephone, please?	*Könnten wir bitte Ihr Telefon benutzen?*
We are lost.	*Wir haben uns verlaufen.*
We are trying to get to…	*Wir versuchen nach….zu kommen.*
Where is the pub?	*Wo ist das Wirtshaus?*
Is there a village shop?	*Gibt es hier einen Dorfladen?*
I am tired.	*Ich bin müde.*
My legs are aching.	*Meine Beine tun mir weh.*
I have a blister.	*Ich habe eine Blase.*
My shoes are rubbing.	*Meine Schuhe drücken.*
I fell over.	*Ich bin hingefallen.*
It's just a graze.	*Es ist nur eine Schramme.*
Have you a sticking plaster / an Elastoplast?	*Hast Du ein Heftpflaster / ein Hansaplast?*
I hurt my foot / leg / hand / arm / back.	*Ich habe mir meinen Fuß / mein Bein / meine Hand / meinen Arm / meinen Rücken verletzt.*
I have sprained my ankle.	*Ich habe mir meinen Knöchel verstaucht.*
I have been stung.	*Ich bin gestochen worden.*
I have been bitten by something.	*Ich bin von etwas gebissen worden*
Have you anything to put on a sting?	*Hast Du irgendwas zum auftragen auf Stiche dabei?*
Have you any insect repellent?	*Hast Du Anti-Mückensalbe dabei?*

WALKS cont.	*WANDERUNGEN Forts.*
LANDMARKS	***ORIENTIERUNGSPUNKTE***

BUILDINGS etc (abc)	***GEBÄUDE usw.***
a chemist's shop	*eine Apotheke*
the church	*die Kirche*
a cottage	*ein Landhaus*
the graveyard	*der Friedhof*
a house	*ein Haus*
the manor house	*das Herrschaftshaus*
a newsagent's shop	*ein Zeitungsladen*
the playground	*der Spielplatz*
the police station	*eine Polizeiwache*
a post box	*ein Briefkasten*
the post office	*die Post*
the railway station	*der Bahnhof*
the recreation ground	*der Sportplatz*
a shop	*ein Laden*
the telephone box	*die Telefonzelle*
the village green	*der Dorfplatz*
the village hall	*das Rathaus*
the village school	*die Dorfschule*
the village shop	*der Dorfladen*

TYPES OF ROAD	***STRASSENARTEN***
a signpost	*ein Hinweisschild*
to point the way to..	*den Weg nach....anzeigen*
a road	*eine Straße*
a main road	*die Hauptstraße*
a "B" road / a minor road	*eine Landstraße / eine Nebenstraße*
a lane	*ein Feldweg*
a bridleway	*ein Reitweg*
a rough track	*ein Holperweg*
a footpath	*ein Gehweg*

WALKS cont.   *WANDERUNGEN Forts.*

OBSTACLES		*HINDERNISSE*	
a stile	*eine Zaunsteige*	a bog	*ein Sumpf*
a gate	*ein Tor*	a cowpat	*eine Kuhflade*
a wall	*eine Mauer*	a railway	*eine Eisenbahn*
a cattle grid	*ein Kuhgatter*	a railway bridge	*ein Eisenbahnbrücke*

FARMS	*BAUERNHÖFE*
a farmhouse	*ein Bauernhaus*
a farmyard	*ein Bauernhof*
the farmer	*der Bauer*
the dairy / the cowshed	*die Molkerei / der Kuhstall*
a hen coop	*ein Hühnerstall*
a hen / an egg	*ein Huhn / eine Henne / ein Ei*
to collect the eggs / a basket	*die Eier einsammeln / ein Korb*
the barn / a hayloft	*die Scheune / der Heuboden*
a stable / a trough	*ein Stall / ein Trog*

WATER	*WASSER*
a river / a stream / a ford	*ein Fluß / ein Strom / eine Furt*
a canal / a barge	*ein Kanal / ein Kanalboot*
a lock / the lock keeper	*eine Schleuse/der Schleusenwärter*
the towpath	*der Schlepperweg*
a lake / an island	*ein See / eine Insel*
a pond	*ein Teich*
a puddle	*eine Pfütze*
a waterfall	*ein Wasserfall*
rapids / the current	*Stromschnellen / die Strömung*
strong / fast	*stark / schnell*
dangerous	*gefährlich*

WALKS cont. *WANDERUNGEN Forts.*

CROSSING WATER *WASSER ÜBERQUEREN*

stepping stones	*Trittsteine*
slippery / wobbly	*glitschig / wacklig*
to tread on / to jump	*drauftreten / springen*
a bridge	*eine Brücke*
a footbridge	*eine Fußgängerbrücke*
to cross	*überqueren*

PADDLING *IM WASSER PLANSCHEN*

Shall we paddle?	*Sollen wir im Wasser planschen?*
Take off your socks and shoes.	*Zieh' Deine Strümpfe und Schuhe aus.*
Have you got a towel?	*Hast Du ein Handtuch?*
Dry your feet here.	*Trockne hier Deine Füße:*
It's freezing / quite warm.	*Es ist kalt / warm.*
It's deep / shallow.	*Es ist tief / flach.*
It's pebbly / muddy.	*Es ist steinig / schlammig.*

HIGH GROUND *ANHÖHEN*

a mountain / to climb	*ein Berg / klettern*
to go to the top	*auf den Gipfel gehen*
to see the view	*die Aussicht genießen*
panorama / spectacular	*ein Panorama / spektakulär*
Can you see..?	*Kannst Du...sehen?*
on the horizon / in the distance	*am Horizont / in der Ferne*
over there	*dort drüben*
a steep slope	*ein Steilhang*
to be careful	*vorsichtig sein*
a hill / a gentle slope	*ein Hügel / ein sanfter Hang*
a valley	*ein Tal*
a tunnel / to hide	*ein Tunnel / verstecken*
a cave / dark /	*eine Höhle / dunkel*
to echo	*ein Echo hören*

WALKS cont. *WANDERUNGEN Forts.*

FIELDS etc.		FELDER usw.	
a meadow	*eine Wiese*	unploughed	*ungepflügt*
a field	*ein Feld*	sown	*besät*
ploughed	*gepflügt*	a valley	*ein Tal*

WALKING CONDITIONS		WANDERBEDINGUNGEN	
muddy	*schlammig*	tiring	*anstrengend*
slippery	*rutschig*	boring	*langweilig*
steep	*steil*	good	*gut*
flooded	*überschwemmt*	perfect	*perfekt*

WEATHER CONDITIONS *WITTERUNG*

Hot	Heiß
It's very sunny.	*Es ist sehr sonnig.*
It's stuffy.	*Es ist schwül.*
It may thunder.	*Ein Gewitter könnte aufziehen.*
It is too hot for me.	*Es ist zu heiß für mich.*
Can we go into the shade for a bit?	*Können wir eine Weile im Schatten gehen?*
I am boiling.	*Ich bin glühendheiß.*

Cold	Kalt
It's freezing.	*Es ist kalt.*
It's icy.	*es ist eisig.*
It's rather slippery.	*Es ist etwas rutschig.*
Shall we slide on the ice?	*Sollen wir auf dem Eis schlittern?*
I am frozen.	*Ich friere*

WALKS cont.   *WANDERUNGEN Forts.*

WEATHER CONDITIONS cont.   *WITTERUNG Forts.*

Wet	*Naß*
It's beginning to rain.	*Es fängt an zu regnen.*
It's drizzling.	*Es nieselt.*
It's pouring down.	*Es schüttet.*
Everywhere is very muddy.	*Überall ist es sehr schlammig.*
I am soaked.	*Ich bin durchnäßt.*
My feet are wet.	*Meine Füße sind naß.*
It may stop raining soon.	*Vielleicht hört es bald auf zu regnen.*
Shall we shelter here until it stops raining?	*Sollen wir uns hier unterstellen, bis der Regen aufhört?*

Thunder	*Gewitter*
Did you hear the thunder?	*Hast Du den Donner gehört?*
I think there's going to be a thunderstorm.	*Ich glaube ein Gewitter zieht auf.*
It just lightened.	*Es hat gerade geblitzt.*
Count how long between the flash and the thunder.	*Zähle die Sekunden zwischen Blitz und Donner.*
It's a long way away.	*Es ist noch weit weg.*
It's very close.	*Es ist sehr nah.*
We had better get back.	*Wir sollten lieber zurückgehen.*

TREES   *BÄUME*

a forest	*ein großer Wald*
a wood	*ein Wald*
a tree	*ein Baum*
a bush	*einen Busch*

WALKS cont.   *WANDERUNGEN Forts.*

Parts of Trees	**Teile des Baumes**
the trunk	*der Stamm*
massive / strong	*massiv / kräftig*
a hollow trunk / rotten	*ein hohler Stamm / verfault*
a branch / a twig / a leaf	*ein Ast / ein Zweig / ein Blatt*

Climbing trees		**Auf Bäume klettern**	
to climb up	*hoch klettern*	to grasp	*greifen*
to swing from	*schwingen von*	to get a foothold	*Fuß fassen*

TYPES OF TREES	*BAUMARTEN*		
deciduous	*Laubbaum*	ivy	*Efeu (m)*
evergreen	*Immergrün*	mountain ash	*Bergesche (f)*
ash	*Esche (f)*	oak	*Eiche (f)*
beech	*Buche (f)*	pine	*Kiefer(f)*
birch	*Birke (f)*	silver birch	*Silberburke (f)*
Christmas	*Weihnachtsbaum- m*	spruce	*Rottanne (f)*
fir	*Fichte (f)*	sycamore	*Platane (f)*
hawthorn	*Hagedorn (m)*	weeping willow	*Trauerweide (f)*
holly	*Stechpalme (f)*	yew	*Eibe (f)*

WALKS cont.   *WANDERUNGEN Forts.*

ANIMALS (abc)	*TIERE*
a badger	*ein Dachs*
a cow / a bull	*eine Kuh / ein Bulle*
a bullock / a calf	*ein Ochse / ein Kalb*
a herd of cows	*eine Kuhherde*
a dog	*ein Hund*
a fox	*ein Fuchs*
a goat	*eine Ziege*
a hare	*ein Hase*
a rabbit / a rabbit hole	*ein Kaninchen/ ein Kaninchenloch*
a burrow / a rabbit warren	*ein Bau / ein Kaninchenstall*
a sheep / a ram	*ein Schaf / ein Widder*
a ewe / a lamb	*ein Mutterschaf / ein Lamm*
a flock	*eine Schafherde*

BIRDS (abc)	*VÖGEL*
a blackbird	*eine Amsel*
a duck / a drake	*eine Ente / ein Enterich*
a duckling	*ein Entchen*
a goose / a gosling	*eine Gans / ein Gänschen*
a hen / a cock	*eine Henne / ein Hahn*
a chicken	*ein Huhn*
a kingfisher	*ein Eisvogel*
a peacock / a peahen	*ein Pfau / eine Pfauhenne*
tail feathers / to display	*Pfauenfeder / entfalten*
a robin	*ein Rotkehlchen*
a swallow	*eine Schwalbe*
a swan / a cygnet	*ein Schwan / ein junger Schwan*
a thrush	*eine Drossel*

WALKS cont.   *WANDERUNGEN Forts.*

BIRDS & THEIR ACTIONS	*VÖGEL & IHRE GEWOHNHEITEN*
to fly / to learn to fly	*fliegen / das Fliegen lernen*
to sing / to whistle / to chirp	*singen / pfeifen / zwitschern*
to build a nest / to lay an egg	*ein Nest bauen / ein Ei legen*
to hatch out	*ausschlüpfen*

FEEDING BIRDS	*VÖGEL FÜTTERN*
Shall we take some bread for the birds?	*Sollen wir etwas Brot für die Vögel mitnehmen?*
Did you bring some bread?	*Hast Du Brot dabei?*
Would you like to give them some?	*Möchtest Du ihnen etwas geben?*
to throw	*werfen*

INSECTS		*INSEKTEN*	
an ant	*eine Ameise*	a spider	*eine Spinne*
a bee	*eine Biene*	a spider's web	*ein Spinnennetz*
to sting	*stechen*	a fly	*eine Fliege*
to buzz	*summen*	a wasp	*eine Wespe*

FRUIT PICKING	*OBST PFLÜCKEN*
Would you like to go fruit picking?	*Möchtest Du gerne Obst pflücken gehen?*
I want to make jam.	*Ich möchte Marmelade machen.*
to pick	*pflücken*
Pick one's that are ripe/ sweet / sour.	*Pflücke welche, die reif / süß / sauer sind*
I don't want them too ripe / unripe.	*Ich mag sie nicht, wenn sie zu reif / unreif sind.*

WALKS cont.   *WANDERUNGEN Forts.*

FRUIT PICKING cont.   *OBST PFLÜCKEN Forts.*

to put in a basket	*in einen Korb legen*
How many have you got?	*Wieviele hast Du?*
I think we need a few more.	*Ich glaube, wir brauchen noch mehr.*
That is probably enough now.	*Das reicht wahrscheinlich.*
There are a lot over here.	*Dort drüben gibt es viele.*
Don't eat too many.	*Iß nicht zu viele.*

Kinds of Fruit	***Obstsorten***
apples	*Äpfel (m)*
blackberries	*Brombeeren (f)*
blackcurrants	*Schwarze Johannisbeeren (f)*
cherries	*Kirschen (m)*
gooseberries	*Stachelbeeren (f)*
raspberries	*Himbeeren (f)*
redcurrants	*Rote Johannisbeeren (f)*
strawberries	*Erdbeeren (f)*

PHOTOGRAPHY
FOTOGRAFIEREN UND FILMEN

TAKING PHOTOGRAPHS	*FOTOS MACHEN*
May I take a picture of you, please?	*Darf ich bitte ein Foto von Dir machen?*
Could you take a picture of me, please?	*Kannst Du bitte ein Foto von mir machen?*
Can you wait for a second while I take a photograph?	*Kannst Du eine Sekunde warten, während ich das Foto mache?*
Can you stand / sit over there, please?	*Stell / setz' Dich bitte dort drüben hin.*
Could you move a little closer together, please?	*Könnt ihr bitte etwas mehr zusammenrücken?*
Could you try to smile?	*Bitte lächeln!*
Can you try to keep still, please?	*Nicht bewegen, bitte!*
Should I bring my camera with me?	*Soll ich meine Kamera mitnehmen?*
Could you look after my camera for me, please?	*Kannst Du bitte auf meine Kamera aufpassen?*
Don't you like having your photo taken?	*Magst Du es nicht fotografiert zu werden?*
I like / hate having my photo taken.	*Ich mag / hasse es fotografiert zu werden.*
I am not photogenic.	*Ich bin nicht fotogen.*
I would like to take a photo of you all to show my family.	*Ich möchte gerne ein Foto von euch machen, um es meiner Familie zu zeigen.*
May I take a photo of your house?	*Darf ich ein Foto von eurem Haus machen?*

PHOTOGRAPHY cont.   *FOTOGRAFIEREN Forts.*

LOOKING AT PHOTOS	FOTOS ANSCHAUEN
Have you any photos of when you were young?	*Hast Du Kinderfotos von Dir?*
Can I look at your photo album?	*Kann ich mir Dein Fotoalbum angucken?*
That photo of you is very good.	*Das ist ein sehr gutes Foto von Dir.*
That one doesn't look at all like you.	*Dieses hier sieht Dir überhaupt nicht ähnlich.*
You have changed a lot.	*Du hast Dich sehr verändert.*
You haven't changed much.	*Du hast Dich kaum verändert.*
Have you got photos of your holiday?	*Hast Du Fotos von Deinem Urlaub?*
Are you in the photo?	*Bist Du auf dem Fotos?*
It's a very good photo.	*Das ist ein sehr gutes Foto.*
in the foreground..	*Im Vordergrund....*
in the background..	*Im Hintergrund...*
This photograph is of..	*Dieses Foto ist von...*
This photo was taken two years ago.	*Dieses Foto wurde vor zwei Jahren aufgenommen.*
That's where we used to live.	*Früher haben wir hier mal gelebt.*
That one is of me as a baby.	*Das bin ich als Baby.*

CAMERAS   *KAMERAS*

TYPES OF CAMERA	KAMERATYPEN
Polaroid	*Polaroid*
instant	*Sofort-Bild*
automatic	*automatische*
manual	*manuelle*
disposable	*Einweg*

PHOTOGRAPHY cont.   *FOTOGRAFIEREN Forts.*

USING A CAMERA	*KAMERABENUTZUNG*
a button / to press	*ein Knopf / drücken*
a lever / to pull	*ein Hebel / ziehen*
a switch / to switch	*ein Schalter / schalten*
the lens cap / to remove / to replace	*Die Schutzkappe / abnehmen / aufsetzen*
the lens / normal / wide angle / zoom	*Das Objektiv / Normal / Weitwinkel / Tele*
to clean	*säubern*
the viewfinder	*der Sucher*
to focus	*scharf stellen*
in focus / out of focus	*scharf / unscharf*
auto-focus	*Auto-Focus*
clear / blurred	*klar / verschwommen*
the aperture / the aperture setting	*die Blende / die Blendeneinstellung*
the shutter / the shutter speed	*die Verschlußklappe / die Verschlußzeit*
the flash	*der Blitz*
Did you use a flash?	*Hast Du einen Blitz benutzt?*
I need a new flash bulb.	*Ich brauche eine neue Blitzlichtbirne.*

CAMERA ACCESSORIES	*KAMERA AUSSTATTUNG*
a camera case	*eine Kamerahülle*
a camera bag	*eine Kameratasche*
a strap	*ein Trageriemen*
a camera stand	*ein Kameraständer*
a tripod	*ein Stativ*
a photo album	*ein Fotoalbum*

Your German Exchange

PHOTOGRAPHY cont.   *FOTOGRAFIEREN Forts.*

BUYING FILMS   *FILME KAUFEN*

Do you sell films here? *Verkaufen Sie Filme?*

Could I have a colour / black and white film, please? *Kann ich bitte einen Farb- / Schwarzweißfilm haben?*

What sort would you like? *Welche Sorte möchten Sie?*

Two hundred / three hundred / four hundred? *Zweihundert / dreihundert / vierhundert usw.?*

How many would you like? *Wieviele Bilder soll er haben?*

Twelve / twenty four / thirty six, please. *Zwölf / vierundzwanzig / sechsunddreißig, bitte.*

thirty five millimetre format *Fünfunddreißig Millimeter*

to load *einlegen*

How do you load the film? *Wie legt man den Film ein?*

Could you help me to load the film, please? *Könnten Sie mir bitte dabei helfen, den Film einzulegen?*

to rewind *zurückspulen*

automatic rewind *automatische Rückspulung*

to remove the film *den Film rausholen*

GETTING FILMS DEVELOPED *DEN FILM ENTWICKELN LASSEN*

Could you develop these for me, please? *Können Sie bitte diese Filme entwickeln?*

I would like them in one hour if possible. *Ich möchte sie wenn möglich in einer Stunde abholen?*

I would like to collect them in four hours / tomorrow. *Ich möchte sie in vier Stunden / morgen abholen.*

Can you develop black and white film here? *Entwickeln Sie hier Schwarz-Weißfilme?*

Do you want just one set of prints? *Möchten Sie jeweils einmal Abzüge haben?*

I would like an extra set of prints. *Ich möchte noch Extraabzüge haben.*

These are under-exposed / over-exposed. *Diese sind unterbelichtet / überbelichtet.*

VIDEO CAMERA RECORDERS (CAMCORDERS)

VIDEOKAMERA-REKORDER (CAMCORDERS)

THE VIDEO CAMERA	*DIE VIDEOKAMERA*
a camcorder case	*eine Camcorderhülle*
to get the video camera out	*die Videocamera rausholen*
a grip strap	*ein Halteriemen*
to hold	*halten*

TAPES		BÄNDER	
a tape	*ein Band*	to insert	*eingeben*
a cassette	*eine Kassette*	to eject	*herausholen*
a blank tape	*ein Leerband*	to label	*beschriften*
a used tape	*eine gebrauchte Kassette*	to record on	*aufnehmen auf*

BATTERIES	*BATTERIEN*
a battery pack	*eine Packung mit Batterien*
a battery charger	*ein Batterie-Aufladegerät*
to charge up the battery	*die Batterie aufladen*
Plug it into the mains.	*An die Stromleitung anschließen.*
The battery is fully charged.	*Die Batterie ist vollgeladen.*
It is getting weak.	*Sie wird schwach.*
The battery has run down.	*Die Batterie ist alle.*
Do you have an adaptor for this?	*Hast Du dafür einen Adaptor?*
to attach the battery to the camcorder	*Die Batterie an dem Camcorder anbringen.*
to slide / to push	*schieben / drücken*
to click into place	*In die richtige Stellung einrasten*

251

CAMCORDERS cont.   *CAMCORDERS Forts.*

THE LENS	*DAS OBJEKTIV*
a lens hood	*ein Objektivverdeck*
to remove	*abnehmen*
to replace	*aufsetzen*
to clean the lens	*das Objektiv säubern*

TURNING THE CAMCORDER ON AND RECORDING	*DEN CAMCORDER ANSCHALTEN UND AUFNEHMEN*
the power switch	*der Netzschalter*
to switch on / off	*an- ausschalten*
a flashing light	*ein Blinklicht*
a warning light	*ein Hinweislicht*
ready to record	*bereit aufzunehmen*
standby	*auf "aufnahmebereit" bleiben*
record mode	*Aufnahmemodus*
Are you ready?	*Bist Du bereit?*
I am about to record now.	*Ich nehme jetzt gleich auf.*
the viewfinder	*der Sucher*
to focus	*scharf stellen*
to adjust	*einstellen*
to zoom	*zoomen*

GETTING THE SOUND RIGHT	*DEN TON RICHTIG EINSTELLEN*
the microphone	*das Mikrofon*
Can you speak up a bit, please?	*Kannst du bitte etwas lauter sprechen?*
That wasn't loud enough.	*Das war nicht laut genug.*
That was too loud.	*Das war zu laut.*

CAMCORDERS cont.   *CAMCORDERS Forts.*

PLAYING BACK	***ZURÜCKSPIELEN***
to switch between camera and player	*Aufnehmen oder Abspielen einschalten*
to playback	*abspielen*
the playback switch	*der Abspielschalter*
to rewind	*zurückspulen*
to fast forward	*vorspulen*
to stop	*anhalten*
to pause	*unterbrechen*

EDITING	***ÜBERARBEITEN***
to edit	*überarbeiten*
to cut	*schneiden*
to record over	*überspielen*
the counter reset button	*der Zählwerkzurückstell-Schalter*
to zero the counter	*den Zähler auf Null stellen*
to insert a marker	*einen Anzeiger eingeben*

SPORT
SPORT

TENNIS   *TENNIS*

DO YOU PLAY TENNIS?	*SPIELST DU TENNIS?*
Would you like to play tennis?	*Möchtest Du gerne Tennis spielen?*
Shall we just knock up for a while?	*Sollen wir uns noch etwas einspielen?*
Is the net the right height?	*Hat das Netz die richtige Höhe?*
Shall we check the height of the net?	*Sollen wir die Höhe des Netzes überprüfen.*
It's too low / too high.	*Es ist zu niedrig / zu hoch.*
Up a bit / down a bit / O.K.	*Etwas höher / etwas niedriger / O.K.*

EQUIPMENT	*AUSRÜSTUNG*
a tennis racket	*ein Tennisschläger*
Which racket would you prefer?	*Mit welchem Schläger möchtest Du am liebsten spielen?*
What weight of racket would you like?	*Was für ein Gewicht soll Dein Schläger haben?*
a tennis ball	*ein Tennisball*
new balls	*neue Bälle*
a racket press	*eine Schlägerpresse*
a holdall	*eine Schlägertasche*
a sportsbag	*eine Sporttasche*
a towel	*ein Handtuch*

TENNIS cont.   *TENNIS Forts.*

CLOTHES	*KLEIDUNG*
I haven't got any tennis clothes with me.	*Ich habe meine Tenniskleider nicht dabei.*
You can borrow some clothes.	*Du kannst Dir Kleider ausleihen.*
You can wear anything.	*Du kannst tragen was Du willst.*
shorts / a T shirt	*Tennishosen (n) / ein T-Shirt*
a tennis skirt	*ein Tennisrock*
a tennis dress	*ein Tenniskleid*
tennis shoes / socks	*Tennisschule (m) / Strümpfe (n)*
a sweatband / a headband	*ein Schweißband / ein Stirnband*
a sun visor	*ein Sonnenvisier*
a track suit	*ein Trainingsanzug*

THE TENNIS COURT	*DER TENNISPLATZ*
the net	*das Netz*
the base line	*die Grundlinie*
the service line	*die Aufschlaglinie*
the centre line	*die Mittellinie*
the tramlines	*die Linien des Doppelspielfelds*
the side netting	*die Seitenbenetzung*
the service box	*das Aufschlagfeld*
the changing room	*die Umkleidekabine*
a locker	*ein Spind*

STARTING A GAME	*EINE PARTIE ANFANGEN*
Do you want to carry on knocking up?	*Willst Du Dich noch weiter einspielen?*
Shall we start to play now?	*Sollen wir jetzt anfangen zu spielen?*
How many sets shall we play?	*Wieviele Sätze sollen wir spielen.*

TENNIS cont.　　　　　　*TENNIS Forts.*

STARTING A GAME cont.　　*EINE PARTIE ANFANGEN Forts.*

to toss up	*eine Münze werfen*
Let's toss for it.	*Laß uns eine Münze werfen.*
Toss a coin.	*eine Münze werfen.*
Heads or tails? It's heads / tails.	*Kopf oder Zahl? Kopf / Zahl.*
You serve first.	*Du schlägst als Erster auf.*
Which end do you prefer?	*Auf welcher Seite möchtest Du spielen?*
I prefer this / that end.	*Ich möchte auf dieser / dieser Seite spielen.*
The sun is in my / your eyes.	*Ich spiele gegen die Sonne / Du spielst gegen die Sonne.*

SERVING	***AUFSCHLAG***
to serve	*aufschlagen*
to hold one's serve	*seinen Aufschlag behalten*
to break someone's serve	*den Aufschlag von jemandem durchbrechen*
to serve an ace	*ein As servieren*
first / second service	*erster / zweiter Aufschlag*
It's your service.	*Du hast Aufschlag.*

TENNIS cont.   *TENNIS Forts.*

IN OR OUT?	*AUF DER LINIE ODER AUS?*
Was that in / out?	*War er auf der Linie / war er im Aus?*
Out! The ball was definitely out.	*Aus! Der Ball war auf jedem Fall im Aus.*
In! The ball was just in.	*Auf der Linie! Der Ball war gerade so auf der Linie.*
I'm not sure.	*Ich bin mir nicht sicher.*
I didn't see it land.	*Ich habe ihn nicht aufspringen sehen.*
It touched the line.	*Er hat die Linie berührt.*
Shall we play it again?	*Sollen wir ihn nochmal spielen?*

FAULTS	*FEHLER*
a fault	*ein Fehler*
a double fault	*ein Doppelfehler*
a foot fault	*ein Fußfehler*

LET BALLS	*WIEDERHOLUNGSBÄLLE*
to play a let	*einen Wiederholungsball spielen*
Should we play a let?	*Sollen wir einen Wiederholungsball spielen?*

KEEPING THE SCORE	*DEN SPIELSTAND BEHALTEN*
What's the score?	*Wie steht es?*
I've forgotten what the score is.	*Ich weiß nicht mehr, wieviel es steht*
The score is	*Es steht*
• love all	• *null beide*
• love fifteen	• *null fünfzehn*
• fifteen love	• *fünfzehn null*
• fifteen all	• *fünfzehn beide*

TENNIS cont.	*TENNIS Forts.*
KEEPING THE SCORE cont.	*DEN SPIELSTAND BEHALTEN Forts.*

•	thirty forty	•	*dreißig vierzig*
•	deuce	•	*Einstand*
•	That's deuce.	•	*Das ist Einstand*
•	Advantage.	•	*Vorteil*
•	My / our / your advantage.	•	*Mein / Unser / Dein Vorteil.*
•	Game.	•	*Spiel*
•	Game to you.	•	*Das Spiel geht an Dich.*
•	That's game.	•	*Das ist Spiel.*
•	Change ends	•	*Die Seiten wechseln.*

Three games to two, first set.	*Drei zu zwei Spiele, erster Satz.*
Match point?	*Match Point?*
Game, set and match.	*Spiel, Satz und Sieg.*
a tie-breaker	*ein Tie-Break*
a sudden-death-tie-breaker	*ein Sudden-Death-Tie-Break*
Shall we play another game?	*Sollen wir nochmal spielen?*

STROKES	*SCHLAGARTEN*
forehand / backhand	*Vorhand / Rückhand*
a forehand drive / volley	*ein Vorhandschlag/volley*
a backhand drive / volley	*ein Rückhandschlag/volley*
to lob / a high lob / a top spin lob	*lobben / ein hoher Lobball/ ein Top-Spin-Lob*
a smash / an overhead smash	*ein Schmetterball / ein Überkopf-Schmetterball*
a service	*ein Aufschlag*
first / second service	*erster / zweiter Aufschlag*
an ace	*ein As*
a drop shot	*ein Stoppball*
a slice	*ein angeschnittener Ball / ein Slice*
a volley / a half volley	*ein Volley / ein halber Volley*
a slam	*ein Schlag*

TENNIS cont.　　　　　*TENNIS Forts.*

LOSING THE BALL	*DEN BALL VERLIEREN*
Did you see where the ball went?	*Hast Du gesehen, wo der Ball geblieben ist?*
We've lost the ball.	*Wir haben den Ball verloren.*
It went somewhere here.	*Er muß irgendwo hier sein.*
I can't find it.	*Ich kann ihn nicht finden.*
I've found it.	*Ich habe ihn gefunden.*
Let's look for it later.	*Laß' uns später nach ihm suchen.*
Have you any more balls?	*Hast Du noch mehr Bälle?*

THE OFFICIALS	*DIE OFFIZIELEN*
an umpire	*der Schiedsrichter*
Will you be umpire?	*Machst Du den Schiedsrichter?*
the referee	*der Oberschiedsrichter*
the net judge	*der Netzrichter*
the foot-fault judge	*der Fußfehlerrichter*
the line judge	*der Linienrichter*
a ball boy / a ball girl	*ein Balljunge / ein Ballmädchen*

TYPES OF TENNIS	*TENNIS SPIELVARIANTEN*
singles	*Einzel*
ladies' singles / men's singles	*Dameneinzel / Herreneinzel*
doubles	*Doppel*
ladies' doubles / men's doubles	*Damendoppel / Herrendoppel*
mixed doubles	*gemischtes Doppel*
lawn tennis	*Rasentennis*
tennis on a hard surface	*Tennis auf hartem Untergrund*
to play tennis on grass	*Tennis auf Rasen spielen*

TENNIS cont.   *TENNIS Forts.*

TENNIS TOURNAMENTS	*TENNISTURNIERE*
the first round	*die erste Runde*
the second round	*die zweite Runde*
the quarter final	*das Viertelfinale*
a semi final	*ein Halbfinale*
the final	*das Finale*
the championship	*die Meisterschaft*
the grand slam	*der Grand Slam*
a seeded player	*ein gesetzter Spieler*
first seed	*auf Nummer eins gesetzt*
He was seeded third.	*Er wurde auf Nummer drei gesetzt.*

HOW WELL YOU PLAYED	*WIE GUT DU SPIELST*
You play well.	*Du spielst gut.*
Well played! / Good shot!	*Gut gespielt! / Toller Schlag!*
Bad luck!	*Pech gehabt!*
I haven't played for ages.	*Ich habe schon seit Ewigkeiten nicht mehr gespielt.*

RIDING
REITEN

CAN YOU RIDE? / *KANNST DU REITEN*

How long have you ridden?	*Wie lange reitest du schon?*
I have ridden for five years.	*Ich reite seit fünf Jahren.*
Would you like to have a riding lesson with me?	*Soll ich Dir eine Reitstunde geben?*
Shall we go for a ride?	*Sollen wir reiten?*
You ride well.	*Du reitest gut.*
Who are you riding?	*Welches Pferd reitest Du?*
What is your horse's name?	*Wie heißt Dein Pferd?*

CLOTHES AND EQUIPMENT / *KLEIDUNG UND AUSRÜSTUNG*

a riding hat	*ein Reithut*	riding boots	*Reitschuhe*
a riding jacket	*eine Reitjacke*	a whip	*eine Peitsche*
jodhpurs	*Reithosen*	gloves	*Handschuhe*

THE STABLE / *DER STALL*

the stable yard	*die Stallungen*
the tackroom	*die Sattelkammer*
a gate	*ein Tor*
a mounting block	*ein Steigklotz*
the school	*die Reitschule*
a barn	*die Scheune*
a horse box	*eine Pferdebox*

RIDING TERMS / *REITAUSDRÜCKE*

to hold the reins	*die Zügel halten*
to give someone a leg up	*Jemandem hinaufhelfen*

RIDING TERMS cont.   *REITAUSDRÜCKE Forts.*

to mount / to dismount	*besteigen / absteigen*
to ride	*reiten*
to walk / to trot	*in Schritt gehen lassen / traben*
to canter	*Kanter / kurzer Galopp*
to gallop	*galoppieren*
to jump	*springen*
to kick	*ausschlagen*
to rein back	*die Zügel anziehen*
to fall off	*herunterfallen*
to rear / to buck / to shy	*aufbäumen / bocken / scheuen*
to walk a horse	*ein Pferd führen*
to neigh	*wiehern*

HACKING   *PFERDEVERLEIH*

a hack / to go for a hack	*ein Mietpferd / mit einem Mietpferd ausreiten*
a road	*eine Straße*
a lane	*ein Weg*
a bridleway	*ein Reitweg*
a footpath	*ein Fußweg*
a ditch	*ein Graben*
a field	*ein Feld*
a gate / to open / to shut / to jump	*ein Tor / öffnen / schließen / springen*
private land	*Privatgrundstück*

RIDING cont.

REITEN Forts.

TACK	DAS GESCHIRR
to saddle up / the saddle	aufsatteln / der Sattel
the flaps / the girth	die Lasche / der Gurt
to tighten / to loosen	befestigen / lockern
a buckle / a hole	eine Schnalle / ein Loch
the fasten	der Verschluß
the seat / the pommel	der Sitz / der Sattelknauf
the stirrups	der Steigbügel
to lengthen / to shorten	verlängern / verkürzen
even / uneven	gleich / ungleich
the bridle / the bit	das Zaumzeug / die Gebißstange
the headstall	das Kopfgestell
the reins / a leading rein	die Zügel / die Führungszügel
a head collar	ein Kummet
a blanket	eine Decke

GROOMING A HORSE	EIN PFERD STRIEGELN
to groom / to rub down	striegeln / abreiben
to brush	bürsten
a currycomb	ein Striegel
a dandybrush	eine Kardätsche
soft / hard	weich / hart
a bucket / water	ein Eimer / Wasser
a tap	ein Wasserhahn
a sponge / to sponge	ein Schwamm / wischen

HOOF PROBLEMS	HUFPROBLEME
a hoof pick / a stone / lame	eine Hufnagel / ein Stein / lahmen
a horseshoe / a blacksmith	ein Hufeisen / ein Hufschmied
to shoe	beschlagen
to lose a shoe	ein Hufeisen verlieren

RIDING cont.   *REITEN Forts.*

TYPES OF HORSE	*PFERDEARTEN*
a thoroughbred	*ein Vollblut*
a racehorse	*ein Rennpferd*
a mare / a stallion	*eine Stute / ein Hengst*
a foal / a colt	*ein Fohlen / ein Füllen*
a pony / a Shetland pony	*ein Pony / ein Shetland Pony*
a carthorse	*ein Zugpferd*
a shirehorse	*ein schweres Zugpferd*

DESCRIBING HORSES	*PFERDE BESCHREIBEN*
How old is your horse?	*Wie alt ist Dein Pferd?*
He / she is three years old.	*Er / sie ist drei Jahre alt.*
How tall is he / she?	*Wie groß ist er / sie?*
She is … hands.	*Er / sie ist……handbreit (vier englische Zoll) groß.*
What colour is your horse?	*Welche Farbe hat Dein Pferd?*
grey / bay / chestnut	*Grau / Braun / dunkler Fuchs*
palomino	*Palomino*
dappled	*gepfleckt*
piebald / skewbald	*scheckig / gescheckt*
broken / unbroken	*zugeritten / nicht zugeritten*
the coat	*das Fell*
the mane / the tail	*die Mähne / der Schwanz*
the hindquarters	*die Hinterhand*
the temperament	*das Temperament*
frisky // gentle	*lebhaft // zahm / sanft*
lazy / fast	*faul / schnell*
nervous	*nervös*
temperamental	*temperamentvoll*

RIDING cont.   *REITEN Forts.*

COMPETITIONS	REITTURNIERE
hunter trials	*ein Jagdwettbewerb*
equitation	*Reiten*
a three day event	*eine Dreitagetreffen*
dressage	*Dressur (f)*
collection / collected trot	*Versammlung / versammelter Trab*
extension	*Verstärkung (f)*
extended trot	*Verstärkung des Trab*
cross country	*querfeldein*
show jumping	*Schau-Springen*
to jump / a jump	*springen / ein Sprung*
height / three feet high	*Höhe (f) / ein Meter hoch*
a water jump / a ditch	*ein Wassersprung / ein Graben*
a fence / a pole	*ein Hindernis / eine Stange*
a gate / a double	*ein Torgitter / ein Doppel*
a fault / a double fault	*ein Fehler / ein Doppelfehler*
a time fault / a penalty	*ein Zeitfehler / ein Strafe*
a time limit	*ein Zeitliche-begrenzung*
a race against time	*ein Rennen gegen die Zeit*
to start the clock	*die Zeit laufen lassen*
a refusal	*eine Verweigerung*
three refusals	*drei Verweigerungen*
to disqualify	*disqualifizieren*
to have a clear round	*eine fehlerfreie Runde haben*
a jump-off	*ein Absprung*

RIDING cont.   *REITEN Forts.*

USEFUL EXPRESSIONS	*NÜTZLICHE AUSDRUCKSWEISEN*
You can borrow a hat at the riding school.	*Man kann sich Hüte in der Reitschule ausleihen*
Does that hat fit you properly?	*Paßt Dir der Hut gut?*
Put your feet in the stirrups.	*Stell Deine Füße in die Steigbügel.*
Use your whip.	*Benutze Deine Peitsche.*
Kick harder.	*Fester treten.*
Can you trot / canter / gallop?	*Kannst Du traben / kantern / galoppieren?*
Would you like to try a jump?	*Möchtest Du mal einen Sprung versuchen?*
What height can you jump?	*Welche Höhe kannst Du überspringen?*

SKIING
SKIFAHREN

CLOTHES	*KLEIDUNG*
a ski suit	*ein Skianzug*
a salopette	*eine Lifthose*
a ski jacket / a hood	*eine Skijacke / eine Kapuze*
gloves / mittens	*Handschuhe / Fausthandschuhe*
thermal underwear	*Thermal-Unterwäsche*
sunglasses	*eine Sonnenbrille*

EQUIPMENT	*AUSRÜSTUNG*
skis / ski bindings	*Skier / eine Skibindung*
ski boots	*Skischuhe*
fastens / clasps	*Verschlüsse / Schnallen*
to tighten / to loosen	*enger machen / locker machen*
ski poles / handgrips / straps	*Skistöcke / Griffe / Riemen*
a ski pass / a photo	*ein Skipass / ein Foto*
suntan cream	*Sonnencreme*

USEFUL EXPRESSIONS	*NÜTZLICHE AUSDRÜCKE*
Don't forget your...	*Vergiß nicht Dein....*
Have you got your...?	*Hast Du Dein / Deine.....?*
May I borrow..?	*Kann ich mir....leihen?*
I can't find my..	*Ich kann mein / meine....nicht finden.*
I've forgotten where I left my...	*Ich weiß nicht mehr, wo ich mein / meine......habe.*

SKIING cont.   *SKIFAHREN forts.*

SKI HIRE	***SKIVERLEIH***
I would like to hire boots / skis / poles, please?	*Ich möchte bitte Schuhe / Skier / Stöcke ausleihen.*
What size boots are you?	*Welche Schuhgröße hast Du?*
Try these.	*Probier' diese mal an.*
Are those comfortable?	*Sind diese bequem?*
Where do they feel tight / loose?	*Wo fühlen sie sich zu eng / zu weit an.*
How do you adjust them?	*Wie stellt man sie ein?*
You can adjust the fastens like this..	*Du kannst die Verschlüsse so einstellen ....*
What length skis do you normally wear?	*Welche Skilänge benutzt Du normalerweise?*
How tall are you?	*Wie groß bist Du?*
What do you weigh? I weigh..	*Wieviel wiegst Du? Ich wiege...*
How experienced are you?	*Wieviel Erfahrung has Du?*
I'm a beginner.	*Ich bin Anfänger.*
I'm intermediate.	*Ich bin mittelgut.*
I'm experienced.	*Ich habe viel Erfahrung.*
Try these poles.	*Versuche diese Stöcke.*
Choose poles with yellow handles.	*Suche Dir Stöcke mit gelben Griffen aus.*
These poles are too short / too long.	*Diese Stöcke sind zu kurz / zu lang.*
Bring the boots back if the are uncomfortable.	*Wenn die Schuhe unbequem sind, bring sie zurück.*
Can I change my boots, please?	*Kann ich bitte meine Schuhe umtauschen?*
They are too narrow.	*Sie sind zu schmal.*
They squash my toes.	*Sie drücken an meinen Zehen.*
They hurt here.	*Sie tun hier weh.*
Can you sharpen my skis, please?	*Können Sie bitte meine Skier schleifen?*

SKI HIRE cont.   *SKIVERLEIH Forts.*

Can you wax my skis, please?	*Können Sie bitte meine Skier wachsen?*
Can I hire..?	*Kann ich mir....*
• a monoski	• *einen Monoski*
• a toboggan	• *einen Rodelschlitten*
• skating boots	• *Schlittschuhe*
• a crash helmet	• *einen Sturzhelm*
• a ski board	• *ein Snowboard .....ausleihen?*

WEATHER CONDITIONS	*WITTERUNG*
Have you heard the weather forecast?	*Hast Du die Wettervorhersage gehört?*
It's raining.	*Es regnet.*
It's cloudy.	*Es ist bewölkt.*

SNOW	*SCHNEE*
It's snowing.	*Es schneit.*
There's no snow.	*Es gibt keinen Schnee.*
It's snowing heavily.	*Es schneit sehr stark.*
The snow is a metre deep.	*Der Schnee ist einen Meter hoch.*
fresh snow	*Neuschnee*
powder	*Pulver*
The snow is powdery.	*Es ist Pulverschnee*
It's very icy.	*Er ist sehr vereist.*
The snow is slushy.	*Der Schnee ist matschig.*
a blizzard	*ein Schneesturm*
danger of avalanche	*Lawinengefahr*

TEMPERATURE	*TEMPERATUR*
It's below freezing point.	*Es ist unter dem Gefrierpunkt.*
It's six degrees below zero.	*Es ist sechs Grad unter null.*
It's freezing.	*Es ist eiskalt.*
It's thawing.	*Es taut.*
The snow is melting.	*Der Schnee schmilzt.*

SKIING cont.   *SKIFAHREN forts.*

VISIBILITY	*DIE SICHT*
The visibility is poor.	*Die Sicht ist schlecht.*
It's foggy.	*Es ist nebelig.*
It's misty.	*Es ist dunstig.*
It's difficult to see far.	*Es ist schwierig, in die Ferne zu sehen.*
freezing fog.	*Eisnebel*

THE SKI RUNS	*DIE SKIPISTEN*
a map of the ski area	*eine Karte des Skigebiets.*
the level of difficulty	*der Schwierigkeitsgrad*
nursery slopes	*Anfängerhügel*
easiest runs	*Anfängerpisten*
easy / average runs	*leichte / mittlere Pisten*
most difficult runs	*schwierige Pisten*
off-piste / dangerous	*außerhalb der Piste / gefährlich*
narrow / wide / gentle	*schmal / weit / leicht*

SKI LIFTS	*SKILIFTE*
What time do the lifts open / close?	*Um wieviel Uhr öffnen / schließen die Skilifte?*
Where do I buy a ski pass?	*Wo kann ich mir einen Skipass kaufen?*
You will need a photograph.	*Du wirst ein Paßfoto brauchen.*
Where is there a photo booth?	*Wo ist hier ein Fotoautomat?*
What coins does it take?	*Was für Münzen nimmt er?*
It takes…	*Er nimmt...*
a tow bar	*eine Schleppstange*
a drag lift / a chair lift	*ein Schlepplift / ein Sessellift*
a cable car / a gondola	*eine Drahtseilbahn / eine Gondel*
a safety bar	*eine Sicherheitsstange*
a foot rest	*eine Fußstütze*
a ski rack	*ein Skiständer*

271

SKIING cont.   *SKIFAHREN forts.*

QUEUEING	*SICH ANSTELLEN*
to form a queue	*eine Schlange bilden*
to queue up	*sich anstellen*
crowded	*gedrängt*
a short / long queue	*eine kurze / lange Schlange*
a queue jumper	*ein Vordrängler*
Wait your turn.	*Warte bis Du dran bist.*
He pushed in front of me.	*Er hat sich vorgedrängt.*

SKI SCHOOL	*SKISCHULE*
Where is the ski school meeting place?	*Wo ist der Treffpunkt für die Skischule?*
a ski instructor	*ein Skilehrer*
a ski class	*eine Skiklasse*
Which class are you in?	*In welcher Klasse bist Du?*
Which class should I join?	*In welche Klasse soll ich gehen?*
How much skiing have you done?	*Wie oft bist Du schon Ski gefahren?*
I have been skiing three times.	*Ich war bisher dreimal Skifahren.*
I have only been skiing on a dry ski slope.	*Ich bin bisher nur auf einer Trockenpiste gefahren*
I am a beginner / intermediate / experienced.	*Ich bin Anfänger / mittelgut / erfahrend.*
I only began skiing last year.	*Ich habe erst letztes Jahr mit dem Skifahren angefangen.*
You have to do a ski test.	*Man muß eine Skiprüfung machen.*
Show me how you ski.	*Zeig' mir wie Du Skifahren kannst.*
Go and join that group over there.	*Geh' und schließe Dich der Gruppe dahinten an.*
Join that class.	*Schließe Dich dieser Klasse an.*

LEARNING TO SKI   *SKIFAHREN LEHRNEN*

Put on your skis.	*Ziehe Deine Skier an.*
The bindings need to be open.	*Die Bindung muß offen sein.*
Sidestep up the hill.	*Gehe mit Seitenschritten den Hügel hoch.*
Have you ever used a drag lift?	*Bist Du schon einmal Schlepplift gefahren?*
to ski	*skifahren*
to fall down	*stürzen*
to get up	*aufstehen*
to turn round	*sich umdrehen*
to traverse	*den Hang überqueren*
to snow plough	*Schneepflug fahren*
a snowplough turn	*ein Schneepflug-Schwung*
a stem turn	*ein Stemmbogen*
a parallel turn	*ein Parallelschwung*
Can you ski over / round moguls?	*Kannst Du eine Buckelpiste fahren*
a mogul field	*eine Buckelpiste*
hot dogging	*Freestyle*
to mono-ski	*Monoski fahren*
to ski board	*Snowboard fahren*
slalom racing	*Slalom fahren*
the course	*die Rennstrecke*
the poles / the flags	*die Stöcke / die Flaggen*
the gates	*die Tore*

FALLING DOWN   *STÜRZEN*

Can you do an emergency stop?	*Kannst Du eine Vollbremsung machen?*
to fall down	*stürzen*
Are you hurt?	*Bist Du verletzt?*
I'm fine.	*Mir geht's gut.*
I hurt here..	*Mir tut es hier weh.*
I can't get up.	*Ich kann nicht aufstehen.*

LEARNING TO SKI cont.   *SKIFAHREN LEHRNEN Forts.*

FALLING DOWN cont.   *STÜRZEN Forts.*

How do you get up from a fall?	*Wie stellt man sich nach einem Sturz wieder auf?*
Sort out your skis.	*Sortiere Deine Skier auseinander.*
Edge your skis.	*Kante Deine Skier.*
Plant your poles and push.	*Stecke Deine Stöcke in den Schnee und drücke sie an.*
Stand up.	*Stehe auf.*
Take your skis off.	*Ziehe Deine Skier aus.*
Put the lower ski on first.	*Ziehe zuerst den Talski an.*
Push the inside edge into the snow.	*Drücke die Innenkante in den Schnee.*

APRES SKI   *APRES SKI*

a bar / a restaurant	*eine Bar / ein Restaurant*
a disco / a nightclub (See 201-203)	*eine Disco / ein Nachtclub*
expensive / cheap	*teuer / billig*
a skating rink (See 282-283)	*eine Schlittschuhbahn*
to ice skate	*schlittschuhlaufen*
to toboggan	*Bob fahren*
to go for a sleigh ride	*eine Schlittenfahrt machen*
a sleigh	*ein Pferdeschlitten*

ACCIDENTS   *UNFÄLLE*

There has been an accident.	*Es gab einen Unfall.*
Someone is hurt.	*Es hat sich jemand verletzt.*
Where do you hurt? (See 237, 411, 420)	*Wo tut es weh ?*
Don't move him / her.	*Bewege ihn / sie nicht.*
Can you stand up?	*Kannst Du aufstehen?*
Fetch the rescue service.	*Hole den Rettungsdienst.*
Help / Get help.	*Hilfe / Hole Hilfe.*
Warn other people.	*Warne die anderen Leute.*

SKIING cont.   *SKIFAHREN forts.*

RESCUE SERVICES	*RETTUNGSDIENST*
a helicopter / a stretcher	*ein Hubschrauber / eine Trage*
a blood wagon	*ein Wundversorgungswagen*
to air lift	*auf dem Luftweg befördern*
a doctor	*ein Arzt*
a broken arm / leg	*ein gebrochener Arm/ ebrochenes Bein*
What is your name?	*Wie heißen Sie?*
Where are you staying?	*Wo wohnen Sie?*
Are you insured?	*Sind Sie verletzt?*

HOW ARE YOU FEELING?	*WIE GEHT ES JEMANDEM?*
I am cold / hot.	*Mir ist kalt / warm.*
I am tired / feel fine.	*Ich bin müde / Mir geht es gut.*
I am thirsty / hungry.	*Ich habe Durst / Hunger.*
I want to stop now.	*Ich will jetzt nicht mehr weiter.*
I want to carry on.	*Ich will weiter machen.*
I can't do this./ I am scared	*Ich kann das nicht/Ich habe Angst.*
This is good fun.	*Das macht Spaß.*
Can we do it again?	*Können wir das nochmal machen?*
My legs hurt.	*Meine Beine tun weh.*
My boots are rubbing.	*Meine Schuhe drücken.*
Can we stop for lunch soon?	*Können wir bald etwas zu Mittag essen?*
I would like a drink.	*Ich möchte gerne etwas trinken.*
I need the toilet.	*Ich muß auf's Klo.*
Let's go to that mountain café.	*Laß uns zum Bergcafé gehen.*
Shall we stop for a few minutes?	*Sollen wir für ein paar Minuten Pause machen?*
I'd like to go back to the hotel / chalet now.	*Ich möchte jetzt gerne ins Hotel / ins Apartment zurück.*
I have to be back at four o'clock.	*Ich muß um vier Uhr zurück sein.*
Shall we meet again after lunch?	*Sollen wir uns nach dem Mittagessen wiedertreffen?*
Where / when shall we meet?	*Wo / wann sollen wir uns treffen?*

FOOTBALL
FUßBALL

THE PITCH	*DAS SPIELFELD*
the goal / the goal posts	*das Tor / die Torpfosten*
the cross bar / the netting	*die Querlatte / das Tornetz*
the goal area / the goal line	*der Dreimeter-Raum / die Torlinie*
the penalty area / the touch line	*der Strafraum / die Seitenlinie*
the corner / mid-field	*die Ecke / Mittelfeld*
offside	*Abseits*
the terrace / a stand	*der Rang / ein Stehplatz*
the bench	*die Bank*
floodlighting	*Flutlicht*
muddy	*schlammig*

THE PLAYERS (abc)	*DIE SPIELER*
an amateur	*ein Amateur*
to award a free kick	*einen Freistoß / Elfmeter geben*
the away team	*die Auswärtsmannschaft*
to be on the bench	*auf der Bank sitzen*
to blow the whistle	*pfeifen*
a coach	*ein Trainer*
a defender	*ein Abwehrspieler*
the favourites	*die Favoriten*
a footballer	*ein Fußballer*
a forward	*ein Stürmer*
a goal keeper	*der Torhüter*
the home team	*die Heimmannschaft*
a manager	*ein Manager*
a mid-fielder	*ein Mittelfeldspieler*

FOOTBALL cont. *FUßBOL Forts.*

THE PLAYERS cont. (abc) *DIE SPIELER Forts.*

an opponent	*ein Gegenspieler*
a professional	*ein Profi*
a referee	*ein Schiedsrichter*
a striker	*eine Spitze*
the strong side	*die bessere Mannschaft*
a substitute	*ein Auswechselspieler*
to be substituted on / off	*ein-/ausgewechselt sein*
a sweeper	*ein Libero*
the teams	*die Mannschaften*
a transfer	*eine Ablöse / ein Transfer*
a transfer fee	*eine Ablösesumme*
the weak side	*die schlechtere Mannschaft*

THE SPECTATORS	*DIE ZUSCHAUER*
a spectator	*ein Zuschauer*
a fan	*ein Fan*
a supporter	*ein Anhänger*
the crowd	*die Menge*
a ticket holder	*ein Karteninhaber*
a tout	*ein Schwarzmarkthänlder*
to cheer	*jubeln*
to shout	*schreien*
to chant	*Sprechchöre anbringen*
to sing	*singen*
the national anthem	*die Nationalhymne*
a football hooligan	*ein Fußball-Hooligan*

FOOTBALL cont. *FußBALL Forts.*

PLAY	*SPIELEN*
a kick / to kick off	*ein Schuß / den Anstoß machen*
a free kick / a goal kick	*ein Freistoß / ein Torabschlag*
an indirect free kick	*ein indirekter Freistoß*
a corner kick	*ein Eckball*
to pass / to dribble	*passen / dribbeln*
to head / a header	*köpfen / ein Kopfball*
to throw in	*einwerfen*
to tackle	*draufgehen*
to intercept	*abfangen*
to challenge	*dagegenhalten*
a good challenge	*gut dagegengehalten*
a bad challenge	*schlecht dagegengehalten*
to take a corner	*einen Eckball treten*
to be offside	*in Abseits stehen*
to be sent off	*vom Platz gestellt werden*
to be shown the red / yellow card	*die rote / gelbe Karte gezeigt bekommen*
tactics	*die Taktik*
the rules / the rule book	*die Regeln / das Regelbuck*
against the rules	*gegen die Regeln*
foul play / a foul	*unfaires Spiel / ein Foul*
a penalty	*ein Elfmeter*
the penalty spot	*der Elfmeterpunkt*
a penalty goal	*ein Elfmetertor*
a penalty shoot out	*ein Elfmeterschießen*

THE SCORE	*DER SPIELSTAND*
an aggregate score	*ein Gesamtergebnis*
What is the score?	*Wie steht es?*
to score an own goal	*ein Eigentor schießen*
to equalize / to win	*ausgleichen / gewinnen*

Your German Exchange

FOOTBALL cont.   *FußBALL Forts.*

THE RESULT	DAS RESULTAT
a win / to win	*ein gewonnenes Spiel / gewinnen*
a victory / a walk over	*ein Sieg / ein leichter Sieg*
a draw / to draw	*ein Remis / Remis spielen*
a defeat	*eine Niederlage*
to be defeated	*besiegt werden*
to lose	*verlieren*
a tie	*ein Unentschieden*
to tie	*unentschieden spielen*
a replay	*ein Wiederholungs-spiel*
a match	*ein Spiel*
a friendly	*ein Freundschafts-spiel*
no score	*keine Tore*

STAGE OF THE GAME	SPIELPHASEN
first half / second half	*erste Halbzeit / zweite Halbzeit*
half time / full time	*Halbzeit / neunzig Minuten*
extra time	*Verlängerung*
injury time	*Nachspielzeit*

GENERAL TERMS	ALLGEMEINE AUSDRÜCKE
soccer	*Fußball*
the football season	*die Fußballsaison*
the football league	*die Fußballliga*
divisions	*Liga / Division*
first / second / third division	*erste / zweite / dritte Liga*
League Division One	*die League Division One (In Germany: die zweite Liga)*
the Premier League	*die Premier League (In Germany: die Bundesliga)*
a cup	*ein Pokal*
a trophy	*eine Trophäe*

279

FOOTBALL cont.   *FußBALL Forts.*

EQUIPMENT	AUSRÜSTUNG
a football	*ein Fußball*
kit	*Trikot*
home kit	*Heimtrikot*
away kit	*Auswärtstrikot*
team strip	*Mannschaftsstreifen*
shorts	*Hosen*
a shirt	*ein Hemd*
socks	*Strümpfe*
football boots	*Fußballschuhe*
a sweatband	*ein Schweißband*

USEFUL EXPRESSIONS	NÜTZLICHE AUSDRÜCKE
Who's playing?	*Wer spielt gegen wen?*
What's the score?	*Wie steht es?*
There's no score yet.	*Es sind noch keine Tore gefallen.*
They are in injury time.	*Es wird schon überzogen.*
They won by five goals to nil.	*Sie haben fünf zu null gewonnen.*
They failed to score.	*Es sind keine Tore gefallen.*
It was a draw.	*Sie haben Unentschieden gespielt.*
They took the lead in the second half.	*In der zweiten Halbzeit sind sie in Führung gegangen.*

RUGBY
RUGBY

THE PLAYERS	*DIE SPIELER*
the forwards	*der Stürmer*
the back row	*die hintere Reihe*
the front / second row	*die vordere / zweite Reihe*
a hooker / a flanker	*ein Hakler / ein "Flanker"*
the half backs	*die Läufer*
scrum half	*Gedränge-halbspieler*
fly half	*Halbspieler*
three quarter backs / fullback	*Dreivierteläufer / Verteidiger*
wing three quarter	*Dreiviertelflügel*

THE FIELD	*DAS SPIELFELD*
the goal / the goal posts	*das Tor / die Torpfosten*
the uprights	*die senkrechten Pfosten*
the cross bar	*die Querlatte*
halfway line	*die Mittellinie*
the goal line / the dead-ball line	*die Torlinie /die Feldauslinie*
the twenty two line	*Zweiundzwanzigerlinie*

THE PLAY (abc)	*DAS SPIEL*
to bounce	*aufspringen*
converted	*verwandeln*
to drop kick	*ein Dropkick machen*
a free kick	*ein Freistoß*
to hook	*häkeln*
a line out / mark	*eine Gasse / decken*
a penalty / a penalty try	*ein Strafstoß / ein Strafversuch*
a scrummage / scrum	*ein offenes Gedränge/ Gedränge*
to touch down	*ein Versuch / ein "Touchdown" machen*

ICE SKATING
SCHLITTSCHUHLAUFEN

WOULD YOU LIKE TO GO ICE SKATING?	*MÖCHTEST DU GERNE SCHLITTSCHUHLAUFEN?*
Can you skate?	*Kannst Du Schlittschuhlaufen?*
How long have you skated?	*Wie lange läufst Du schon Schlittschuh?*
Would you like to have a go at it?	*Möchtest Du es mal versuchen?*

THE ICE RINK	*DIE SCHLITTSCHUHBAHN*
the ticket office	*der Kartenschalter*
Could we have four tickets, please?	*Können wir bitte vier Karten haben?*
Have you got your own boots?	*Hast Du Deine eigenen Schuhe?*
Do you want to hire boots?	*Möchtest Du Dir welche ausleihen?*
Could I have two tickets for the ice rink and we would like to hire boots, please.	*Ich hätte gerne zwei Karten für die Schlittschuhbahn und wir möchten uns bitte Schuhe ausleihen.*

BOOT HIRE	*SCHLITTSCHUHVERLEIH*
What size of shoe do you take?	*Welche Schuhgröße brauchst Du?*
I am size six	*Ich habe Größe sechs.*
I am a continental size forty.	*Ich habe Größe vierzig.*
You take your shoes off and hand them in at the boot hire shop.	*Du ziehst Deine Schuhe aus und gibst sie beim Schuhausleih ab.*
Try your skates on.	*Probiere Deine Schlittschuhe aus.*
How do you fasten them?	*Wie bindet man sie zu?*
You fasten them like this.	*Du bindest sie so zu.*
Are they comfortable?	*Sind sie bequem?*
These boots hurt.	*Sie tun weh.*
Can I change my boots, please?	*Kann ich bitte meine Schuhe umtauschen?*

ICE SKATING cont.

SCHLITTSCHUHLAUFEN
Forts

ON THE ICE	AUF DEM EIS
Hold on to the handrail at first.	*Halte Dich erst einmal an dem Gelände fest.*
Should we skate round the edge until you're used to it?	*Sollen wir erst einmal am Rand ein wenig rumfahren, bis du Dich daran gewöhnt hast?*
to fall over	*stürzen*
to get knocked down	*umgestoßen werden*
Someone pushed me over.	*Jemand hat mich umgestoßen.*
Can you help me to get up, please?	*Kannst Du mir bitte helfen aufzustehen?*
Are you O.K.?	*Bist Du O.K.?*
You're doing really well.	*Du machst das sehr gut.*
I think I'll just watch for a bit.	*Ich glaube, ich schaue nur ein wenig zu.*

TYPES OF SKATING	SCHLITTSCHUHLAUFARTEN
speed skating	*Eisschnellauf*
figure skating	*Eiskunstlaufen*
ice dancing	*Eistanz*
solo skating	*Sololauf*
pair skating	*Paarlauf*
a leap	*ein Satz*
a spiral	*eine Schraube*
a jump	*ein Sprung*
a spin	*eine Drehung*

TABLE TENNIS
TISCHTENNIS

CAN YOU PLAY TABLE TENNIS?	*KANNST DU TISCHTENNIS SPIELEN?*
Would you like to play table tennis / ping pong?	*Möchtest Du Tischtennis / Ping Pong spielen?*
Do you have a table tennis table?	*Hast Du eine Tischtennisplatte?*
Do you play much?	*Spielst Du oft?*
I haven't played for ages.	*Ich habe schon lange nicht mehr gespielt.*
I've forgotten how to play.	*Ich weiß nicht mehr wie man es spielt.*
Shall I teach you how to play?	*Soll ich Dir es beibringen?*

EQUIPMENT	*AUSRÜSTUNG*
a table tennis table	*eine Tischtennisplatte*
the white line	*die weiße Linie*
the net	*das Netz*
the edge of the table	*die Tischkante*
a bat	*ein Schläger*
Which bat do you prefer?	*Welchen Schläger möchtest Du am liebsten haben?*
I'll take this one.	*Ich nehme diesen.*
a table tennis ball	*ein Tischtennisball*
Have you got any more balls?	*Hast Du noch mehr Bälle?*
This ball isn't bouncing properly.	*dieser Ball springt nicht richtig auf.*

PLAYING	*SPIELEN*
Let's choose ends.	*Laß' uns die Seiten wählen.*
Spin the racket.	*Drehe den Schläger.*
Toss for it.	*Wirf' eine Münze.*
We change ends every game.	*Wir wechseln nach jedem Spiel Seiten.*

TABLE TENNIS cont.   *TISCHTENNIS Forts.*

DOUBLES	*DOPPEL*
In doubles the players take alternate shots.	*Beim Doppel wechseln sich die Spieler mit dem Schlagen ab.*
You have to serve from the right to the right.	*Man schlägt von rechts nach rechts auf.*
Each player receives service for five points.	*Jeder Spieler erhält Aufschlag für fünf Punkte.*

SINGLES	*EINZEL*
You serve first.	*Du schlägst zuerst auf.*
You change service every five points.	*Man wechselt den Aufschlag alle fünf Punkte.*
Whose service is it?	*Wer hat Aufschlag?*
It's mine / yours.	*Meiner / Deiner.*
It's your service now because five points have been scored.	*Da wir fünf Punkte gemacht haben, hast Du jetzt Aufschlag.*

SHOTS	*SCHLÄGE*
to hit forehand	*mit der Vorhand schlagen*
to hit backhand	*mit der Rückhand schlagen*
to serve	*aufschlagen*
You hit the net.	*Du hast ins Netz geschlagen.*
Where did the ball land?	*Wo ist der Ball aufgekommen?*
Was it in or out?	*Hat er die Platte berührt / nicht berührt?*
It was in / out.	*Es war in / aus.*
It didn't land on the table.	*Er hat die Platte nicht berührt.*
It was a let.	*Das war ein Wiederholungsball.*
Play it again.	*Spiel ihn nochmal.*
Can you find the ball?	*Kannst Du den Ball finden?*
Did you see exactly where it went?	*Hast du genau gesehen, wo er hingesprungen ist?*

TABLE TENNIS cont.   *TISCHTENNIS Forts.*

SCORING	*ERGEBNIS*
What's the score?	*Wieviel steht es?*
Love all.	*Null zu null.*
One love.	*Eins zu null.*
Three, two.	*Drei, zwei.*
Twenty, twenty.	*Zwanzig, zwanzig.*
The service changes every point now.	*Es gibt jetzt einen Aufschlagswechsel bei jedem Punkt.*
The winner is the first person to score twenty one points.	*Wer als erster einundzwanzig Punkte erzielt, hat das Spiel gewonnen.*
You have to get two points ahead of me to win.	*Du mußt mit zwei Punkten Abstand gewinnen.*
You won easily.	*Du hast mühelos gewonnen.*
Well played! / Bad luck!	*Gut gespielt / Pech gehabt.*
It was a close game.	*Es war ein knappes Spiel.*
Shall we play the best of three games?	*Sollen wir spielen: wer die meisten von drei Spielen gewinnt?*

GOLF
GOLF

THE GOLF COURSE		DER GOLFPLATZ	
the links		*ein Golfplatz an der Küste*	
a hole	*ein Loch*	thirteenth	*dreizehntes*
first	*erstes*	fourteenth	*vierzehntes*
second	*zweites*	fifteenth	*fünfzehntes*
third	*drittes*	sixteenth	*sechzehntes*
fourth	*viertes*	seventeenth	*siebzehntes*
fifth	*fünftes*	eighteenth	*achtzehntes*
sixth	*sechstes*	a tee	*ein Tee*
seventh	*siebtes*	the fairway	*das Fairway*
eighth	*achtes*	the rough	*das Rauh*
ninth	*neuntes*	the green	*das Grün*
tenth	*zehntes*	the putting green	*das Grün*
eleventh	*elftes*	a flag	*eine Fahne*
twelfth	*zwölftes*	the hole	*das Loch*

OBSTACLES		HINDERNISE (n)	
a hazard	*ein Hindernis*	sand	*Sand (m)*
long grass	*langes Gras (n)*	a ditch	*ein Graben*
bushes	*Büsche (m)*	a pond	*ein Teich*
trees	*Bäume (m)*	a lake	*ein See*
a bunker	*ein Bunker*		

OTHER PARTS OF THE GOLF CLUB	ANDERE BEREICHE DES GOLFCLUBS
the club house / the bar	*das Clubhaus / die Bar*
the practice ground / green	*der Übungsplatz / das Grün*
miniature golf	*Miniatur-Golf*
crazy golf	*Mini- Golf*

GOLF cont.   *GOLF Forts.*

THE EQUIPMENT	DIE AUSRÜSTUNG
a golf bag	*eine Golftasche*
a caddie / to caddie	*ein Caddie / Caddie sein*
a set of golf clubs	*ein Golfschlägerset*
the woods	*die Holzschläger*
a driver	*ein Driver*
one / two / three	*Einer / Zweier / Dreier*
four / five	*Vierer / Fünfer*
the irons / the long irons	*die Eisen / die langen Eisen*
six / seven / eight / nine	*Sechse /Siebener/ Neuner/ Zehner*
the putter	*der Putter*
the sand wedge	*der Sandschläger*
the pitching wedge	*der Einlochschläger*
a golf ball / a tee	*ein Golfball / ein Tee*

THE STROKES	DIE SCHLÄGE
You must shout "Fore!".	*Du mußt "Achtung!" schreien.*
to tee up / to strike	*den Ball aufs Tee legen / schlagen*
to drive	*einen Treibball spielen*
a beautiful drive	*ein schöner Treibball*
to hook	*ein Kurvball (nach links)*
to slice	*anschneiden*
to make an approach shot	*einen Schlag zwischen Abschlag und Grün machen*
to putt	*einlochen*
a putt	*ein Schlag, mit dem man einlocht*
to tap / to hole	*leicht schlagen / einlochen*
a shot	*ein Schlag*
a long shot / a chip shot	*ein weiter Schlag / ein Chip*
a low / high shot	*ein niedriger / hoher Schlag*
to swing	*schwingen*
a short / long swing	*ein kurzer / langer Schwung*

GOLF cont.   *GOLF Forts.*

THE SCORING	DAS PUNKTEN
par / under par / over par	*Par / Unter-Par / Über-Par*
a birdie	*ein Birdie*
an eagle / a double eagle	*ein Eagle / ein Doppel-Eagle*
a hole in one	*ein Hole in One*
a bogey / a double bogey	*ein Bogey / ein Doppel-Bogey*
a handicap	*ein Handicap*
What is your handicap?	*Was ist Dein Handicap?*

MOTOR RACING
AUTORENNEN

THE COURSE	*DER STRECKENVERLAUF*
the starting line	*die Startlinie*
the finishing line	*die Ziellinie*
the chequered flag	*die Zielfahne*
the track	*die Strecke*
a lane	*eine Spur*
the inside / outside lane	*die Innen- / Außenspur*
a lap / to do a lap	*eine Runde / eine Runde fahren*
to lap someone	*jemanden überrunden*
to do a lap of honour	*eine Ehrenrunde fahren*
a five lap course	*eine Fünf-Runden-Strecke*
a circuit	*eine Rundstrecke*
a bend	*eine Kurve*
a double bend	*eine Doppelkurve*
a hairpin bend	*eine Haarnadelkurve*
He took the bend too fast.	*Er ist zu schnell in die Kurve gegangen.*
a chicane	*eine Schikane*
the pits	*die Boxen*
a crash barrier	*eine Leitplanke*

THE PEOPLE	*DIE LEUTE*
a racing driver	*ein Rennfahrer*
a champion	*ein Meister*
an ex-champion	*ein Ex-Meister*
a winner	*ein Gewinner*
a runner-up	*der Zweite*
a loser	*ein Verlierer*
a spectator	*ein Zuschauer*
a mechanic	*ein Mechaniker*
a co-driver	*ein Kopilot*

MOTOR RACING cont.

AUTORENNEN Forts.

THE RACING CAR	*DAS RENNAUTO*
the steering wheel	*das Steuerrad*
the accelerator / the brakes	*das Gaspedal / die Bremsen*
the tyres / new tyres	*die Reifen / neue Reifen*
a puncture / to change the tyres	*ein Platten / die Reifen wechseln*
the bumper	*die Stoßstange*
the chassis	*das Fahrgestell*
the body	*die Karosserie*
the make of car	*der Autohersteller*
the engine size	*die Motorgröße*
the horse power	*die Pferdestärke (PS)*
the speed	*die Geschwindigkeit*

THE VERBS (abc)	*DIE VERBEN*
to accelerate	*beschleunigen*
to be out of control	*nicht unter Kontrolle haben*
to brake	*bremsen*
to collide / to crash	*dagegenstoßen / zusammenstoßen*
to correct a skid	*gegensteuern*
to drive	*fahren*
to finish	*das Rennen beenden*
to lap	*eine Runde fahren*
to lose	*verlieren*
to overtake	*überholen*
to race	*rasen*
to show the chequered flag	*die Zielflagge zeigen*
to skid / leave skid marks	*schleudern / Bremsspuren hinterlassen*
to slow down	*abbremsen*
to start	*anfahren*
to steer	*steuern*
to overtake on the inside	*auf die Innenspur überhohlen*
to win	*gewinnen*

ATHLETICS
LEICHTATHLETIK

THE KIT	*DIE AUSSTATTUNG*
a track suit / a sweat shirt	*ein Trainingsanzug/ ein Sweatshirt*
shorts	*eine kurze Hose/ Shorts*
a shirt	*ein Hemd*
a skirt	*ein kurzer Rock*
a leotard	*ein Gymnastik-Body*
trainers / spikes	*Turnschuhe / Spikes*
a sports bag / a towel	*eine Sporttasche / ein Handtuch*

THE ATHLETES	*DIE ATHLETEN*
a jogger / to jog	*ein Jogger / joggen*
I go jogging.	*Ich gehe joggen.*
to keep fit	*sich fit halten*
a sprinter / to sprint / to run	*ein Sprinter / sprinten / rennen*
to race against	*wettlaufen*
a middle distance runner	*ein Mittelstrecken- Läufer*
a marathon runner	*ein Marathon- Läufer*

JUMPERS	*SPRINGER*
to jump	*springen*
a hurdler	*ein Hürdenläufer*
to hurdle / a hurdle	*hürdenlaufen / eine Hürde*
a high jumper	*ein Hochspringer*
a long jumper	*ein Weitspringer*
a pole vaulter	*ein Stabhochspringer*
to vault	*stabhochspringen*

THROWERS	*WERFER*
a discus thrower / to throw	*ein Diskuswerfer / werfen*
a javelin thrower	*ein Speerwerfer*
a shot putter	*ein Kugelstoßer*

ATHLETICS cont.   *LEICHTATHLETIK Forts.*

OTHER SPORTSMEN AND WOMEN	*ANDERE SPORTLER UND SPORTLERINNEN*
a gymnast	*ein Turner / eine Turnerin*
a decathlete	*ein Zehnkämpfer*
a heptathlete	*ein Siebenkämpferin*
an amateur	*ein Amateur / eine Amateurin*
a professional	*ein Profi*
a coach	*ein Trainer / eine Trainerin*

RECORD HOLDERS	*REKORDHALTER*
to break the record	*den Rekord brechen*
a record breaker	*ein Rekordbrecher*
Well inside the record time.	*Weit über der Rekordzeit.*
Just inside the record time.	*Knapp über der Rekordzeit.*
a world record holder	*ein Weltrekordhalter*
a champion	*ein Meister*
to run one's personal best	*seine eigene Bestzeit laufen*

EVENTS	*WETTBEWERBE*
a meeting	*ein Treffen*
warm-up exercises / to warm up	*Aufwärmübungen / aufwärmen*
track events	*Laufdisziplinen*
runs / walks	*Wettläufe / Gehwettbewerbe*
field events	*Technische Disziplinen*
jumps / throws	*Sprungdisziplinen/ Wurfdisziplinen*
short races / sprints	*Kurzstreckenläufe/ Sprints*
one hundred metres	*Einhundertmeter*
middle distance races	*Mittelstreckenläufe*
one thousand five hundred metres	*Eintausendfünfhundertmeter*
long distance races	*Langstreckenläufe*
the half marathon	*der Kurzstrecken-Marathon*
the marathon	*der Marathon*
a steady pace	*ein gleichbleibendes Tempo*
a final spurt	*ein Endspurt*

ATHLETICS cont.

LEICHTATHLETIK Forts.

RELAY RACES	*STAFFELLÄUFE*
the baton / a hand over	*der Stab / ein Stabwechsel*
a leg	*eine Etappe*
the first / last leg	*die erste / letzte Etappe*

HURDLING	*HÜRDENLÄUFE*
hurdles / to hurdle	*Hürden / hürdenlaufen*
to clear	*überspringen*

LONG JUMP	*WEITSPRUNG*
distance	*die Sprungweite*
the take off	*der Absprung*
the landing	*die Aufsprung*

HIGH JUMP	*HOCHSPRUNG*
the cross bar	*die Querstange*
the height	*die Höhe*
to raise	*erhöhen*
to attempt	*versuchen*
to clear	*überspringen*
three attempts	*drei Versuche*
the first / second / third attempt	*der erste / zweite / dritte Versuch*
the final attempt	*der letzte Versuch*
to be disqualified	*disqualifiziert sein*

TRIPLE JUMP	*DREISPRUNG*
a hop / a skip / a jump	*ein erster / ein zweiter / ein dritter Sprung*

ATHLETICS cont.

LEICHTATHLETIK Forts.

POLE VAULTING	*STABHOCHSPRUNG*
the pole / the cross bar	*der Stab / die Querstange*
a height increase	*Latte erhöhen*
to dislodge the bar	*die Latte reißen*
three misses / to disqualify	*drei Fehlversuche/ disqualifizieren*

SHOT PUT	*KUGELSTOßEN*
the longest throw	*der weiteste Wurf*
the discus throw	*der Diskuswurf*
the javelin throw	*der Speerwurf*

GYMNASTICS

TURNEN

Qualities needed (abc)		*Erforderliche Fähigkeiten*	
agility	*Flinkheit*	grace	*Anmut*
balance	*Gleichgewicht*	rhythm	*Rhythmus*
flexibility	*Biegsamkeit*	strength	*Kraft*

The Moves (abc)	*Die Bewegungen*
a balance	*Gleichgewicht haben*
a cartwheel	*ein Radschlag*
a drop / a back drop	*eine Rolle / eine Rückwärtsrolle*
a front drop	*eine Vorwärtsrolle*
a tuck	*ein Hocksprung*
the floor exercises	*die Bodenübungen*
the grip changes	*der Griffwechsel*
a handstand	*ein Handstand*
a jump	*ein Sprung*
a landing	*auf dem Boden aufkommen*
a leap / a skip	*ein Satz / ein Hüpfer*
a turn / a half turn	*eine Drehung/ eine halbe Drehung*
a full turn	*eine volle Drehung*
a vault	*einen Scherensprung machen*

GYMNASTICS cont.   *TURNEN Forts.*

THE APPARATUS	*DIE GERÄTE*
a horizontal bar / a horse vault	*ein Reck / ein Pferd*
the parallel bars / the rings	*der Barren / die Ringe*
the side horse	*der Bock*
a springboard	*ein Sprungbrett*
a trampoline	*ein Trampolin*
the uneven bars	*der Stufenbarren*

THE STADIUM	*DAS STADION*
the arena / the track	*die Arena / die Laufbahn*
the lanes / the inside lane	*die Bahnen / die Innenbahn*
the outside / middle lane	*die Außenbahn / die Mittelbahn*
the starting line / starting block	*die Startlinie / der Startblock*
the starting pistol	*die Startpistole*
a false start	*ein Fehlstart*
On your marks, get ready, go!	*Auf die Plätze, fertig, los!*

MEDALS	*MEDALLIEN*
a Gold medal	*eine Goldmedaille*
a Silver medal	*eine Silbermedaille*
a Bronze medal	*eine Bronzemedaille*
to be awarded	*ausgezeichnet werden*
to win	*gewinnen*
to be presented	*überreicht werden*

THE OLYMPICS	*DIE OLYMPISCHEN SPIELE*
an Olympic medal	*eine olympische Medaille*
the Olympic games	*die olympischen Spiele*
the Olympic torch	*die olympische Fackel*
to light / to carry / to burn	*anzünden / tragen / brennen*
an Olympic Champion	*ein Olympiasieger*
the next Olympics	*die nächsten olympischen Spiele*
the last Olympics	*die letzten olympischen Spiele*

CRICKET
KRICKET

Although cricket is not generally played on the Continent, this section may be useful to help your foreign exchange to understand the game when he/she visits England.	*Kricket wird nicht sehr oft in Europa gespielt, aber folgendes könnte helfen es etwas den Austauschschülern, wenn Sie England besuchen, verständlicher zu machen.*

CLOTHES	*KLEIDUNG (f)*
cricket whites	*die weißen Kricket Klamotten*
leg pad	*Schützer (m) für die Beine*
a pullover	*ein Pullover*
trousers	*Hosen (f)*
a shirt	*ein Hemd*
gloves	*Handschuhe (m)*

EQUIPMENT	*AUSRÜSTUNG (f)*
a cricket bat	*ein Kricketschlagholz (n)*
a cricket ball	*ein Kricketball*
the wickets / the stumps	*drei Holzstäbe (m)*
the bails	*zwei horizontale Holzteile*

THE CRICKET FIELD	*SPIELFELD (n)*
the pitch	*das Spielfeld*
the wickets	*drei Holzstäbe*
the boundary	*das Spielfeld limit / die Spielfeldgrenze*

CRICKET cont.   *KRICKET Forts.*

THE FIELDERS' POSITIONS	*BALLFÄNGER POSITIONEN*
slip	*slip - ein Ballfänger der in der Nähe des Wicket Keeeper steht*
second slip	*zweite slip*
gully	*gully*
point	*point*
cover point	*cover point*
mid off	*halb nach rechts*
mid on	*halb nach links*
mid wicket	*halb wegs*
legside	*linke Seite*
offside	*rechte Seite*

THE PLAYERS	*DIE SPIELER*
the captain	*der Kapitän*
the umpires	*die Schiedsrichter*
the teams	*die Manschaften*
the batsman	*der Spieler*
the bowler	*der Werfer*
the fielders	*die Ballfänger - steht hinter dem "wicket"*

PLAYING CRICKET	*SPIELEN KRICKET*
to toss a coin	*eine Münze werfen*
to win / lose the toss	*gweinnen / verlieren*
to position the fielders	*die Ballfänger positionieren*

CRICKET cont.   *KRICKET Forts.*

BOWLING	***WERFEN***
to bowl	*werfen*
overarm	*überarm werfen / mit gestrecktem Arm*
underarm	*unterarm werfen*
to bowl out	*das "wicket" treffen / ausscheiden*
to throw	*werfen*
a wide	*schlecht werfen*
to spin the ball	*ein drehender Ball / ein Ball mit Drall*
an over (= six balls)	*sechs Wurfe*
a fast bowler	*ein schneller Werfer*
a spin bowler	*ein Werfer der die Bäll zum drehen bringt*

BATTING	***SCHLAGEN***
to bat / to hit	*den Ball schlagen*
He is batting now.	*Er schlägt jetzt.*
She is a good batter.	*Sie schlägt gut.*
to be out	*ausgeschieden*
to be bowled out	*ausgeschieden - der Schlagmann trifft den Ball nicht aber der Ball trifft das "wicket"*
to be caught out	*ausgeschieden - der Schlagmann trifft den Ball und ein Ballfänger fängt den Ball*

CRICKET cont.   *KRICKET Forts.*

BATTING cont.   *SCHLAGEN Forts.*

to be out for a duck	*ausgeschieden ohne Punkte / keine*
(= to score no runs)	*Punkte bekommen*
to score	*schießen*
What's the score?	*Wie steht es? / Wie sieht es aus?*
to keep the score	*Punkte zählen*
a run	*ein Lauf / durch laufen einen Punkt bekommen*
a four (= hit the ball to the boundary)	*eine Vier = vier Punkte bekommen durch den Schlag des Balls bis zum Feldlimit*
a six (= as a four but without the ball bouncing)	*eine Sechs = wie oben bei Vier aber der Ball darf nicht in Feld der Boden berühren*
a century (=one hundred runs)	*ein Jahrhundert (=ein Hundert Punkte)*

FIELDING	***AUFFANGEN UND ZURÜCKWERFEN***
the fielding side / team	*aufs Feld / auf den Platz schicken*
to field	*auffangen*
to catch	*fangen*
to drop a catch	*fallen lassen / nicht fangen*
a good catch	*ein guter Fang*

AN INNINGS	***EINE INNENRUNDE***
He has had a good innings.	*Er war lange an der Reihe.*
first / second	*erste / zweite*
to retire	*aufgeben*

SWIMMING
SCHWIMMEN

DO YOU LIKE SWIMMING?	*SCHWIMMST DU GERNE?*
Yes, I love swimming.	*Ja, ich schwimme gern.*
No, I'm sorry, but I can't swim.	*Nein, tut mir leid, ich kann nicht schwimmen.*
Would you like to go swimming?	*Möchtest Du gerne Schwimmen gehen?*
I don't really like swimming.	*Ich schwimme eigentlich nicht so gerne.*

TYPES OF POOL	*SCHWIMMBADARTEN*
a public swimming pool	*ein öffentliches Bad*
a private pool	*ein Swimming Pool*
an indoor / outdoor pool	*ein Hallenbad / ein Freibad*
a heated / unheated pool	*ein beheiztes / unbeheiztes Bad*
an aquatic park	*ein Erlebnisbad*

CLOTHES AND EQUIPMENT	*KLEIDUNG UND AUSRÜSTUNG*
a swimming costume	*ein Badeanzug*
a bikini	*ein Bikini*
trunks	*eine Badehose*
shorts	*eine kurze Hose / Shorts*
a swimming hat	*eine Badekappe*
a towel	*ein Handtuch*
goggles	*eine Taucherbrille*
a snorkel	*ein Schnorchel*
flippers	*Schwimmflossen*
a rubber ring	*ein Schwimmreifen*
armbands	*Schwimmflügel*
a lilo	*eine Luftmatratze*
a float	*ein Floß*

SWIMMING cont.   *SCHWIMMEN Forts.*

BUYING TICKETS	*KARTEN KAUFEN*
an adult's ticket	*eine Erwachsenenkarte*
a child's ticket	*eine Kinderkarte*
a swimmer's ticket	*eine Badekarte*
a spectator's ticket	*eine Zuschauerkarte*
Could I have tickets for two children, please?	*Kann ich bitte zwei Kinderkarten haben?*
Could I have two adult spectator tickets, please?	*Kann ich bitte zwei Zuschauerkarten für Erwachsene haben?*
Are there tubes at this swimming pool?	*Gibt es in diesem Schwimmbad Wasserrutschen?*
Could we have tickets to go down the tubes, please?	*Könnten wir bitte zwei Karten für die Wasserrutsche haben?*

TIMES OF SESSIONS	*BADEZEITEN*
When does this session start?	*Wann fängt diese Badezeit an?*
When does this session end?	*Wann hört diese Badezeit auf?*
When does our session end?	*Wann hört unsere Badezeit auf?*
They blow a whistle at the end of the session.	*Am Ende der Badezeit, wird gepfiffen.*
When does the next session start?	*Wann fängt die nächste Badezeit an?*
What time does the pool open on Saturday?	*Um wieviel Uhr öffnet das Bad am Samstag?*
What time does the pool close?	*Um wieviel Uhr macht das Bad zu?*

SWIMMING cont.	*SCHWIMMEN Forts.*
THE PARTS OF THE POOL	*DIE BADEBEREICHE*

NON-SWIMMING AREAS	*DER ALLGEMEINE BEREICH*
The Spectator Area I think I will sit and watch, if you don't mind.	*Der Zuschauerbereich* *Wenn es Dir nichts ausmacht werde ich mich hinsetzen und gucken.*
The Café I shall go and get something to eat and drink.	*Das Café* *Ich werde etwas zu Essen und zu Trinken holen gehen.*
The Drinks Machine What change does the drinks machine take?	*Der Getränkeautomat* *Welche Münzen nimmt der Getränkeautomat an?*

THE CHANGING ROOMS	*DIE UMKLEIDEKABINEN*
Where are the changing rooms? Is there a family changing room?	*Wo sind die Umkleidekabinen?* *Gibt es Familien-Umkleidekabinen?*
They are all individual cubicles. There are separate changing rooms for men and women.	*Es sind alles Einzelkabinen.* *Es gibt getrennte Umkleidekabinen für Frauen und Männer.*
The changing rooms are for both sexes.	*Die Umkleidekabinen sind für Frauen und Männer.*

SWIMMING cont.   *SCHWIMMEN Forts.*

GETTING CHANGED	UMZIEHEN
Shall we get changed together?	*Sollen wir uns gemeinsam umziehen?*
I'll use this cubicle.	*Ich nehme diese Kabine.*
to get undressed	*sich ausziehen.*
to get dressed	*sich anziehen.*
to dry oneself	*sich abtrocknen*
to use talcum powder	*Körperpuder benutzen*
to dry one's hair	*sich seine Haare trocknen*
a coin operated hair dryer	*ein Münzfön*
a hair brush / to brush	*eine Haarbürste / bürsten*
a comb / to comb	*ein Kamm / kämmen*
a mirror / to look in	*ein Spiegel / sich anschauen*

THE LOCKERS	DIE SCHLIESSFÄCHER
What coins do you need for the lockers?	*Welche Münzen braucht man für die Schließfächer?*
How do the lockers work?	*Wie funktionieren die Fächer?*
Don't forget the number of your locker.	*Vergiß' nicht Deine Spindnummer.*
Can you remember our locker number?	*Weißt Du noch unsere Spindnummer?*
I have forgotten the number of my locker.	*Ich habe meine Spindnummer vergessen.*
My locker was somewhere here.	*Mein Spind war irgendwo hier.*
to lock / unlock the door	*die Tür öffnen / schließen*
Don't lose your key.	*Verliere Deinen Schlüssel nicht.*
Put your clothes in here.	*Tu Deine Kleider hierein.*

THE FOOTBATH AND SHOWERS	DAS FUSSBAD UND DIE DUSCHEN
You have to walk through the footbath.	*Man muß durch das Fußbad gehen.*
You are supposed to shower before getting into the pool.	*Bevor man in das Becken geht, sollte man duschen.*

SWIMMING cont.   *SCHWIMMEN Forts.*

THE POOLS   *DIE BECKEN*
the paddling pool   *das Planschbecken*
the children's pool   *das Nichtschwimmerbecken*
the main pool   *das Schwimmerbecken*

PARTS OF THE POOL   *BECKENBEREICHE*
the deep end   *der tiefe Teil*
the shallow end   *der flache Teil*
a length / a width   *eine Länge (Bahn) / eine Breite*
How long is the pool?   *Wie lang ist das Becken?*
How wide is it?   *Wie breit ist das Becken?*
the depth   *die Tiefe*
How deep is it at the deep /   *Wie tief ist es im tiefen Teil/ im*
shallow end?   *flachen Teil*
the diving board   *das Sprungbrett*
the slide   *die Rutsche*

WAVE MACHINES   *WELLENMASCHINE*
Does this pool have a wave   *Hat dieses Becken eine*
machine?   *Wellenmaschine?*
They put the wave machine on at   *Die Wellenmaschine wird in*
intervals.   *bestimmten Zeitabständen*
                                      angestellt.

The waves are just starting.   *Die Wellen fangen gerade an.*
They usually have the waves on   *Normalerweise sind die Wellen für*
for five minutes.   *fünf Minuten an.*
There's also a water spout.   *Es gibt auch einen*
                                      Wassermassagestrahl

SWIMMING cont.   *SCHWIMMEN Forts.*

TUBES	WASSERRUTSCHEN
Pick up a mat.	*Nimm eine Matte.*
This session is using blue / red / yellow mats.	*In diesem Badezeitabschnitt werden blaue / rote / gelbe Matten benutzt.*
You sit on a mat.	*Du setzt Dich auf eine Matte.*
Wait till the tube is clear.	*Warte, bis die Rutsche frei ist.*
You can go down now.	*Jetzt kannst Du losrutschen.*
What is this tube like?	*Wie ist diese Wasserrutsche?*
It's steep.	*Sie ist steil.*
It has a gentle slope.	*Sie hat nur leichtes Gefälle.*
It bends a lot.	*Sie hat starke Kurven.*
There's a corkscrew.	*Es gibt eine Spirale.*
That one is really fast.	*Die ist sehr schnell.*
It's like a water chute.	*Sie ist wie ein Wasserfall.*
Which tube do you like best?	*Welche Wasserrutsche gefällt dir am besten?*
I like this one / that one best.	*Mir gefällt diese / diese am besten.*
Have you been down all the tubes?	*Bist Du schon auf allen Wasserrutschen gewesen?*
I didn't like that one.	*Diese hat mir nicht so gefallen.*
That one was brilliant.	*Diese hier war toll.*

SWIMMING STROKES	SCHWIMMSTILE
to swim / to go for a swim	*schwimmen / schwimmen gehen*
to float on your back / front	*sich auf seinem Rücken / Bauch treiben lassen*
to swim breast stroke	*Brustschwimmen*
back stroke / crawl	*Rückenschwimmen / Kraulen*
side stroke	*Seitenschwimmen*
butterfly stroke	*Schmetterling*
Can you swim back stroke?	*Kannst du Rückenschwimmen?*
I can't do butterfly.	*Ich kann keinen Schmetterling.*

306

SWIMMING cont.   *SCHWIMMEN Forts.*

UNDERWATER SWIMMING	*UNTERWASSER-SCHWIMMEN*
Can you swim under water?	*Kannst Du unter Wasser schwimmen?*
I only like swimming under water with goggles on.	*Ich Schwimme unter wasser nur mit einer Taucherbrille.*
How far can you swim under water?	*Wie weit kannst Du unter Wasser schwimmen?*
to swim between someone's legs	*durch die Beine von jemandem schwimmen.*

RACING	*WETTSCHWIMMEN*
to race	*wettschwimmen*
Let's have a race.	*Laß uns ein Wettschwimmen machen.*
I'll race you to the far end.	*Ich schwimme gegen Dich bis zum anderen Ende.*
I won / you won.	*Ich habe gewonnen / Du hast gewonnen.*
It was a draw.	*Es war ein Unentschieden.*
Let's see who can swim furthest?	*Laß uns herausfinden, wer am weitesten schwimmen kann.*
How many lengths can you swim?	*Wieviele Bahnen kannst Du schwimmen?*

DIVING	*SPRINGEN*
to dive	*springen*
Is it deep enough for diving?	*Ist es tief genug zum springen?*
I can dive but I'm not very good.	*Ich kann springen, aber nicht sehr gut.*
Did I splash a lot then?	*Habe ich eben viel gespritzt?*
What did that dive look like.	*Wie hat der Sprung eben ausgesehen?*

SWIMMING cont.	SCHWIMMEN Forts.

DIVING FOR COINS / *NACH MÜNZEN TAUCHEN*

Should we dive for coins?	*Sollen wir nach Münzen tauchen?*
Have you any coins?	*Hast Du Münzen?*
Will you throw some coins in for us to find?	*Würdest Du ein paar Münzen ins Wasser schmeißen, damit wir sie suchen.*

SAFETY / *SICHERHEIT*

a lifeguard	*ein Bademeister*
the First Aid post	*die Erste Hilfe Station*
Can you life save?	*Kannst Du Rettungsschwimmer?*
Don't go out of your depth.	*Geh´ nicht zu tief ins Wasser.*
Don't run in case you slip.	*Renne nicht, damit Du nicht ausrutschst.*
You shouldn't swim just after eating.	*Nach dem Essen sollte man nicht schwimmen.*
I sometimes get cramp.	*Ich bekomme manchmal Krämpfe.*
I have got cramp in my right / left leg.	*Ich habe einen Krampf in meinem rechten / linken Bein.*

GETTING OUT OF THE POOL / *AUS DEM BECKEN GEHEN*

They just blew the whistle to get out.	*Sie haben gerade zum Rausgehen gepfiffen.*
It's the end of our session now.	*Unsere Badezeit ist jetzt zu Ende.*
Shall we get out just before the end of our session so the changing rooms won't be so busy?	*Sollen wir kurz vor dem Ende unserer Badezeit rausgehen, damit die Umkleidekabinen nicht so voll sind?*
My mother said we have to get out now.	*Meine Mutter hat gesagt, daß wir jetzt rausgehen müssen.*
You're shivering / looking cold.	*Du zitterst / siehst verfroren aus.*
I think we should get out now.	*Ich glaube wir sollten jetzt besser rausgehen.*
Can't we have five more minutes?	*Können wir nicht fünf Minuten länger bleiben?*

THE BEACH
DER STAND

THE SEA		*DAS MEER*	
the tide	*die Gezeiten*	to go out	*fallen*
high tide	*Flut*	a wave	*eine Welle*
low tide	*Ebbe*	to break	*brechen*
to come in	*steigen*	spray	*Schaum*

THE BEACH	*DER STRAND*
the sand	*der Sand*
a rock / a rock pool	*ein Fels / ein Felsenbecken*
a starfish	*ein Seestern*
a pebble / shingle	*ein Kieselstein / Kiesstrand*
the cliffs / a sand dune	*die Klippen / eine Sanddüne*
a jellyfish / seaweed	*eine Qualle / Seetang*

CLOTHES AND EQUIPMENT	*KLEIDUNG UND AUSRÜSTUNG*
a swimming costume	*ein Badeanzug*
a bikini / trunks	*ein Bikini / eine Badehose*
to get changed / to get dressed	*sich umziehen / sich anziehen*
to dry oneself / a towel	*sich abtrocknen / ein Handtuch*
a rubber ring	*ein Schwimmreifen*
armbands	*Schwimmflügel*
a surfboard / an inflatable	*ein Surfbrett / ein Schlauchboot*
a lilo	*eine Luftmatratze*
to have a turn on / with	*an der Reihe sein mit*
to float	*sich treiben lassen*
a deckchair / a beach mat	*ein Liegestuhl / eine Strandmatte*
a wind break / a parasol	*ein Windschutz / ein Sonnenschirm*

SWIMMING AND SNORKELLING	SCHWIMMEN UND SCHNORCHELN
Swimming - see pages 301-308	*Schwimmen*
to float	*sich treiben lassen*
to ride on the waves	*auf den Wellen reiten*
Snorkelling	*Schnorcheln*
to snorkel	*schnorcheln*
a mask	*eine Maske*
a snorkel	*ein Schnorchel*
a mouthpiece	*ein Mundstück*
a tube	*ein Schlauch*
flippers	*Schwimmflossen*
goggles	*eine Taucherbrille*

BUILDING SANDCASTLES	SANDBURGEN BAUEN
a bucket / a spade	*ein Eimer / ein Spaten*
a sandcastle / a flag	*eine Sandburg / eine Fahne*
battlements / a drawbridge	*Zinnen / eine Zugbrücke*
a moat / a tunnel	*ein Graben / ein Tunnel*
a mound / a tower	*ein Erdhügel / ein Turm*
to build / to dig	*bauen / graben*
to collect shells	*sammeln Muscheln*
to decorate with pebbles	*ausschmücken mit Kieselsteinen*
to fill	*füllen*
to jump on	*draufspringen*
to knock down	*umschmeißen*
to make	*machen*
to pat	*klopfen*
to smooth	*glätten*
to tunnel	*einen Tunnel bauen*
to turn out	*einen Eimer entleeren*
to wait for the tide to come in	*auf die Flut warten*

THE BEACH cont.   *DER STRAND Forts.*

WALKING ON THE BEACH	*AM STRAND SPAZIERENGEHEN*
to go for a walk	*spazierengehen*
along the beach	*den Strand entlang*
on the cliffs	*auf den Klippen*
over the rocks	*über die Felsen*
at the edge of the sea	*am Meer entlang*

COLLECTING SHELLS	*MUSCHELN SAMMELN*
an unusual one	*eine ungewöhnliche*
a different type	*eine andere Sorte*
a pretty one	*eine schöne*
broken	*kaputt*
to wash the sand off	*den Sand wegspülen*
to put in a bucket	*in einen Eimer legen*

SHRIMPING	*GARNELEN FANGEN*
a fishing net	*ein Fischernetz*
to catch	*fangen*
to look at the rock pools	*beim Felsenbecken gucken*
a crab	*ein Krebs*
a shrimp	*ein Garnele*

CRICKET AND FRENCH CRICKET	*KRICKET UND FRANZÖSISCHES KRICKET*
Cricket - see 297-300	*Kricket*
French cricket	*Französisches Kricket*
a bat / a ball	*ein Schläger / ein Ball*
to bat / to bowl / to field	*schlagen / werfen / fangen*
to throw / to catch / to drop	*werfen / fangen / fallen lassen*
to get hit by the ball below the knee	*unterhalb der Knie vom Ball getroffen werden*
to swivel round	*umdrehen*

THE BEACH cont.

DER STRAND Forts.

FRENCH CRICKET cont.

FRANZÖSISCHES KRICKET Forts.

to stand still	*stillstehen*
You're not allowed to move your feet.	*Man darf nicht die Füße bewegen.*
to hit the ball into the sea	*den Ball ins Meer schlagen*
to hit the ball a long way	*den Ball weit weg schlagen*
to be out	*draußen sein*
It's your turn to bat now.	*Du bist dran zu schlagen.*
Well caught!	*Gut gefangen!*
Out!	*Draußen!*

DONKEY RIDES	***ESEL REITEN***
to have a ride on a donkey	*auf einem Esel reiten*
to put your feet in the stirrups	*seine Füße in die Steigbügel tun*
to hold on to the reins	*die Zügel halten*
to sit in the saddle	*im Sattel sitzen*
to pat / to stroke	*streicheln*
to walk / to trot	*laufen / trotten*

OTHER ACTIVITIES	***ANDERE AKTIVITÄTEN***
to paddle / to get wet	*paddeln / naß werden*
to play boules	*Boule spielen*
to play catch	*Fangen spielen*
to play pig in the middle	*"Schweinchen in der Mitte" spielen*
to play with a beach ball	*mit einem Strandball spielen*
to ride	*reiten*
to run into the water	*ins Wasser rennen*
to stay at the edge	*am Rand stehen*
to swim a long way out	*weit raus schwimmen*
to surf	*surfen*

THE BEACH cont.

DER STRAND Forts.

EATING ON THE BEACH	AM STRAND ETWAS ESSEN
to have something to eat	etwas zu Essen haben
a stick of rock	eine Zuckerstange
an ice cream	ein Eis
an iced lolly	ein Eis am Stiel
a cold drink	ein kaltes Getränk
a picnic - see 235-236	ein Picknick
a sandwich	ein Sandwich
a barbecue - see 184-185	etwas grillen
a disposable barbecue	ein Einweggrill
to gather firewood	Brennholz suchen
driftwood	Treibholz
to build a wind shield	einen Windschutz bauen

WATER SKIING	WASSERSKI
to have a water skiing lesson	Unterricht im Wasserski bekommen
a motorboat	ein Motorboot
to tow / to be towed	ziehen / gezogen werden
a towrope	ein Schleppseil
a handle	ein Griff
skis / bindings	Skier / Bindungen
a life-jacket	eine Schwimmweste
to crouch	hocken
to hold the towrope	das Schleppseil halten
to accelerate	beschleunigen
to stand upright	aufrecht stehen
the surface of the water	die Wasseroberfläche
to skim	gleiten
to zigzag	im Zickzack fahren
to cross the wake	das Kielwasser überqueren
to fall	fallen
to get back up again	wieder aufstehen

WINDSURFING	*WINDSURFING*
to windsurf	*windsurfen*
to surfboard	*surfen*
a surfboard	*ein Surfbrett*
the crest of a wave	*der Wellengipfel*
a big / small wave	*eine große / kleine Welle*
a breaking wave	*eine Brecher*
There's a huge wave coming.	*Da kommt eine riesige Welle.*

PROBLEMS	*PROBLEME*
Take care, there is…	*Paß auf, dort ...*
• broken glass	• *sind Glasscherben*
• a jellyfish / sewage	• *ist eine Qualle / ist Abwasser*
• a steeply shelving beach	• *ist ein steiler abschüssiger Strand*
• a strong current	• *ist eine starke Strömung*

WARNING AND SAFETY SIGNS	*WARN- UND SICHERHEITSSCHILDER*
Bathing Forbidden	*Baden verboten*
Unsupervised Bathing	*Unbeaufsichtiges Baden*
First Aid Post / Lifebuoy	*Erste Hilfe Station / Rettungsboje*
Lifeguard	*Rettungsschwimmer / Bademeister*

BOATS	*BOOTE*
to have a ride on a speed boat	*fahren auf ein Rennboot*
a rowing boat / to row	*ein Ruderboot / rudern*
an oar	*ein Mannschafts-ruderboot*
a yacht / to go yachting	*eine Yacht / mit der Yacht fahren*
to sail / a sail	*segeln / ein Segel*
the crew / to race	*die Mannschaft / Wettrennen*
to win / to lose	*gewinnen / verlieren*
a canoe / a paddle / to paddle	*ein Kanu / ein Paddel / paddeln*
a pedal-boat	*ein Tretboot*
to pedal	*treten*
to hire	*ausleihen*

CRUISES	SEEFAHRTEN
to go for a cruise	*eine Seefahrt machen*
to pay the fare	*die Fahrt bezahlen*
a short / long cruise	*eine kurze / lange Fahrt*
a two hour cruise	*eine Zwei-Stunden-Rundfahrt*
the captain / the crew	*der Kapitän / die Mannschaft*
a sailor	*ein Seemann*
to go aboard	*an Bord gehen*
to go on deck	*aufs Deck gehen*
to get soaked by the spray	*von der Gischt durchnäßt werden*
to go back inside	*wieder reingehen*
to get out of the wind	*aus dem Wind gehen*
to have a drink in the bar	*etwas in der Bar trinken*
to feel seasick	*sich seekrank fühlen*

THE HARBOUR	DER HAFEN		
the quay	*der Kai*	the nets	*die Netze*
the lighthouse	*der Leuchtturm*	the catch	*der Fang*
a flashing light	*ein Blinklicht*	the fishes	*die Fische*
a warning siren	*eine Warnsirene*	to anchor	*ankern*
the fishing boats	*die Fischerboote*	an anchor	*ein Anker*

SUNBATHING
SONNENBADEN

SUNBATHING EQUIPMENT	*SONNENBADEARTIKEL*
a sunbed	*eine Sonnenliege*
a deckchair	*ein Liegestuhl*
a mat / a rug	*eine Matte / eine Decke*
a cushion / a sunshade	*ein Kissen / eine Markise*
suntan cream	*Sonnenschutz-creme*
suntan lotion	*Sonnenschutz-lotion*
suntan oil	*Sonnenschutzöl*
coconut	*Kokosnuß*
water resistant	*wasserab-weisend*
after sun lotion	*After Sun Lotion*
a sun bed / a sun lamp	*ein Sonnenbett / eine Sonnenlampe*

USEFUL EXPRESSIONS	*NÜTZLICHE AUSDRUCKWEISEN*
Can you put some cream on my back, please?	*Kannst Du bitte meinen Rücken mit Sonnencreme einschmieren?*
May I borrow some suntan cream, please?	*Kann ich mir bitte etwas Sonnencreme leihen?*
What factor is your cream?	*Welchen Lichtschutzfaktor hat Deine Creme?*
It's too hot for me.	*Mir ist es zu heiß.*
I am going to move into the shade for a bit.	*Ich gehe eine Weile in den Schatten.*
I am going to cool off in the swimming pool / sea.	*Ich gehe mich im Schwimmbecken / Meer abkühlen.*
I don't like to sunbathe in the middle of the day.	*Mittags sonne ich mich nicht gerne.*

SUNBATHING cont.	*SONNENBADEN Forts.*

USEFUL EXPRESSIONS cont.	*NÜTZLICHE AUSDRUCKWEISEN Forts.*

Can you see the mark where my strap was?	*Kannst Du die Markierung sehen, wo mein Halter war?*
Is my back looking brown?	*Sieht mein Rücken braun aus?*
I have got sunburnt.	*Ich habe einen Sonnenbrand.*
My skin is peeling.	*Meine Haut schält sich.*
I am sore.	*Ich bin verbrannt.*
Have you any calamine lotion?	*Hast Du eine Salbe gegen Sonnenbrand?*
Insects keep biting me.	*Immerzu beißen mich Insekten.*
I don't want skin cancer.	*Ich will keinen Hautkrebs bekommen.*
You are looking rather red.	*Du siehst ziemlich rot aus.*

THE WEATHER	*DAS WETTER*
The sun has gone in.	*Die Sonne ist verschwunden.*
I wish the sun would come out again.	*Ich wünschte, die Sonne käme bald wieder raus.*
The sun is about to go behind that cloud.	*Die Sonne wird gleich hinter der Wolke verschwinden.*
There's not a cloud in the sky.	*Es ist kein Wölkchen am Himmel.*

FAMILY AND FRIENDS
FAMILIE UND FREUNDE

IMMEDIATE FAMILY	*NÄCHSTE VERWANDTSCHAFT*
mother / Mum / Mummy	*Mutter / Mama / Mami*
father / Dad / Daddy	*Vater / Papa / Papi*
a sister	*eine Schwester*
an older sister	*eine ältere Schwester*
the oldest sister	*die älteste Schwester*
a younger sister	*eine jüngere Schwester*
the youngest sister	*die jüngste Schwester*
brother	*Bruder*
an older brother	*ein älterer Bruder*
the oldest brother	*der älteste Bruder*
a younger brother	*ein jüngerer Bruder*
the youngest brother	*der jüngste Bruder*
a twin	*Zwillinge*
identical twins	*eineiige Zwillinge*
non-identical twins	*zweieiige Zwillinge*
a daughter	*eine Tochter*
a son	*ein Sohn*

COMMON QUESTIONS	*ALLGEMEINE FRAGEN*
How many brothers and sisters have you?	*Wieviele Geschwister hast Du?*
I have one of each.	*Ich habe einen Bruder und eine Schwester.*
I have two sisters and one brother.	*Ich habe zwei Schwestern und einen Bruder.*
Are you the eldest / the youngest?	*Bist Du der älteste / jüngste?*

FAMILY AND FRIENDS cont.   *FAMILIE UND FREUNDE Forts.*

COMMON QUESTIONS   *ALLGEMEINE FRAGEN*

How old is your sister / brother?	*Wie alt ist Deine Schwester / Dein Bruder?*
What are your brothers and sisters called?	*Wie heißen Deine Geschwister?*
The oldest / youngest is called..	*Die / der älteste / jüngste heißt...*
The next one is thirteen and is called..	*Die / der danach ist dreizehn und heißt...*

THE GENERATIONS   *DIE GENERATIONEN*

the older generation	*die ältere Generation*
the younger generation	*die jüngere Generation*
my / our / your generation	*meine / unsere / Deine Generation*
the generation gap	*die Generationslücke*

CLOSE RELATIVES   *NAHE VERWANDTE*

a grandmother / granny / grandma	*eine Großmutter / Oma / Großmama*
a great-grandmother	*eine Urgroßmutter*
a grandfather / granddad /grandpa	*ein Großvater / Opa / Großpapa*
a great-grandfather	*ein Urgroßvater*
a granddaughter	*eine Enkelin*
a great-granddaughter	*eine Urenkelin*
a grandson	*ein Enkel*
a great-grandson	*ein Urenkel*
an aunt / uncle	*eine Tante / ein Onkel*
a great-aunt / a great-uncle	*eine Großtante / ein Großonkel*
a niece / a nephew	*eine Nichte / ein Neffe*
a cousin	*ein Vetter / eine Kusine*
a first / second cousin	*ein erster / zweiter Vetter / eine erste / zweite Kusine*
a cousin once / twice removed	*ein Vetter / eine Kusine ersten / zweiten Grades*

FAMILY AND FRIENDS cont.   *FAMILIE UND FREUNDE Forts.*

RELATIVES BY MARRIAGE	*ANGEHEIRATETE VERWANDTSCHAFT*
a wife	*eine Ehefrau*
a husband	*ein Ehemann*
a mother-in-law	*eine Schwiegermutter*
a father-in-law	*ein Schwiegervater*
a daughter-in-law	*eine Schwiegertochter*
a son-in-law	*ein Schwiegersohn*
a sister-in-law	*eine Schwägerin*
a brother-in-law	*ein Schwager*

SEPARATION AND DIVORCE	*TRENNUNG UND SCHEIDUNG*
to decide to separate	*beschließen sich zu trennen*
to have a trial separation	*gerichtlich getrennt sein*
My parents are separated.	*Meine Eltern leben getrennt.*
to divorce	*sich scheiden lassen*
a divorce	*eine Scheidung*
My parents are divorced.	*Meine Eltern sind geschieden.*
to decide where the children will live	*entscheiden, bei wem die Kinder leben werden*
I live with my father in the holidays.	*In den Ferien lebe ich bei meinem Vater.*
I live with my mother in term time.	*Während der Schulzeit lebe ich bei meiner Mutter.*
I spend alternate weekends with each parent.	*Ich verbringe die Wochenenden abwechselnd mit einem Elternteil.*
a one parent family	*eine Ein-Eltern-Familie*
to have access to the children	*Zugang zu den Kindern haben*
to pay maintenance	*Unterhaltskosten zahlen*
to spend the holidays with	*meine Ferien mit....verbringen*

FAMILY AND FRIENDS cont.

FAMILIE UND FREUNDE Forts.

SEPARATION AND DIVORCE cont.

TRENNUNG UND SCHEIDUNG Forts.

My father / mother has re-married.	*Mein Vater / meine Mutter hat wieder geheiratet.*
My father and mother have both re-married.	*Mein Vater und meine Mutter haben beide wieder geheiratet.*
a stepmother / a stepfather	*eine Stiefmutter / ein Stiefvater*
a stepdaughter / a stepson	*eine Stieftochter / ein Stiefsohn*
a stepsister / a stepbrother	*eine Stiefschwester / ein Stiefbruder*

FRIENDS

FREUNDE

an acquaintance	*eine Bekanntschaft*
a friend of the family	*ein Freund der Familie*
a god parent	*ein Pate / eine Patin*
to become friends	*sich anfreunden*
a good friend / a best friend	*ein guter Freund / ein bester Freund*
a friend of mine	*ein Freund von mir*
a boyfriend / a girlfriend	*ein Freund / eine Freundin*
a group of friends	*eine Gruppe von Freunden*
I go around with a group of people.	*Ich mache etwas mit einer Gruppe von Leuten.*
I don't have one particular boyfriend / girlfriend.	*Ich habe keinen bestimmten Freund / keine bestimmte Freundin.*
I have a boyfriend. His name is..	*Ich habe einen Freund. Er heißt...*
My girlfriend is called..	*Meine Freundin heißt...*
a fiancée	*ein Verlobter / eine Verlobte*
a lover	*ein Liebhaber / eine Geliebte*
to live with	*mit....zusammenleben*

FAMILY AND FRIENDS cont. *FAMILIE UND FREUNDE Forts.*

LIKING / NOT LIKING PEOPLE *LEUTE MÖGEN / NICHT MÖGEN*

LIKING	*LEUTE MÖGEN*
to like	*mögen*
to get on well with	*sich gut verstehen mit*
to make friends with	*befreundet sein mit*
to fancy	*gefallen*
to chat up	*anmachen*
to get off with	*weggehen mit*
to have a date with	*eine Verabredung haben mit*
to go out with	*ausgehen mit*
to flirt with	*flirten mit*
to fall for	*sich verknallen in*
to fall in love	*sich verlieben in*
to love	*lieben*
to adore	*anbeten*

NOT LIKING	*NICHT MÖGEN*
not to get on well together	*sich nicht gut verstehen*
to fall out	*brechen mit*
to have a row	*einen Streit haben*
to dislike / to get fed up with	*nicht mögen / genug haben von*
to hate	*hassen*
to break up with	*sich trennen von*
to finish a relationship	*Schluß machen*

FAMILY AND FRIENDS cont.   *FAMILIE UND FREUNDE*
                               Forts.

PHYSICAL RELATIONSHIPS	*KÖRPERLICHE BEZIEHUNGEN*
to hold hands	*Hände halten*
to put your arm round someone	*um jemanden den Arm legen*
to cuddle	*umarmen*
to kiss / to snog	*küssen / knutschen*
to go to bed together	*miteinander ins Bett gehen*
to make love	*sich Lieben*
to have sex	*Sex haben*
to be faithful / unfaithful	*treu / untreu sein*
to live with	*leben mit*
to use contraception	*Verhütungsmittel benutzen*
to have safe sex	*"Safer Sex" machen*
to use a condom	*ein Kondom benutzen*
to be on the pill	*die Pille nehmen*
to sleep around	*mit jeder / jedem ins Bett gehen*
the morning after pill	*die Pille danach*
AIDS	*AIDS*
VD	*Geschlechtskrankheiten*
a late period	*eine verspätete Periode*
a missed period	*eine ausgebliebene Periode*
to do a pregnancy test	*einen Schwangerschaftstest machen*
to be pregnant	*schwanger sein*
a urine sample	*eine Urinprobe*
to see the doctor	*zum Arzt gehen*
to go to the family planning clinic	*zur Familienberatung gehen*
to get advice	*sich beraten lassen*
to decide on a termination	*sich zu einem Abbruch entschließen*
to have a baby	*ein Baby bekommen*

FAMILY AND FRIENDS cont.　　*FAMILIE UND FREUNDE*
　　　　　　　　　　　　　　　Forts.

BABIES	*BABIES*
birth	*Geburt*
to be born	*geboren werden*
What time were you born?	*Um wieviel Uhr wurdest Du geboren?*
Where were you born?	*Wo wurdest Du geboren?*
a baby / twins / triplets / quads	*ein Baby / Zwillinge / Drillinge / Vierlinge*
When is your birthday?	*Wann hast Du Geburtstag?*
My birthday is..	*Ich habe am....Geburtstag.*
I am adopted.	*Ich bin adoptiert.*

BABIES' PROBLEMS	*BABIE-PROBLEME*
to cry / to be hungry	*weinen / Hunger haben*
to need the nappy changed	*die Windeln wechseln müssen*
disposable nappies	*Einwegwindeln*
towelling nappies	*Stoffwindeln*
a safety pin	*eine Sicherheitsnadel*
plastic pants	*Windelhosen*
to be tired / to sleep	*müde sein / schlafen*
to have wind	*Blähungen haben*

FEEDING BABIES	*BABIES FÜTTERN UND STILLEN*
to need a feed	*gefüttert / gestillt werden müssen*
to have a feed / to feed	*gefüttert/gestillt werden / füttern/stillen*
breast fed / bottle fed	*Bruststillen / Flaschennahrung*
to sterilize the bottles	*die Flaschen sterilisieren*
to warm a bottle	*eine Flasche erwärmen*
demand feeding	*füttern / stillen nach Bedarf*
to be fed four hourly	*alle vier Stunden gefüttert / gestillt werden*
milk / solid food	*Milch / feste Nahrung*

FAMILY AND FRIENDS cont.   *FAMILIE UND FREUNDE Forts.*

BABY EQUIPMENT	*BABYAUSSTATTUNG*
a carry cot / a cot	*ein tragbares Kinderbettchen / ein Kinderbettchen*
a pram	*ein Kinderwagen*
a baby sling	*ein Tragetuch*
a baby seat for the car	*ein Autobabysitz*
a high chair	*ein Babystuhl*
a play pen	*ein Laufställchen*
a changing mat	*eine Windelunterlage*
a bib	*ein Lätzchen*
toys / a musical box / a mobile	*Spielzeug / eine Spieldose / ein Mobile*

YOUNG CHILDREN	*KLEINKINDER*
to learn to roll over / to crawl	*lernen sich auf die Seite zu rollen / krabbeln*
to stand up / to walk	*aufstehen / laufen*
for the first time	*zum ersten Mal*
to say his / her first words	*seine / ihre ersten Worte sagen*
to go to nursery school	*in den Kindergarten gehen*
to play	*spielen*
to draw / to colour / to paint	*zeichnen / ausmalen / malen*
to do jigsaws	*Puzzle legen*
to learn the alphabet	*das Alphabet lernen*
to learn to count	*das Zählen lernen*
to learn to read and write	*Lesen und Schreiben lernen*

ADOLESCENCE	*JUGENDLICHE*
to be a teenager	*ein Jugendlicher sein*
to be independent	*unabhängig sein*
to grow up	*aufwachsen*
a social life	*ein soziales Leben*
to go out with friends	*mit Freunden ausgehen*

FAMILY AND FRIENDS cont.

FAMILIE UND FREUNDE
Forts.

ADOLESCENCE cont.

JUGENDLICHE Forts.

to go to parties	*zu Parties gehen*
to go to bed late	*spät ins Bett gehen*
to lie in	*ausschlafen*
to come of age	*die Volljährigkeit erlangen*
to have the right to vote	*das Wahlrecht haben*
to be old enough to drink	*alt genug zum Trinken sein*
to learn to drive - see 397-398	*Autofahren lernen*
to be adult	*erwachsen sein*

MARITAL STATUS

FAMILIENSTATUS

unmarried	*unverheiratet*
a spinster	*eine unverheiratete Frau*
a bachelor	*ein Junggeselle*
to get engaged	*sich verloben*
a fiancé / fiancée	*ein Verlobter / eine Verlobte*
an engagement ring	*ein Verlobungsring*
to announce the engagement	*die Verlobung bekanntgeben*

WEDDINGS

HOCHZEITEN

to decide on a wedding day	*sich auf den Hochzeitstag festlegen*
to send out invitations	*Einladungen verschicken*
to look at a wedding present list	*sich eine Hochzeitsliste ansehen*
to get married in church / in a registry office	*in der Kirche / auf dem Standesamt heiraten*
the bride / bridegroom	*die Braut / der Bräutigam*
the best man	*Trauzeuge*
a bridesmaid / a pageboy	*Brautjungfer / ein Page*
the vicar / the registrar	*der Pfarrer / der Standesbeamte*
the organist / the choir	*der Organist / der Chor*

FAMILY AND FRIENDS cont.   *FAMILIE UND FREUNDE Forts.*

WEDDINGS cont.   *HOCHZEITEN Forts.*

the photographer	*der Fotograf*
to pose for photos / to have photos taken	*sich zum fotografieren aufstellen / Fotos machen*
the guests	*die Gäste*
the wedding dress / the veil / the train / the wedding ring	*das Hochzeitskleid / der Schleier / der Hochzeitszug / der Ehering*
a bouquet / to carry	*ein Bukett / tragen*
to throw / to catch	*werfen / fangen*
a buttonhole	*ein Knopfloch*
the wedding service	*der Hochzeitsgottesdienst*
to walk down the aisle	*das Kirchenschiff durchschreiten*
the father of the bride	*der Brautvater*
to kneel	*knien*
to sing hymns / to pray	*Kirchenlieder singen / beten*
to throw confetti / rice	*Konfetti / Reis werfen*

THE WEDDING RECEPTION   *DER HOCHZEITSEMPFANG*

to shake hands	*Hände schütteln*
to welcome guests	*Gäste willkommen heißen*
to make a speech	*eine Rede halten*
the best man's speech	*die Rede des Trauzeugen*
to make a joke	*einen Witz machen*
to make a toast	*einen Toast bringen*
to raise your glasses	*die Gläser erheben*

THE HONEYMOON   *DIE FLITTERWOCHEN*

to leave the reception	*den Empfang verlassen*
to get changed	*sich umziehen*
to go on honeymoon	*in die Flitterwochen fahren*
to decorate the car	*das Auto ausschmücken*
newly married	*frisch verheiratet*
to throw confetti	*Konfetti werfen*
to wave goodbye	*Auf Wiedersehen winken*

FAMILY AND FRIENDS cont.

FAMILIE UND FREUNDE
Forts.

WEDDING ANNIVERSARIES
a silver wedding
a golden wedding
a diamond wedding
to celebrate a wedding anniversary

HOCHZEITSTAGE
eine silberne Hochzeit
eine goldene Hochzeit
eine diamantene Hochzeit
einen Hochzeitstag feiern

MIDDLE AGE
to be middle aged
to have grown up children
to become a grandparent
to go through the menopause
middle age spread
hormone replacement therapy
to feel depressed
to start getting wrinkles
to have more free time
to take up new interests

MITTLERES ALTER
im mittleren Alter sein
erwachsene Kinder haben
Großvater / Großmutter werden
in den Wechseljahren sein
Wechseljahrbeschwerden
Hormontherapie
sich deprimiert fühlen
Falten bekommen
mehr Freizeit haben
neue Interessen entwickeln

OLD AGE
to retire
to take partial / early retirement
to enjoy retirement
a pension / a senior citizen
to get discounts
to live on one's own
to live with one's family
to go into sheltered housing
a retirement home
to be looked after / to be nursed

DAS ALTER
in den Ruhestand gehen
in Teil- Vorruhestand gehen
den Ruhestand genießen
eine Rente / ein älterer Bürger
Vergünstigungen beziehen
alleine leben
bei seiner Familie leben
in eine Altenwohnanlage ziehen
ein Altersheim
betreut werden / gepflegt werden

FAMILY AND FRIENDS cont.　　*FAMILIE UND FREUNDE*
　　　　　　　　　　　　　　　　Forts.

DEATH	*TOD*
to die	*sterben*
to have a heart attack	*eine Herzattacke habe*
to have a stroke	*einen Schlaganfall habe*
to have cancer	*Krebs haben*
to be unconscious	*nicht bei Bewußtsein sein*
to be unable to talk properly	*unfähig sein, richtig zu sprechen*
to forget things	*Dinge vergessen*
to be in pain	*Schmerzen haben*
to take painkillers	*Schmerzmittel nehmen*
to die in one's sleep	*im Schlaf sterben*
to die peacefully	*friedlich sterben*
to call the doctor	*den Arzt rufen*
to sign the death certificate	*den Totenschein unterzeichnen*
to call the mortuary	*den Leichenwagen bestellen*
the funeral	*die Beerdigung*
a church / a crematorium	*eine Kirche / ein Krematorium*
the coffin / a grave	*der Sarg / ein Grab*
a wreath / flowers	*ein Kranz / Blumen*
to mourn / to weep	*trauern / weinen*
to pray	*beten*
to comfort	*trösten*
a widow / a widower	*eine Witwe / ein Witwer*

CONTACTING PEOPLE
BY POST & BY TELEPHONE

KONTAKTE ZU ANDEREN MIT POST & MIT TELEFON

BY POST   *MIT POST*

STATIONERY   *SCHREIBWAREN*

Notepaper	*Briefpapier*
headed	*mit einer Überschrift versehen*
lined	*liniert*
unlined	*unliniert*
white	*weiß*
cream	*Cremefarben*
azure	*himmelblau*
blue	*blau*
a line guide	*ein Linienpapier*

Postcards	*Postkarten*
a picture postcard	*eine Bildpostkarte*
a funny postcard	*eine Witzpostkarte*
a scenic postcard	*eine Landschafts-postkarte*
a photograph	*eine Fotografie*
an art reproduction	*eine Kunstpostkarte*

**CONTACTING PEOPLE
BY POST cont.**

*KONTAKTE ZU ANDEREN
MIT POST Forts.*

STATIONERY cont.

SCHREIBWAREN Forts.

Envelopes	*Umschläge*
an envelope	*ein Umschlag*
to seal	*schließen*
to lick	*lecken*
to slit open	*aufschlitzen*
to address	*adressieren*
a padded envelope	*ein wattierter Umschlag*
to enclose a stamped addressed envelope (an SAE)	*beilegen ein frankierter Rückumschlag*

Stamps	*Briefmarken*
a stamp / to buy	*eine Briefmarke / kaufen*
a book of stamps	*ein Briefmarkenheft*
a first class stamp	*Schnellpost*
a second class stamp	*Langsamerepost*
to lick / to stick on	*lecken / aufkleben*

USEFUL EXPRESSIONS	*NÜTZLICHE AUSDRUCKWEISEN*
What stamp do I need for ..?	*Welche Briefmarke brauche ich für...?*
How much does it cost to send a letter to America?	*Wieviel kostet ein Brief nach Amerika?*
by the cheapest means possible	*so billig wie möglich.*
as fast as possible	*so schnell wie möglich*
How long will it take to get there?	*Wie lange wird es dauern, bis er ankommt?*
How much does it weigh?	*Wieviel wiegt er?*
Put it on the scales.	*Legen Sie ihn auf die Briefwaage.*

CONTACTING PEOPLE BY POST cont.

KONTAKTE ZU ANDEREN MIT POST Forts.

USEFUL EXPRESSIONS cont.

NÜTZLICHE AUSDRUCKWEISEN Forts.

Guaranteed next day delivery	*Garantierte Zustellung am nächsten Tag.*
to send by recorded delivery	*per Einschreiben schicken*
by air mail	*mit Luftpost*
an international reply coupon	*ein internationales Antwortformular*
to fill in details on a form	*Angaben auf einem Formular ausfüllen*
the sender	*der Absender*
the recipient	*der Adressat*
Surname	*Nachname*
Christian names	*Vornamen*
address and postcode	*Adresse und Postleitzahl*
date	*Datum*
contents	*Inhalt*
value	*Wert*

PARCELS

PÄCKCHEN

to wrap up a parcel	*ein Päckchen einpacken*
wrapping paper / gift wrap	*Einpackpapier / Geschenkpapier*
brown paper / tissue paper	*braunes Papier / Seidenpapier*
corrugated paper / bubble wrap	*Wellpappe / bubble wrap?*
Sellotape / to sellotape	*Tesafilm / mit Tesafilm kleben*
string / to tie a knot	*Schnur / einen Knoten machen*
to put your finger on the knot	*Deinen Finger auf den Knoten legen*
scissors / a knife / to cut	*eine Schere / ein Messer / schneiden*
tape / to stick	*Band / kleben*
to undo	*aufmachen*
Fragile! Handle with Care!	*Zerbrechlich! / Vorsicht!*
This way up!	*Oben!*

CONTACTING PEOPLE BY POST cont.

KONTAKTE ZU ANDEREN MIT POST Forts.

POST BOXES
Is there a post box near here?

to take a letter to the post
What are the collection times?
the first post / the next post

to catch the last post
to miss the post
Local Mail Only
Other Desinations
Working Days
Public Holidays

BRIEFKÄSTEN
Gibt es hier in der Nähe einen Briefkasten?

einen Brief zur Post bringen
Wann sind die Leerungszeiten?
die erste Leerung / die zweite Leerung

die letzte Leerung erwischen
die Leerung verpassen
Nur Ortsbriefe
Andere Bestimmungsorte
Werktage
Sonn- und Feiertage

THE POST OFFICE
to queue up
to wait to be served
to go to the counter

DAS POSTAMT
sich anstellen
warten bis man bedient wird.
an den Schalter gehen

POSTAL DELIVERIES
a postman / a post van
a postal round
What time does the post usually arrive?
Has the post been delivered yet?
Is there a letter for me?

POSTZUSTELLUNG
ein Briefträger / ein Postauto
ein Zustellbezirk
Um wieviel Uhr kommt normalerweise die Post?
Ist die Post schon da gewesen?
Ist ein Brief für mich dabei?

CONTACTING PEOPLE BY POST cont.	*KONTAKTE ZU ANDEREN* *MIT POST Forts.*

WRITING LETTERS   *BRIEFE SCHREIBEN*

Formal letters Dear Sir.......Yours faithfully,.. Dear Mr. / Mrs./ Miss.... .....Yours sincerely **Informal letters** Dear James, ... With best wishes / Affectionately / Love / Lots of love / All my love..	*Offizielle Briefe* *Sehr geehrte Damen und Herren..........Hochachtungsvoll,....* *Sehr geehrter Herr / Frau / Fräulein....* *.......mit freundlichen Grüßen* *Persönliche Briefe* *Lieber Jakob,.....* *Mit den besten Wünschen / mit herzlichen Grüßen / mit Liebe / ganz herzlich / allerherzlichst..*

BY TELEPHONE   *MIT DEM TELEFON*

To telephone England from Germany dial 00, followed by 44 (the U.K. code), followed by your area code minus the first zero and finally the rest of the telephone number.	*Um England von Deutschland aus anzurufen, wähle 00, anschließend 44 (die Vorwahl für GB), anschließend Deine regionale Vorwahlnummer ohne die erste Null, und zum Schluß den Rest der Telefonnummer.*

To telephone to Germany from England dial 00, followed by 49, followed by the area code minus the first 0, followed by the person's telephone number.	*Um Deutschland von England aus anzurufen, wähle 00, anschließend 49, anschließend Deine regionale Vorwahlnummer, ohne die erste Null und zum Schluß die Telefonnummer der Person, die Du erreichen willst.*

CONTACTING PEOPLE BY TELEPHONE cont.

KONTAKTE ZU ANDEREN MIT TELEFON Forts.

British Directory Enquiries = 192	*Die britische Auskunft=192*
International Directory Enquiries = 153	*die internationale Auskunft =153*
German Directory Enquiries =01188	*Die deutsche Auskunft = 01188*
German International Directory Enquiries = 00118	*Die internationale Auskunft = 00118*

Germany's ringing tone consists of tones separated by longer pauses. Germany's engaged tone is similar to the U.K.'s engaged tone but faster.	*Deutsche Klingelzeichen bestehen aus Zeichen, die durch eine längere Pause getrennt sind. Das deutsche Besetztzeichen ist dem britischen Besetztzeichen sehr ähnlich, nur etwas schneller.*

THE TELEPHONE

DAS TELEFON	
the receiver	*der Hörer*
to pick up / to listen	*abnehmen / hören*
The telephone is ringing.	*das Telefon klingelt*
Shall I answer it? I'll get it.	*Soll ich dran gehen? Ich gehe.*
I'll take it in the kitchen.	*Ich nehme es mit in die Küche.*
the dial / to dial a number	*die Wählscheibe / eine Nummer wählen*

CONTACTING PEOPLE BY TELEPHONE cont.
KONTAKTE ZU ANDEREN MIT TELEFON Forts.

THE TONES
DIE ZEICHEN

the dialling tone	*das Wählzeichen*
to get the engaged tone	*das Besetztzeichen hören*
It's engaged. / It's ringing.	*Es ist besetzt. / Es klingelt.*
It's out of order.	*Es funktioniert nicht.*
It's unobtainable.	*Man kann niemanden erreichen.*
There isn't any dialling tone.	*Es gibt kein Wählzeichen.*
Can you help me, please?	*Kannst du mir bitte helfen?*
I was cut off.	*Ich wurde getrennt.*

ANSWERING THE PHONE
DAS TELEFON BEANTWORTEN

Hello, is that Peter?	*Hallo, ist dort Peter?*
Could I speak to your mother?	*Kann ich mit Deiner Mutter sprechen?*
Is Julia there please?	*Ist Julia da?*
Who is that speaking?	*Wer spricht dort?*
Who do you want to talk to?	*Wen möchten Sie sprechen?*
To whom do you want to speak?	*Mit wem möchten Sie sprechen?*
Hang on.	*Einen Moment?*
I'll just get him / her for you.	*Ich hole ihn / sie für Dich.*
He / she won't be a minute.	*Er / sie kommt gleich.*
I am sorry he / she isn't in at the moment.	*Tut mir leid, aber er / sie ist momentan nicht da.*
When will he / she be back?	*Wann kommt er / sie zurück?*
Can you say I rang?	*Können Sie ausrichten, ich hätte angerufen?*
Could you give him / her a message, please?	*Könnten Sie bitte ihm /ihr eine Nachricht hinterlassen?*
I will ring again another time.	*Ich rufe noch mal an.*
We are just about to eat. Can we ring you later?	*Wir fangen gerade mit dem Essen an. Können wir dich später zurückrufen?*
What is your number?	*Wie ist Deine Nummer?*
Can I take a message?	*Kann ich etwas ausrichten?*
Whom shall I say called?	*Wer hat angerufen?*

**CONTACTING PEOPLE
BY TELEPHONE cont.**

*KONTAKTE ZU ANDEREN
MIT TELEFON Forts.*

FINDING TELEPHONE NUMBERS	*TELEFONNUMMERN HERAUSBEKOMMEN*
a telephone directory	*eine Telefonbuch*
an address book	*ein Adreßbuch*
to look up a number	*nach einer Nummer schauen*
What is their name?	*Wie heißen die?*
How do you spell it?	*Wie buchstabiert man ihn?*
What is their initial?	*Wie sind die Initialien?*
What is their address?	*Wie ist deren Adresse?*
Yellow Pages	*Branchenbuch*
Directory Enquiries	*Telefonauskunft*

USING A PUBLIC CALL BOX	*EINE ÖFFENTLICHE TELEFONZELLE BENUTZEN*
I need some change.	*Ich brauche Kleingeld.*
What coins does it take?	*Welche Münzen passen rein?*
a telephone token	*eine Telefonmarke*
Does it take a 'phone card?	*Kann man eine Telefonkarte benutzen?*
a twenty five unit card	*eine Karte mit fünfundzwanzig Einheiten*
Could I reverse the charge, please?	*Könnte ich bitte ein "R"-Gespräch führen?*
out of order	*Außer Betrieb*
How do you use this telephone?	*Wie benutzt man dieses Telefon?*
Can you use a chargecard?	*Kann man eine Kreditkarte benutzen?*

**CONTACTING PEOPLE
BY TELEPHONE cont.**

*KONTAKTE ZU ANDEREN
MIT TELEFON Forts.*

ANSWERPHONES	*ANRUFBEANTWORTER*
to switch on / off	*an- / ausstellen*
Is the answerphone on?	*Ist der Anrufbeantworter an?*
There is a message on the answerphone for you.	*Auf dem Anrufbeantworter ist eine Nachricht für Dich .*
The answerphone is flashing / beeping.	*Der Anrufbeantworter blinkt / piept.*
to play back the tape	*das Band zurückspielen*
to listen to the messages	*die Nachrichten anhören*
to record a message	*eine Nachricht aufnehmen*
to rewind	*zurückspulen*
to reset	*zurückstellen*

SCHOOL AND COLLEGE
SCHULE UND HOCHSCHULE

TYPES OF SCHOOL	*SCHULARTEN*
I go to..	*Ich gehe in...*
• a nursery school	• *einen Kindergarten*
• a primary school	• *eine Grundschule*
• a secondary school	• *eine höhere Schule*
• a private (public) school	• *eine Privatschule*
• a state school	• *eine staatliche Schule*
• a coeducational school	• *eine koedukative Schule*
• a sixth form college	• *ein Oberstufen-Gymnasium*

SCHOOL BUILDINGS AND ROOMS	*SCHULGEBÄUDE UND RÄUME*
the school office	*das Schulbüro*
the staff room	*das Lehrerzimmer*

The assembly hall	***Die Aula***
the platform	*das Podium*
a microphone	*ein Mikrofon*
chairs / to stack	*Stühle / stapeln*
to put out in rows	*in Reihen aufstellen*

The classroom	***Das Klassenzimmer***
a desk / a desk lid	*ein Lehrerpult / ein Pultdeckel*
to open / to close	*öffnen / schließen*
a chair / to sit down	*ein Stuhl / sich setzen*
the blackboard / to write on	*die Tafel / schreiben auf*
chalk / a blackboard duster	*Kreide / ein Tafelschwamm*
to wipe the blackboard	*die Tafel wischen*
the notice board	*das Schwarze Brett*
to pin up	*anstecken*
a notice	*eine Mitteilung*

SCHOOL BUILDINGS AND ROOMS cont.

SCHULGEBÄUDE UND RÄUME Forts.

The dining room	*Der Eßraum*
the canteen	*die Kantine*
to queue up	*sich anstellen*
to take a tray	*ein Tablett nehmen*
to ask for	*fragen nach*
to help yourself	*sich selber bedienen*
self-service	*Selbstbedienung*
Could I have a little…, please?	*Könnte ich bitte ein wenig von.....haben?*
Could I have a lot of…,please?	*Könnte ich bitte viel von....haben?*
to clear the table	*den Tisch abräumen*
to wipe the table	*den Tisch abwischen*

The gymnasium	*Die Turnhalle*
the wall bars	*die Kletterwand*
a vault / a horse	*ein Sprungpferd / ein Pferd*
to vault	*einen Scherensprung machen*
a box	*ein Kasten*
a monkey bar / to balance	*ein Trapez / balancieren*
a rope / to climb / to swing	*ein Seil / klettern / schwingen*
a rope ladder	*eine Strickleiter*
a spring board	*ein Sprungbrett*
a trampoline	*ein Trampolin*
a mat	*eine Matte*
the showers	*die Duschen*
a changing room	*eine Umkleide-kabine*

SCHOOL BUILDINGS AND ROOMS cont.

SCHULGEBÄUDE UND RÄUME Forts.

The music rooms	*Das Musikzimmer*
a practice room	*ein Übungszimmer*
a piano	*ein Klavier*
a music stand	*ein Notenständer*
lockers	*Schließfächer*
soundproofed	*schalldicht*

(See pages 157-158 for music lessons)

The art room	*Der Kunstraum*
an easel	*ein Staffelei*
paints	*Farben*
paintbrushes	*Farbpinsel*
paper	*Papier*
to have a painting on the wall	*ein Bild an der Wand haben*
to be on display	*ausgestellt werden*
an exhibition of work	*eine Werk-Austellung.*

(See page 230 for details of art equipment)

The science block	*Die naturwissenschaftlichen Fächer*
a laboratory	*ein Labor*
an overall	*ein Arbeitsanzug*
safety glasses	*Schutzbrille*
a work bench	*eine Werkbank*
a sink	*ein Waschbecken*
acid / alkali / litmus paper	*Säure- / Alkali- / Lackmuspapier*
the Periodic Table	*das Periodensystem*

SCHOOL BUILDINGS AND ROOMS cont.

SCHULGEBÄUDE UND RÄUME Forts.

THE SCIENCE BLOCK cont.

DIE NATURWISSEN-SCHAFTLICHEN FÄCHER Forts.

Apparatus	Geräte
a beaker	*ein Becherglas*
a Bunsen burner	*ein Bunsenbrenner*
a tripod	*ein Stativ*
gauze	*Gaze*
a burette	*eine Bürette*
a condenser	*ein Kondensator*
a crucible	*ein Schmelztiegel*
a crystallizing dish	*eine Kristallisie-rungsschale*
a delivery tube	*eine Abdampfschale*
an evaporating basin	*eine Zustellröhre*
filter paper	*Filterpapier*
a flask	*ein Kolben*
conical	*kegelförmig*
round bottomed	*runder Boden*
flat bottomed	*flacher Boden*
a fractionating column	*die Bruchreihe*
a funnel	*ein Trichter*
a gas jar	*ein Gasbehälter*
a measuring cylinder	*ein Meßzylinder*
a pair of tongs	*Zangen*
a pipette	*eine Pipette*
scales	*Waagen*
a spatula	*ein Spatel*
a stand	*ein Gestell*
a clamp	*eine Klammer*
a syringe	*eine Spritze*
a test tube	*ein Reagenzglas*
a test tube rack	ein Reagenz-glashalter
a thermometer	*ein Thermometer*

SCHOOL BUILDINGS AND ROOMS cont.

SCHULGEBÄUDE UND RÄUME Forts.

The library	*Die Bibliothek*
the librarian	*der Bibliothekar*
to take a book out	*ein Buch ausleihen*
to return a book	*ein Buch zurückbringen*
to be overdue	*überfällig sein*
to reserve	*reservieren*
to read	*lesen*
a reference book	*ein Nachschlagewerk*
a catalogue	*ein Katalog*
a list of authors	*eine Autorenliste*
a list of titles	*eine Titelliste*
alphabetical	*alphabetisch*
to look up	*nachschauen*

The cloakroom	*Die Garderobe*
a peg / to hang up	*ein Kleiderhaken / aufhängen*
a locker / to lock / to unlock	*ein Spind / schließen / aufschließen*
to put away / to get out	*wegschließen / herausholen*
the toilets / engaged / vacant	*die Toiletten / besetzt / frei*
the washbasin	*das Waschbecken*
to wash one's hands	*sich seine Hände waschen*
to dry one's hands	*sich seine Hände trocknen*
a towel	*ein Handtuch*
a mirror / to look in	*ein Spiegel / reinschauen*
to brush one's hair	*sich seine Haare bürsten*

SCHOOL BUILDINGS AND ROOMS cont.

SCHULGEBÄUDE UND RÄUME Forts.

The medical room	*Der Sanitätsraum*
the nurse	*die Krankenschwester*
to feel ill / to lie down	*sich krank fühlen / sich hinlegen*
to have a headache / to feel sick	*Kopfweh haben / sich übel fühlen*
to take your temperature	*die Temperatur messen*
to have an accident	*einen Unfall haben*
to go to hospital / to go home	*ins Krankenhaus gehen / nach Hause gehen*
to ring your family	*seine Familie anrufen*

For details of illnesses see pages 406-417

THE SCHOOL GROUNDS

DIE SCHULGELÄNDE

the playground	*der Schulhof / der Spielplatz*
the netball courts	*die Netzballplätze*
the tennis courts (See pages 255-261 for vocabulary for playing tennis)	*der Tennisplatz*
the sportsfield	*der Sportplatz*
the hockey / lacrosse pitch	*das Hockeyfeld / das Lacrossefeld*
the swimming pool (See pages 301-308 for vocabulary for swimming)	*das Schwimmbad*

THE STAFF

DAS SCHULPERSONAL

the headmaster / headmistress	*der Direktor / die Direktorin*
the deputy headmaster	*der stellvertretende Direktor*
the deputy headmistress	*die stellvertretende Direktorin*
the head of year	*der für ein Jahre gewählte Leiter*
a head of department	*der Fachbereichsleiter*
the form teacher	*der Klassenlehrer*
a subject teacher	*ein Fachlehrer*
the cooks	*die Köche*
the cleaners	*die Reinigungsangestellten*
the caretaker	*der Hausmeister*

SCHOOL AND COLLEGE cont.

SCHULE UND HOCHSCHULE Forts.

THE PUPILS	DIE SCHÜLER
head boy / head girl	*Klassenbester / Klassenbeste*
a prefect / a monitor	*ein Vertrauensschüler / ein Klassensprecher*
a pupil	*ein Schüler*
a day pupil / a boarding pupil	*ein Ganztagsschüler / ein Internatsschüler*
a weekly boarder	*ein Wochenschüler*
a new girl / a new boy	*ein neues Mädchen / ein neuer Junge*
a first year	*ein Studienanfänger*
a sixth former	*ein Oberstufenschüler*

CLOTHES AND EQUIPMENT	KLEIDUNG, AUSSTATTUNG UND AUSRÜSTUNG
school uniform	*Schuluniform*
an overall	*ein Arbeitsanzug*
Do you have to wear school uniform?	*Mußt Du eine Schuluniform tragen?*
What colour is your school uniform?	*Welche Farbe hat Deine Schuluniform?*
Do you like your uniform?	*Magst Du Deine Uniform?*

SCHOOL AND COLLEGE cont.

SCHULE UND HOCHSCHULE Forts.

A briefcase	*Eine Mappe*
a holdall / a satchel	*ein Riemenhalter / ein Ranzen*
a school bag / a duffle bag	*eine Schultasche / ein Sack*
a text book	*ein Textbuch*
an exercise book	*ein Übungsbuch*
a notebook	*ein Notizbuch*
a file / a folder	*ein Ordner / ein Heft*
filepaper	*Ordnerpapier*
a pencil case / a pen / a pencil	*ein Mäppchen / ein Kugelschreiber / ein Bleistift*
a rubber / a pencil sharpener	*ein Radiergummi / ein Bleistiftspitzer*
a calculator	*ein Taschenrechner*

For detailed stationery vocabulary see pages 359-362.

A sports bag	*Ein Sporttasche*
sports kit	*Sportmontur*
sports shoes	*Sportschuhe*
a towel	*ein Handtuch*

THE SCHOOL DAY

DER SCHULTAG

Registration	*Anmeldung*
to take the register	*sich anmelden*
to be present / absent	*anwesend / abwesend sein*
to give out notices	*Meldungen ausgeben*

SCHOOL ASSEMBLY	*SCHULVERSAMMLUNG*
to sing a hymn / to pray	*eine Hymne singen / beten*
to march in / out	*reinmarschieren/ rausmarschieren*
to walk in single file	*in einzelnen Reihen laufen*

SCHOOL AND COLLEGE cont.

SCHULE UND HOCHSCHULE Forts.

THE LESSONS (abc)		DER UNTERRICHT	
Art	*Kunst*	(English)	*(Englisch)*
Biology	*Biologie*	(French)	*(Französisch)*
Business Studies	*Wirtschaft*	(German)	*(Deutsch)*
Chemistry	*Chemie*	(Italian)	*(Italienisch)*
Design	*Gestaltung*	(Russian)	*(Russisch)*
Domestic Science	*Hauswirtschaft*	(Spanish)	*(Spanisch)*
General Studies	*Studium Generale*	(Literature)	*(Literatur)*
Geography	*Geographie*	(Language)	*(Sprachen)*
Greek	*Griechisch*	(Vocabulary)	*(Vokabular)*
Gymnastics	*Turnen*	(Grammar)	*(Grammatik)*
History	*Geschichte*	(to translate)	*(übersetzen)*
Information Technology	*Informations-technik*	Music	*Musik*
Latin	*Latein*	Needlework	*Handarbeiten*
Mathematics	*Mathematik*	Physical Education	*Sportunterricht*
(Algebra)	*(Algebra)*	Physics	*Physik*
(Geometry)	*(Geometrie)*	Religious Studies	*Religion*
Metalwork	*Metallarbeiten*	Technical Drawing	*Technisches Zeichnen*
Modern Languages	*Moderne Sprachen*	Woodwork	*Holzarbeiten*

THE TIMETABLE	DER STUNDENPLAN
a free period	*eine Freistunde*
the mid-morning break	*die Große pause*
playtime	*Pausenzeit*
lunchtime	*Mittagessenszeit*
afternoon break	*Nachmittagspause*
a bell / to ring	*eine Klingel / klingeln*
the end of the school day	*das Ende des Schultages*
homework	*Hausaufgaben*

SCHOOL AND COLLEGE
cont.

SCHULE UND
HOCHSCHULE Forts.

STUDYING	*STUDIEREN*
to study	*lernen / studieren*
to work	*arbeiten*
to concentrate	*sich konzentrieren*
to do homework	*Hausaufgaben machen*
to read	*lesen*
to write	*schreiben*
to take notes	*Notizen machen*
headings	*Überschriften*
a synopsis	*eine Zusammenfassung*
an abbreviation	*eine Abkürzung*
shorthand	*Stenographieren*

WRITING AN ESSAY	*EIN AUFSATZ / REFERAT SCHREIBEN*
the title	*die Überschrift*
to plan an essay	*ein Aufsatz / ein Referat gliedern*
an introduction	*eine Einführung*
a new paragraph	*ein neuer Absatz*
a conclusion / to sum up	*eine Schlußfolgerung / zusammenfassen*
a quotation	*ein Zitat*
a bibliography	*eine Bibliographie*
to argue / an argument	*argumentieren / ein Argument*
to discuss / a discussion	*erörtern / eine Erörterung*
to describe / a description	*beschreiben / eine Beschreibung*
to look at both sides	*beide Seiten betrachten*
to examine	*untersuchen*
to include facts / dates	*Fakten / Daten einbringen*

SCHOOL AND COLLEGE
cont.

SCHULE UND
HOCHSCHULE Forts.

LEARNING	*LERNEN*
to learn	*lernen*
to memorize	*auswendig lernen*
facts	*Fakten*
dates	*Daten*
a poem	*ein Gedicht*
to revise	*revidieren*
to be tested on	*geprüft werden nach*
to test yourself	*sich selbst prüfen*

EXAMS	*PRÜFUNGEN UND ARBEITEN*
to take an exam	*eine Prüfung machen / eine Arbeit schreiben*
to pass exams	*Prüfungen /Arbeiten bestehen*
to fail exams	*durch Prüfungen / Arbeiten fallen*
to re-take exams	*eine Prüfung / Arbeit wiederholen*
to take a course in	*einen Kurs in....machen*
to wait for the results	*auf das Ergebnis warten*
When do you hear your results?	*Wann bekommst Du Dein Ergebnis?*
The results come on Wednesday.	*Die Ergebnisse kommen am Mittwoch raus.*
How do you get your results?	*Wie bekommst du Dein Ergebnis?*
We have to go into school for them.	*Wie müssen sie uns in der Schule abholen.*
The results come by post.	*Die Ergebnisse kommen mit der Post.*

SCHOOL AND COLLEGE cont.

SCHULE UND HOCHSCHULE Forts.

ASSESSMENTS	*EINSTUFUNGEN*
a school report	*ein Zeugnis*
a mark / a percentage / a grade	*eine Note / eine Prozentzahl / eine Note*
an A grade / a B grade etc.	*eine Eins / eine Zwei usw.*
to be graded	*benotet werden*
a distinction	*eine Auszeichnung*
to come top	*ganz oben sein*
to be about average	*im Durchschnitt liegen*
to be near the bottom	*weit unten sein*
to do one's corrections	*seine Korrekturen machen*
to do better / worse than one had thought	*besser / schlechter abgeschnitten habe, als man dachte*
to be upset	*traurig sein*
to be disappointed	*enttäuscht sein*
to be relieved	*erleichtert sein*
to be delighted	*erfreut sein*

THE SCHOOL YEAR	*DAS SCHULJAHR*
the terms	*die Halbjahre*
the Autumn Term	*die Herbstzeit*
the Spring Term	*die Frühlingszeit*
the Summer Term	*die Sommerzeit*
the holidays	*die Schulferien*
a half-term holiday	*Kurzferien*
the Christmas holidays	*die Weihnachtsferien*
the Easter holidays	*die Osterferien*
the Summer holidays	*die Sommerferien*
Speech Day	*Jahresabschlußfeier*
Founder's Day	*Gründungstag*
a Bank Holiday	*ein National Feiertag*
a public holiday	*ein Feiertag*

SCHOOL AND COLLEGE cont.	SCHULE UND HOCHSCHULE Forts.

USEFUL EXPRESSIONS	NÜTZLICHE AUSDRUCKSWEISEN
My school is:-	*Meine Schule ist*
• co-educational	• *eine koedukative Schule*
• a girls' school	• *eine Mädchenschule*
• a boys' school	• *eine Jungenschule*
• selective	• *mit hohem Leistungsstandard*
• mixed ability	• *mit unterschiedlichen Leistungsstandards*
• streamed	• *mit unterschiedlichen Leistungsstufen*
• large / small	• *groß / klein*
• boarding / day	• *Internat / Ganztagsschule*
My school starts at nine o'clock.	*Meine Schule beginnt um neun Uhr*
My lessons last forty minutes.	*Eine Unterrichtsstunde dauert vierzig Minuten*
We have / don't have school on Saturdays.	*Wir haben / haben keinen Samstagsunterricht.*
We have four Spanish lessons a week.	*Wir haben pro Woche vier Stunden Französisch.*
What's your favourite subject?	*Welches ist Dein Lieblingsfach?*
I like Maths. best.	*Ich mag Mathe am liebsten.*
I hate Latin.	*Ich hasse Latein.*
I think History is really interesting.	*Ich finde Geschichte sehr interessant.*

SCHOOL AND COLLEGE cont.	*SCHULE UND HOCHSCHULE Forts.*

WHAT IS YOUR TEACHER LIKE?	*WIE GEFÄLLT DIR DEIN LEHRER?*
My teacher is..	*Mein Lehrer ist....*
• boring	• *langweilig*
• excellent	• *ausgezeichnet*
• quite good	• *ganz gut*
• strict	• *streng*
• can't keep order	• *kann keine Ordnung halten*
• funny	• *witzig*
• eccentric	• *exzentrisch*
My teacher is...	*Mein lehrer ist..*
• old / young	• *alt / jung*
• male / female	• *eine Frau / ein Mann*

WHAT ARE YOU GOING TO DO WHEN YOU LEAVE SCHOOL?	*WAS WIRST DU TUN, WENN DU DIE SCHULE VERLASSEN HAST*
I am planning to..	*Ich plane aufs / nach....*
I have a place at...	*Ich habe einen Studienplatz in...*
I don't know yet.	*Ich weiß es noch nicht.*

HIGHER EDUCATION	*HÖHERE BILDUNGSWEGE*
to apply for a place at..	*sich für einen Studienplatz in....bewerben*
an interview	*ein Interview*
to be called for an interview	*für ein Interview eingeladen werden*
to do an exam	*eine Prüfung machen*
to get the examination results	*das Prüfungsergebnis bekommen*
the grade	*die Note*
A levels	*Abitur*

SCHOOL AND COLLEGE cont.

SCHULE UND HOCHSCHULE Forts.

HIGHER EDUCATION cont.

HÖHERE BILDUNGSWEGE Forts.

University entrance	*Universitätsaufnahme*
to go to college	*auf die Hochschule gehen*
to go to secretarial college	*auf die Sekretärsschule gehen*
technical college	*Fachhochschule*
a former polytechnic / a new university	*eine frühere Fachhochschule / eine neue Universität*
to get a place at	*einen Studienplatz in.....bekommen*
to read for a degree in	*sich auf ein Studium in......vorbereiten*

LIVING AT COLLEGE	*IN DER UNIVERSITÄT WOHNEN*
to be in your first / second year	*im ersten / zweiten Jahr sein*
to be a fresher	*Student im erstem Jahr sein*
to be in your third / last year	*im dritten / vierten Jahr sein*
to be an undergraduate / a student	*ein Student sein*
to have a place in the hall of residence	*ein Zimmer im Studentenwohnheim haben*
self-catering	*Selbstversorgung*
to live in digs	*in Studentenbuden wohnen*
to rent a flat	*eine Wohnung mieten*
to live with some friends	*mit ein paar Freunden wohnen*
the student union	*die Studentengewerkschaft*
a faculty building	*ein Fakultätsgebäude*
the library	*die Bücherei*

FURTHER EDUCATION cont.   *WEITERE BILDUNGSWEGE*
Forts.

UNIVERSITY DEGREES	*UNIVERSITÄTS-ABSCHLÜSSE*
a first degree	*ein Vordiplom*
a further degree	*ein Diplom / ein Magister*
a doctorate	*ein Doktortitel*
a degree in	*ein Abschluß in*
a graduate	*ein Titel*
What class of degree did you get?	*Welche Abschlußbewertung hast Du bekommen?*
What class are you hoping for?	*Welche Bewertung erhoffst Du Dir?*
a first class degree	*sehr gut*
an upper second	*sehr gut bis gut*
a lower second	*gut*
a third	*befriedigend*
a pass degree	*bestanden*
an honours degree	*mit Auszeichnung*

FURTHER EDUCATION cont. **WEITERE BILDUNGSWEGE Forts.**

DEGREE COURSES		STUDIENGÄNGE	
accountancy	*Buchhaltung*	librarianship	*Bibliothekswesen*
architecture	*Architektur*	literature	*Literatur*
the Arts	geisteswissen-schaftliches Fach	mathematics	*Mathematik*
biochemistry	*Biochemie*	mechanical engineering	*Maschinenbau*
botany	*Botanik*	media studies	*Medienwissen-schaften*
business studies	*Wirtschaftslehre*	medicine	*Medizin*
classics	*Altphilologie*	modern languages	*Moderne Sprachen*
computer sciences	Informatik	philosophy	*Philosophie*
dentistry	*Zahnmedizin*	politics	*Politik*
Divinity	*Theologie*	psychology	*Psychologie*
economics	*Volkswirtschaft / Betriebswirt-schaft*	sociology	*Soziologie*
electrical engineering	*Elektroingenieur*	social sciences	*Sozialwissen-schaften*
engineering	*Ingenieurwesen*	statistics	*Statistiken*
film production	*Film*	theatre production	*Theater*
geography	*Geographie*	theology	*Theologie*
geology	*Geologie*	veterinary science	*Tierärztlich*
history	*Geschichte*	zoology	*Zoologie*
law	*Jura*		

STATIONERY
SCHREIBWAREN

PAPER	*PAPIER (n)*
coloured paper	*buntes Papier*
file paper / ring reinforcers	*Aktenpapier / Lochverstärker*
graph paper	*Graphikpapier*
headed notepaper	*beschriftetes Briefpapier*
lined / unlined paper	*liniertes / unliniertes Papier*
squared paper	*Millimeterpapier*
tracing paper	*Pauspapier*
writing paper	*Schreibpapier*

BOOKS	*BÜCHER (n)*
an exercise book	*ein Übungsbuch*
a rough book	*ein leeres Buch*
a note book	*ein Notizbuch*
a text book	*ein Textbuch*

FILES	*ORDNER (m)*
to file	*in Aktenordner einlegen*
a ringbinder file	*ein Ringbuchordner*
an envelope file	*eine Klarsichthülle*
a folder	*ein Mappe*
a file divider	*ein Ordnertrennblatt*

WRITING EQUIPMENT — *SCHREIBGERÄTE*

A pencil case	*ein Mäppchen*
to open / to close	*öffnen / schließen*
to zip up / to unzip / a zip	*zuziehen / aufziehen / ein Reißverschluß*

STATIONERY cont.   *SCHREIBWAREN Forts.*

Pens	*Stifte (m)*
a ball point pen	*ein Kugelschreiber*
a biro	*ein Kugelschreiber*
a felt-tip pen	*ein Filzstift*
a fine tip	*eine feine Spitze*
a thicker tip	*eine dickere Spitze*
a fountain pen	*ein Füllfederhalter*
a fine nib	*eine feine Schreibfeder*
a medium nib	*eine mittlere Schreibfeder*
a thick nib	*eine dicke Schreibfeder*
a cartridge pen	*ein Tinten-patronenstift*

Ink	*Tinte (f)*
a bottle of ink	*ein Tintenfaß*
to fill the pen	*den Federhalter auffüllen*
to run out of ink	*keine Tinte mehr haben*
a cartridge	*eine Tintenpatrone*
to need a new cartridge	*eine neue Patrone brauchen*
to put a cartridge in	*eine neue Patrone einlegen*
a full / half-full / empty cartridge	*eine volle / halbvolle / leere Patrone*
What type of cartridge does it take?	*Welche Sorte Patronen braucht man?*
an ink eradicator	*ein Tintenlöscher*
a mistake	*ein Fehler*
blotting paper / to blot	*Löschpapier / löschen*
an ink blot	*ein Tintenklecks*
to spill the ink	*die Tinte verschütten*

STATIONERY cont.   *SCHREIBWAREN Forts.*

Pencils	***Bleistifte***
a lead pencil	*ein Bleistift*
a colouring pencil	*ein Buntstift*
hard / soft	*hart / weich*
the point / blunt / sharp	*die Spitze / stumpf / spitz*
to break the lead	*die Spitze abbrechen*
a pencil sharpener	*ein Spitzer*
to sharpen	*spitzen*
to throw away the shavings	*das Abgespitzte wegwerfen*

Rubbers	***Radiergummis (m)***
to make a mistake	*einen Fehler machen*
to rub out	*ausradieren*
an ink rubber	*ein Tintenradierer*

Rulers	***Lineale (n)***
metric / imperial	*metrisch / imperial (nach britischem Maß)*
to measure	*messen*
to draw a straight line	*eine gerade Linie ziehen*
to underline / double underline	*unterstreichen / zweimal unterstreichen*

GEOMETRY EQUIPMENT	***GEOMETRIE-AUSRÜSTUNG (f)***
a compass	*ein Zirkel*
a protractor	*ein Winkelmesser*
a set square	*ein Winkel*
to draw an angle	*einen Winkel zeichnen*
to measure an angle	*einen Winkel messen*

STATIONERY cont.

SCHREIBWAREN Forts.

OTHER EQUIPMENT

ANDERE GERÄTE

Scissors	*Scheren (f)*
to cut	*schneiden*
sharp / blunt	*scharf / stumpf*
to cut along a line	*an einer Linie entlang schneiden*
to cut out	*ausschneiden*

Fastening things together	*Sachen aneinander befestigen*
glue	*Klebstoff*
sellotape	*Tesafilm*
double sided sticky tape	*doppelseitiges-Klebeband*
a stapler / to staple / a staple	*ein Hefter / heften / eine Heftklammer*
to run out of staples	*keine Heftklammern mehr haben*
Have you any more staples?	*Hast Du noch Heftklammern?*
How do you load the staples.	*Wie legt man die Heftklammern in den Hefter?*

Hole punchers	*Locher (m)*
to punch holes	*Lochen*
to use ring reinforcers	*Lochverstärkerer benutzen*

Stencils	*Schablonen (f)*
to stencil / a stencil	*schablonieren / eine Schablone*
an alphabet stencil	*eine Buchstabenschablone*
capital letters / lower case letters	*Großbuchstaben / Kleinbuchstaben*

CURRENT EVENTS
AKTUELLE EREIGNISSE

POLITICS   *POLITIK*

ELECTIONS	*WAHLEN*
to call / hold an election	*eine Wahl ausrufen / halten*
to hold a referendum	*einen Volksentscheid abhalten*
a general election	*eine allgemeine Wahl (in Germany : eine Bundestagswahl)*
to nominate / a nomination	*nominieren / eine Nominierung*
to choose a candidate	*einen Kandidaten wählen*
to stand at an election	*sich einer Wahl stellen*
to canvass opinion	*um Stimmen werben*
to campaign	*einen Wahlkampf abhalten*
to give a speech	*eine Rede halten*
the election day	*der Wahltag*
a polling station / a ballot paper	*ein Wahllokal / ein Stimmzettel*
to put a cross	*ankreuzen*
to vote for / against	*wählen für / gegen*
to vote by secret ballot	*in geheimer Wahl wählen*
a postal vote	*eine Briefwahl*
the results of an election	*das Wahlergebnis*
to announce the result	*das Ergebnis bekanntgeben*
to win an election	*eine Wahl gewinnen*
by a narrow margin	*mit knappem Vorsprung*
by a large majority	*mit großer Mehrheit*
to be elected / to be defeated	*gewählt werden / besiegt werden*
to lose an election	*eine Wahl verlieren*
to demand a re-count	*eine Neuzählung fordern*
How would you vote?	*Wie würdest Du wählen?*
I don't bother to vote.	*Ich wähle nicht.*
I voted for…	*Ich habe für....gewählt.*
private versus public life	*privatesgegen öffentliches Leben*
media attention	*Medienaufmerksamkeit*

CURRENT EVENTS cont.   *AKTUELLE EREIGNISSE*
                                  Forts.

THE ECONOMY	*DIE WIRTSCHAFT*
to pay taxes	*Steuern zahlen*
high / low taxation	*hohe / niedrige Steuern*
V.A.T.	*Mehrwertsteuerfrei*
income tax	*Einkommenssteuerfrei*
exempt from tax	*befreit von Steuern*
the Budget	*der Staatshaushalt*
the recession	*die Rezession*
inflation	*Inflation*
the depression	*die Wirtschaftskrise*
unemployment	*Arbeitslosigkeit*
the Welfare State	*der Wohlfahrtsstaat*

THE WORKERS	*DIE ARBEITER*
a Trades Union	*eine Gewerkschaft*
to call a strike	*einen Streik ausrufen*
to go on strike	*in Streik treten*
to go out in sympathy	*sympathisieren*
to demand	*fordern*
• a pay rise	• *eine Lohnerhöhung*
• better hours	• *bessere Arbeitszeiten*
• better conditions	• *bessere Arbeitsbedingungen*
• equality	• *Gleichheit*
• a minimum wage	• *ein Mindestlohn*
to wave a banner	*ein Transparent wehen lassen*
to picket	*einen Streikposten aufstellen*
a peaceful / violent demonstration	*eine friedliche Demonstration / ein Demonstration mit Ausschreitungen*

CURRENT EVENTS cont.   *AKTUELLE EREIGNISSE*
                                 Forts.

EMERGENCIES   *AUSNAHME-ZUSTÄNDE*

to declare a state of emergency	*einen Ausnahmezustand erklären*
a riot	*ein Aufstand*
the riot police	*die Bereitschaftspolizei*
shields / truncheons / tear gas	*Schilder / Gummiknüppel / Tränengas*
a bomb scare / a car bomb	*ein Bombenalarm / eine Autobombe*
terrorists	*Terroristen*
to evacuate the area	*die Gegend evakuieren*
the bomb disposal squad	*das Bombenräumkommando*

WAR	*KRIEG*
to declare war on	*den Krieg erklären an*
to be at war with	*im Krieg stehen mit*
to fight / to wound	*kämpfen / verwunden*
casualties / the wounded	*Verluste / die Verletzten*
the number of dead	*die Anzahl der Toten*
guerrilla warfare	*Guerillakrieg*
nuclear war / a nuclear explosion	*Atomkrieg / eine Atomexplosion*
radiation / fall out	*Radioaktivität / der Niederschlag*
an anti-nuclear protest	*ein Anti-Atomprotest*
to be a pacifist	*ein Pazifist sein*
to campaign for	*sich einsetzen für*
a protest march	*ein Protestmarsch*
a peaceful demonstration	*eine friedliche Demonstration*
unilateral / multilateral	*einseitige / multilaterale*
disarmament	*Abrüstung*
to declare a truce	*einen Waffenstillstand erklären*
to cease fighting	*die Kämpfe beendigen*

CURRENT EVENTS cont.

AKTUELLE EREIGNISSE Forts.

LAW AND ORDER	*RECHT UND ORDNUNG*
the police	*die Polizei*
a policeman / a policewoman	*ein Polizist / eine Polizistin*
a police car / a siren	*ein Polizeiauto / ein Blaulicht*
to break the law	*das Gesetz brechen*
to break the speed limit	*die Geschwindigkeitsbegrenzung mißachten*
speed cameras	*eine Geschwindigkeitsüberwachung*
to be over the breathalyser limit	*über der Promillegrenze sein*
to be disqualified from driving	*die Fahrerlaubnis entzogen bekommen*
to take illegal drugs	*illegale Drogen nehmen*
to be under age	*nicht volljährig sein*
to caution / to arrest / to imprison	*verwarnen / festnehmen / inhaftieren*
to witness / to give evidence	*bezeugen / aussagen*
to sign a statement	*eine Stellungnahme unterzeichnen*
to telephone your home	*Zuhause anrufen*
to ask for a solicitor	*nach einen Rechtsanwalt fragen*
to remain silent	*keine Aussage machen*

LAW COURTS	*GERICHTSHÖFE*
the judge / the jury	*der Richter / die Schöffen*
to try	*versuchen*
the case for the prosecution	*der Fall für die Staatsanwaltsschaft*
to prosecute	*verurteilen*
the case for the defence	*der Fall für die Verteidigung*
to defend	*verteidigen*
a solicitor	*ein Rechtsanwalt*
a barrister	*ein Anwalt*

CURRENT EVENTS cont.　　*AKTUELLE EREIGNISSE Forts.*

LAW AND ORDER cont.　　*RECHT UND ORDNUNG Forts.*

a summons	*eine Vorladung*
a criminal	*ein Krimineller*
to acquit	*freisprechen*
to get let off	*davon gekommen sein*
to find guilty	*für schuldig befunden werden*
a sentence / a fine / to fine	*ein Urteil / eine Strafe / bestrafen*
to be put on probation	*Bewährung bekommen*
a term of imprisonment	*eine Freiheitsstrafe verbüßen*
censorship / freedom of speech	*Zensur / Redefreiheit*

SEXUALITY	***SEXUALITÄT***
heterosexual	*heterosexuell*
homosexual	*homosexuell*
lesbian / gay	*lesbisch / schwul*
sexually transmitted disease	*durch Geschlechtsverkehr übertragbare Krankheit*
HIV positive	*HIV positiv*
AIDS	*AIDS*
a blood test	*ein Bluttest*
a clinic	*eine Klinik*
confidential	*vertraulich*
pornography	*Pornographie*
prostitution	*Prostitution*
equal opportunities	*Gleichberechtigung*
sexual discrimination	*sexuelle Diskriminierung*

CURRENT EVENTS cont.

AKTUELLE EREIGNISSE Forts.

THE MONARCHY	*MONARCHIE*
the King / the Queen	*der König / die Königin*
the Prince / the Princess	*der Prinz / die Prinzessin*
the heir to the throne	*der Thronfolger*
the Queen Mother	*die Königinmutter*
to be a member of the royalty	*ein Angehöriger des Königshauses sein*
What do you think of the future of the monarchy?	*Wie schätzt Du die Zukunft der Monarchie ein?*
Do you think we should become a republic?	*Glaubst Du wir sollten eine Republik werden?*
Are you glad you have a royal family?	*Bist Du froh, eine königliche Familie zu haben?*
Do you wish you had a royal family?	*Hättest Du gerne eine königliche Familie?*
Have you ever met any of the royal family?	*Hast Du schon einmal jemanden von der königlichen Familie gesehen?*
I saw the Queen once.	*Ich habe einmal die Königin gesehen.*

CURRENT EVENTS cont.

THE NATIONAL LOTTERY	*DIE STAATLICHE LOTTERIE*
to buy a lottery ticket	*einen Lottoschein kaufen*
to buy an instant lottery ticket	*ein Rubbellos kaufen*
to choose your numbers	*seine Zahlen auswählen*
a bonus number	*eine Zusatzzahl*
to watch the lottery draw	*die Lotterieziehung anschauen*
The first ball / the final ball is...	*Die erste Kugel / die letzte Kugel ist...*
The results of the lottery were..	*Die Zahlen der Ziehung waren..*
The jackpot is..	*Der Jackpot ist...*
No-one won the lottery.	*Niemand hat im Lotto gewonnen.*
a ten pound prize	*ein fünfundzwanzig Mark Gewinn*
a syndicate	*eine Wettgemeinschaft*
to share the winnings	*den Gewinn teilen*
How much is the lottery jackpot this week?	*Wie hoch ist der Lotto-Jackpot in dieser Woche?*
Do you approve of the lottery?	*Hältst Du die Lotterie für gut?*
The charities are suffering because of the lotteries.	*Die Wohlfahrtsverbände leiden unter der Lotterie.*
It gives people an interest.	*Es gibt den Menschen eine Bedeutung.*
It's just good fun.	*Es macht einfach Spaß.*
Some people get addicted to it.	*Manche Leute werden davon abhängig.*
What would you do if you won the lottery?	*Was würdest Du machen, wenn Du gewinnst?*
I only got two numbers right.	*Ich habe nur zwei Zahlen richtig.*

TRAVEL
REISEN

SIGNS   *HINWEISS-CHILDER*

TOILETS	*TOILETTEN*
Ladies / Gentlemen	*Damen / Herren*
vacant / engaged	*frei / besetzt*
out of order	*außer Betrieb*
hot water / cold water	*warmes Wasser / kaltes Wasser*

ENTRANCES	*EINGÄNGE*
push / pull / no entry	*drücken / ziehen / kein Eingang*

EXITS	*AUSGÄNGE*
Fire Exit	*Notausgang*
Fire Escape	*Feuertreppe*

LIFTS	*AUFZÜGE*
up / down	*hoch / runter*
It's coming	*Er kommt*
Push the button.	*Drück den Knopf.*
Which floor do you want?	*In welchen Stock möchten Sie?*
I want the third floor.	*Ich möchte in den dritten Stock.*
Which floor is it for..?	*In welchem Stock ist...?*
the top floor / the ground floor	*der letzte Stock / das Erdgeschoß*
the basement	*das Untergeschoß*
Excuse me, I want to get out here.	*Entschuldigung, ich möchte hier aussteigen.*

SIGNS cont.　　　　　　　　*HINWEISS-CHILDER Forts.*

ESCALATORS	*ROLLTREPPEN*
the up escalator	*die Aufwärtsrolltreppe*
the down escalator	*die Abwärtsrolltreppe*
Hold on to the hand rail.	*Halte Dich am Geländer fest.*
Stand in the middle.	*Bleib' in der Mitte.*
Take care.	*Sei vorsichtig.*
Mind your feet.	*Paß auf wo Du hintrittst.*

OPEN	*GEÖFFNET*
When do you open?	*Wann öffnen Sie?*
We open at..	*Wir öffnen um...*
Opening hours	*Öffnungszeiten*
Open from...	*Geöffnet von...*
Open until...	*Geöffnet bis...*

CLOSED	*GESCHLOSSEN*
When do you close?	*Wann schließen Sie?*
We shut at..	*wir schließen um...*
We are just about to close.	*Wir schließen gerade.*

SALE	*AUSVERKAUF*
Great reductions!	*Hohe Ermäßigung!*
10% off everything.	*10% Ermäßigung für jede Ware.*
One third off.	*Ein Drittel Ermäßigung*
Half price.	*Zum halben Preis.*
a bargain	*ein Sonderangebot*
Closing down sale.	*Räumungsverkauf*
Sale ends on...	*Der Ausverkauf endet am....*

PRIVATE	*PRIVAT*
No Admittance	*Kein Zutritt*
Strictly Private	*Eintritt strengstens verboten*
Staff Only	*Nur für Angestellte*
Trespassers Will Be Prosecuted.	*Widerrechtliches Betreten wird strafrechtlich verfolgt*

TRAVEL - SIGNS cont.   *REISEN - HINWEISS-*
                                          CHILDER Forts.

NO SMOKING	*NICHT RAUCHEN*
BEWARE OF THE DOG.	*VORSICHT VOR DEM HUND*

TRAVELLING BY TRAIN   *MIT DEM ZUG REISEN*

AT THE STATION	*AUF DEM BAHNHOF*
the entrance	*der Eingang*
the main concourse	*die Bahnhofshalle*
Shall we meet by the..	*Sollen wir uns am....treffen?*
the book stall	*der Bücherstand*
the newspaper kiosk	*das Zeitungskiosk*
the big clock	*die Bahnhofsuhr*

THE BUFFET	*DER STEHIMBISS*
to buy	*kaufen*
a sandwich	*ein Sandwich*
a coffee / a cup of tea	*ein Kaffee / eine Tasse Tee*
a bottle of water	*eine Flasche Wasser*

THE WAITING ROOM	*DER AUFENTHALTSRAUM*
Toilets - see page 61 for using the loo & page 371 for public toilets	*Toiletten*

TRAVELLING BY TRAIN cont.   *MIT DEM ZUG REISEN Forts.*

THE LEFT LUGGAGE OFFICE	*DIE GEPÄCKAUFGABE*
I have lost my..	*Ich habe mein / meine....verloren.*
Has my wallet been handed in?	*Ist meine Brieftasche abgegeben worden?*
Can I leave my suitcase here?	*Kann ich meinen Koffer hier lassen?*
Do you have lockers?	*Haben Sie Schließfächer?*
How much are they?	*Wieviel kosten sie?*
What coins do they take?	*Was für Münzen braucht man für sie?*
Do you have any change?	*Können Sie mir wechseln?*
How do they work?	*Wie funktionieren sie?*

THE TAXI RANK	*DER TAXISTAND*
Shall we take a taxi?	*Sollen wir ein Taxi nehmen?*
There is a very long queue.	*Da ist eine sehr lange Schlange.*
to give a tip	*ein Trinkgeld geben*
How much would it cost for a taxi to…?	*Wieviel kostet ein Taxi nach...?*

THE ENQUIRY OFFICE	*DIE AUSKUNFT*
Could I have a timetable for..?	*Kann ich einen Fahrplan für....haben?*
What time is the next train for..?	*Um wieviel Uhr geht der Zug nach...?*
Is it a through train?	*Ist es ein durchgehender Zug?*
Do I have to change?	*Muß ich umsteigen?*
Where do I have to change?	*Wo muß ich umsteigen?*
Is there a good connection?	*Gibt es dort einen guten Anschlußzug?*

TRAVELLING BY TRAIN cont.   *MIT DEM ZUG REISEN Forts.*

THE ENQUIRY OFFICE cont.   *DIE AUSKUNFT Forts.*

What time is the connection?	*Um wieviel Uhr fährt der Anschlußzug?*
What time does it arrive at..?	*Um wieviel Uhr kommt er in....an?*
What time is the one after that?	*Um wieviel Uhr geht der übernächste Zug?*
How long does it take?	*Wie lange fährt er?*
What platform does it leave from?	*Von welchem Gleis fährt er ab?*

THE TICKET OFFICE	***DER FAHRKARTENSCHALTER***
May I have..?	*Kann ich...haben?*
How much is..?	*Wieviel kostet....?*
• a return ticket	• *eine Rückfahrkarte*
• a day return ticket	• *eine Tages- Rückfahrkarte*
• returning tomorrow / next week	• *eine Rückfahrkarte für morgen / nächste Woche*
• returning next month	• *eine Rückfahrkarte für nächsten Monat*
• a single ticket	• *eine einfache Karte*
• first / second class	• *die erste / zweite Klasse*
• a child rate ticket	• *eine Kinderkarte*
• a student rate ticket	• *eine Studentenkarte*
• a season ticket	• *eine Zeitkarte*
• for a week / a month	• *für eine Woche / einen Monat*
• a book of tickets	• *eine Zehnerkarte*
May I reserve a seat on..?	*Kann ich ein Platz für den....reservieren?*
Is there a reduction for students?	*Gibt es eine Ermäßigung für Studenten?*
Do you have a student card?	*Haben Sie eine Studentenkarte?*
Do you have proof of your age?	*Können Sie Ihr Alter nachweisen?*

TRAVELLING BY TRAIN cont.   *MIT DEM ZUG REISEN Forts.*

THE ARRIVALS / DEPARTURES BOARD	ANKUNFTSTAFEL / ABFAHRTSTAFEL
due to arrive / depart at..	*voraussichtliche Ankunft / Abfahrt um...*
delayed by ten minutes	*um zehn Minuten verspätet*
on time	*pünktlich*
early	*zu früh*
just arrived	*gerade eingefahren*
leaving from Platform Nine	*von Gleis Neun abfahren*
now boarding	*sofort einsteigen*

ANNOUNCEMENTS	DURCHSAGEN (f)
What was that announcement?	*Wie lautete die Durchsage?*
I didn't hear what he / she said.	*Ich habe nicht verstanden, was er / sie gesagt hat.*
The next train to depart from Platform One is the three forty five for Paddington, calling at all stations.	*Der nächste Zug in Richtung Paddington fährt ab um drei Uhr fünfundvierzig von Gleis Eins. Der Zug hält an jeder Station.*
The train just arriving at Platform Four is the two thirty from Edinburgh.	*Auf Gleis Vier fährt ein der Zug aus Edinburgh, Ankunftszeit zwei Uhr vierzig.*
We apologize for the delay.	*Wir bedauern die Verspätung.*

THE TICKET PUNCHING MACHINE	DER FAHRKARTENENTWERTER
to punch your ticket	*seine Karte lochen lassen*
You have to punch your ticket before boarding the train.	*Bevor man den Zug besteigt muß man seine Karte lochen.*

TRAVELLING BY TRAIN cont.   *MIT DEM ZUG REISEN Forts.*

THE PLATFORM	*DAS GLEIS*
a barrier	*eine Absperrung*
a ticket inspector	*ein Fahrkartenschaffner*
to catch / miss the train	*den Zug erreichen / verpassen*
a seat	*ein Platz*
to sit down	*sich setzen*
a luggage trolley / a porter	*ein Gepäckwagen / ein Gepäckträger*

TYPES OF TRAIN	*ZUGARTEN*
an intercity	*ein Intercity Expreß (I.C.E.)*
an express train	*ein Expreßzug*
a local train	*ein Regionalzug*
a sleeper	*ein Nachtzug mit Schlafwagen*
British Rail system (B.R.)	*Britisches Eisenbahn System*
German Railway system	*Deutsche Bundesbahn (D.B.)*
a German inter-regional train	*ein Inter-Regio*
a German slow or stopping train	*ein Bummelzug*

THE CHANNEL TUNNEL TRAIN	*DER KANALTUNNEL ZUG*
to drive on	*auffahren*
to drive off	*runterfahren*
to sit in your car	*in seinem Auto sitzen*

BOARDING A TRAIN   *IN DEN ZUG EINSTEIGEN*

THE CARRIAGES	DIE WAGEN
the front / rear carriage	*der vordere / hintere Wagen*
a compartment	*ein Abteil*
No Smoking / Smoking	*Nichtraucher / Raucher*
First Class / Second Class	*Erste Klasse / Zweite Klasse*
the buffet	*das Büffet*
the dining car	*der Speisewagen*
the bar	*die Bar*
a snacks trollet	*ein Imbißwagen*
the sleeping compartment	*das Schlafabteil*
the Guard's van	*das Schaffnerabteil*

The door	Die Tür
to open / to close	*öffnen / schließen*
Press the button to open the door.	*zum öffnen der Tür Knopf drücken.*

The windows	Die Fenster
Do you mind if I open / shut the window?	*Macht es Ihnen / Dir etwas aus, wenn ich das Fenster öffne / schließe?*

The corridor	Der Gang
to walk along / to look for a seat	*entlang laufen / nach einem Platz suchen*

The communication cord	Die Notbremse
to pull	*ziehen*
an emergency	*ein Notfall*
to stop the train	*den Zug anhalten*

TRAVELLING BY TRAIN cont.   *MIT DEM ZUG REISEN Forts.*

The seats	*Die Plätze*
Is this seat taken?	*Ist dieser Platz besetzt?*
May I sit here?	*Darf ich mich hier hinsetzen?*
I'm sorry, someone is sitting here.	*Es tut mir leid, dieser Platz ist besetzt.*
That is a reserved seat.	*Das ist ein reservierter Platz.*
Would you like to sit by the window?	*Möchtest Du gerne am Fenster sitzen?*
Do you prefer to face the way we are going?	*Möchtest du lieber in Fahrtrichtung sitzen?*
Shall we sit together?	*Sollen wir uns nebeneinander setzen?*

The luggage rack	*Die Gepäckablage*
Can I help you to put your case up?	*Kann ich Ihnen / Dir helfen, den Koffer hoch zu legen?*
Can you manage to get your coat down?	*Schaffst Du es den Mantel runterzubekommen?*

THE PASSENGERS AND RAILWAY STAFF   *DIE PASSAGIERE UND BAHNANGESTELLTEN*

a commuter	*ein Pendler*
the driver / the guard	*der Zugführer / der Schaffner*

The ticket inspector	*der Fahrkartenschaffner*
Tickets please.	*Die Karten, bitte.*
Could I see your ticket, please?	*Kann ich bitte Ihre Karte sehen?*
I didn't have time to buy one, I'm afraid.	*Ich fürchte, ich hatte keine Zeit eine zu lösen.*
Can I pay now, please?	*Kann ich bitte jetzt bezahlen?*
The ticket office was shut.	*Der Fahrkartenschalter war geschlossen.*
I can't find my ticket.	*Ich kann meine Karte nicht finden.*
to be fined	*eine Strafe bezahlen.*
to be surcharged	*einen Zuschlag bezahlen*
to pay extra	*zusätzlich bezahlen*

TRAVELLING BY UNDERGROUND

MIT DER UNTERGRUNDBAHN (U-BAHN) FAHREN

COMMON EXPRESSIONS	*ALLGEMEINE AUSDRUCKSWEISEN*
Shall we go by tube?	*Sollen wir mit der U-Bahn fahren?*
Which lines is this station on?	*Welche U-Bahn Linien fahren von dieser Haltestelle aus ab?*
Which line do we need to take?	*Welche U-Bahn müssen wir nehmen?*
What is this line called?	*Wie heißt diese U-Bahn?*
What is this line number?	*Wie ist die Nummer?*
Let's look at a plan of the underground.	*Laß' uns auf den Fahrplan gucken.*
We are here.	*Wir sind hier.*
We need to go there.	*Dort müssen wir hin.*
Which line do I take for Buckingham Palace?	*Welche U-Bahn geht zum Buckingham Palace?*
Take this line.	*Diese hier können Sie nehmen.*
Where do I get off for ..?	*Wo muß ich austeigen, um nach / zu / zum.....zu kommen?*

CHANGING TRAINS	*UMSTEIGEN*
You need to change at Euston.	*Du mußt / Sie müssen in Euston umsteigen.*
We will have to change here.	*Wir müssen hier umsteigen.*
a connecting station	*ein Umsteigebahnhof*

ZONES	*ZONEN*
the central zone	*die Kernzone*
an outer zone	*eine Außenzone*
zone one / two / three	*Zone eins / zwei / drei*

TRAVELLING BY UNDERGROUND cont.	*MIT DER U-BAHN FAHREN Forts.*

BUYING TICKETS AT THE TICKET OFFICE	*AM FAHRKARTENSCHALTER FAHRKARTEN LÖSEN*
Please could I have two tickets for..	*Kann ich bitte zwei Karten nach....*
to buy..	*kaufen....*
• a single / a return	• *eine einfache / eine Rückfahrkarte*
• a child's ticket	• *eine Kinderkarte*
• an adult's ticket	• *eine Erwachsenenkarte*
• a student's ticket	• *eine Studentenkarte*
• a daily pass	• *eine Tageskarte*
• a weekly pass	• *eine Wochenkarte*
• a book of ten tickets	• *eine Zehnerkarte*
Can you use the passes on the buses too?	*Gelten die Tages- Wochenkarten auch für Busse?*
Is it more expensive at certain times of the day?	*Ist es an bestimmten Tageszeiten teurer?*
When does the cheap rate start?	*Wann fängt der Billigtarif an?*
There is a flat rate fare.	*Es gibt einen Einheitstarif*

AT THE TICKET BARRIER	*AN DER FAHRKARTEN-ABSPERRUNG*
Put your ticket in here.	*Die Karte hier einführen.*
Take your ticket out there.	*Die Karte hier rausnehmen.*
You have to show your ticket.	*Du mußt Deine Karte zeigen.*
The barrier isn't working.	*Die Absperrung funktioniert nicht.*

ESCALATORS	*ROLLTREPPEN*
a down / up escalator	*eine Aufwärts- / Abwärts-Rolltreppe*
to read the advertisements	*die Werbung lesen*
to stand on the right	*rechts stehen*

TRAVELLING BY BUS *MIT DEM BUS FAHREN*

BUS STOPS	*BUSHALTESTELLEN*
Which buses stop here?	*Welche Busse halten hier?*
Is this the right bus stop for..?	*Ist dies die richtige Haltestelle um nach / zu / zum....zu kommen?*
How often do the buses run?	*Wie oft fahren die Busse?*
Have I just missed a bus?	*Habe ich eben einen Bus verpaßt?*
How long have you been waiting?	*Wie lange warten Sie schon?*
to look at the timetable	*auf den Fahrplan schauen*
a request stop	*eine Bedarfshaltestelle*
the next stop	*die nächste Haltestelle*
You have to put your arm out to stop the bus.	*Man muß dem Bus winken, damit er anhält.*
This is the bus you want.	*Diesen Bus mußt Du / müssen Sie nehmen.*
to get on / off the bus	*in den Bus ein- aussteigen*

TYPES OF BUS	*BUSARTEN*
a single / double decker	*ein einfacher Bus / Doppeldecker*
a coach	*ein Reisebus*

GETTING ON THE BUS	*IN DEN BUS STEIGEN*
Do you want to sit upstairs or downstairs?	*Möchtest Du oben oder unten sitzen?*
Shall we go upstairs?	*Sollen wir hoch gehen?*
Press the button to stop the bus.	*Drück den Knopf um auszusteigen.*
You pay the driver / conductor.	*Man bezahlt beim Fahrer / Schaffner.*

TRAVELLING BY BUS cont.　*MIT DEM BUS FAHREN Forts.*

TICKETS	KARTEN
Could I have a single ticket to..?	*Kann ich eine einfache Karte nach....haben?*
a return ticket to..	*Kann ich eine Rückfahrkarte nach...haben?*
I have a bus pass.	*Ich habe eine Dauerkarte.*

TRAVELLING BY AIR　*MIT DEM FLUGZEUG REISEN*

AIRPORTS　*FLUGHÄFEN*

THE TERMINAL	DER TERMINAL
Which terminal does Lufthansa use?	*Von welchem Terminal fliegt Lufthansa?*
British Airways flights use Terminal…	*British Airways Flüge fliegen von Terminal....ab.*
Which airline are you flying with?	*Mit welcher Fluggesellschaft fliegst Du?*

THE CAR PARK	DAS PARKHAUS / DER PARKPLATZ
a short stay car park	*ein Kurzzeitparkplatz*
a long stay car park	*ein Langzeitparkplatz*
to get a ticket	*einen Parkschein holen*
You pay before leaving.	*Man zahlt bevor man fährt.*
How much is the ticket?	*Wieviel kostet der Parkschein?*
Can we take a bus to the terminal?	*Können wir einen Bus zum Terminal nehmen?*

TRAVELLING BY AIR cont. *MIT DEM FLUGZEUG REISEN Forts.*

LUGGAGE TROLLEYS *GEPÄCKWAGEN*
Can you find a luggage trolley? *Kannst Du einen Gepäckwagen finden?*
to push / to pull *schieben / ziehen*
to steer / to brake *lenken / bremsen*

AT THE TERMINAL *IM TERMINAL*
automatic doors *automatische Türen*
an escalator / a lift *eine Rolltreppe / ein Fahrstuhl*
a moving floor *ein Rollsteg*
the shops *die Läden*
the toilets *die Toiletten*
a restaurant / a bar *ein Restaurant / eine Bar*

THE ARRIVALS / DEPARTURES BOARD *DIE ANKUNFTTAFEL / ABFLUGTAFEL*
destination *Bestimmungsort*
due to arrive at *voraussichtliche Ankunft um...*
just arrived / delayed *gerade gelandet / verspätet*
about to depart *im Begriff abzufliegen*
last call *Letzter Aufruf*
now boarding *jetzt an Bord gehen*

THE INFORMATION DESK *DER INFORMATIONSSCHALTER*
Can you tell me..? *Können Sie mir sagen...?*
Has flight number .. arrived yet? *Ist der Flug....schon gelandet?*
Is the flight delayed? *Hat der Flug Verspätung?*
How late is it likely to be? *Wie groß wird die Verspätung sein?*
Why is it so late? *Warum ist er verspätet?*
Is there a problem? *Gibt es ein Problem?*

TRAVELLING BY AIR cont.	*MIT DEM FLUGZEUG REISEN Forts.*
THE INFORMATION DESK cont.	*DER INFORMATIONSSCHALTER Forts.*

Where is the meeting point?	*Wo ist der Treffpunkt / Meeting Point?*
I am supposed to meet a passenger called….but I can't find him / her.	*Ich soll einen Fluggast treffen der ….heißt, aber ich kann ihn nicht finden.*
Have there been any messages left for me?	*Wurden irgendwelche Nachrichten für mich hinterlassen?*
My name is…	*Mein Name ist...*
Can you put a message out on the tannoy for me, please?	*Können Sie bitte eine Nachricht für mich ausrufen lassen?*

THE CHECK-IN DESK	*DER ABFERTIGUNGS-SCHALTER*
to queue	*anstellen*
Can you put your luggage on the scales, please?	*Können Sie bitte ihr Gepäck auf die Waage stellen?*
to lift a suitcase up	*einen Koffer hochheben*
How many suitcases do you have?	*Wieviele Koffer haben Sie?*
Is this one yours?	*Ist das ihrer?*
the baggage allowance	*das erlaubte Gewicht*
excess baggage	*Übergewicht*
to pay a surcharge	*einen Zuschlag zahlen*
hand luggage	*Handgepäck*
Did you pack your suitcase yourself?	*Haben Sie Ihren Koffer selber gepackt?*
Are there any prohibited articles in your luggage?	*Gibt es irgendwelche verbotenen Gegenstände in Ihrem Koffer?*
Your hand luggage is too large.	*Ihr Handgepäck ist zu groß.*
It will have to be put in the hold.	*Ich muß es aufgeben.*
Could I see your ticket, please?	*Kann ich bitte Ihren Flugschein sehen?*

TRAVELLING BY AIR cont.	*MIT DEM FLUGZEUG REISEN Forts.*

THE CHECK-IN DESK cont.	*DER ABFERTIGUNGS-SCHALTER Forts.*
Do you prefer smoking or non-smoking?	*Möchten sie lieber Raucher oder Nichtraucher?*
This child is travelling alone and needs looking after.	*Auf dieses Kind muß aufgepaßt werden, da es alleine fliegt.*
Could I have a seat with extra leg room, please?	*Kann ich bitte ein Platz mit extra Raum für meine Beine haben?*
Could I possibly have an aisle / a window seat?	*Kann ich, wenn möglich, einen Sitz am Gang / einen Fensterplatz haben?*
Here is your boarding card.	*Hier ist Ihre Bordkarte*
Go to passport control when you are ready.	*Wenn Sie so weit sind, gehen Sie zur Ausweiskontrolle.*

PASSPORT CONTROL	*AUSWEISKONTROLLE*
to show your passport	*seinen Paß / Ausweis zeigen*
to put your hand luggage on the conveyor belt	*sein Handgepäck auf's Fließband legen*
to walk through the detector	*durch den Radardetektor gehen*
to be stopped / to be searched	*angehalten werden / durchsucht werden*
to have your bag searched	*seine Tasche durchsuchen lassen*

THE DEPARTURE LOUNGE	*DIE ABFLUGSHALLE*
the duty free shop	*der Duty-Free Shop*
your duty free allowance	*die erlaubte Anzahl an Duty-Free-Waren*
to buy	*kaufen*
• perfume	• *Parfüm*
• cigarettes	• *Zigaretten*
• alcohol	• *Alkohol*

TRAVELLING BY AIR cont.   *MIT DEM FLUGZEUG REISEN Forts.*

THE BOARDING GATE	DER FLUGSTEIG
Our flight has been called.	*Unserer Flug ist aufgerufen worden.*
Now boarding.	*Jetzt an Bord gehen.*
Last call.	*Letzter Aufruf.*
They are boarding at gate..	*Am Flugsteig ....gehen sie an Bord.*
to show your boarding pass	*seine Bordkarte zeigen*
Seats numbered.... board first / next.	*Fluggäste mit den Sitznummern.....gehen zu erst / als nächstes an Bord.*
Please board from the front / rear of the aircraft.	*Bitte steigen Sie im vorderen / im hinteren Teil des Flugzeuges ein.*
Excuse me, could I get to my seat, please.	*Entschuldigen Sie, kann ich bitte zu meinem Platz gehen.*

THE SATELLITE	DER FLUGSTEIG
Our flight is leaving from the satellite.	*Unserer Flug geht vom Flugsteig aus ab.*
We have to take the monorail / a bus.	*Wir müssen mit der Einschienenbahn / mit dem Bus fahren.*

THE FLIGHT   *DER FLUG*

THE CREW	DIE CREW
the Captain	*der Kapitän*
the steward	*der Steward*
the stewardess	*die Stewardeß*
an air hostess	*eine Flug-Hosteß*

TRAVELLING BY AIR cont.

MIT DEM FLUGZEUG REISEN Forts.

SAFETY	*SICHERHEIT*
to fasten your seatbelt	*anschnallen*
to keep your seatbelt fastened	*angeschnallt bleiben*
to remain seated	*sitzen bleiben*
to call the stewardess	*die Stewardeß rufen*
to undo your seatbelt	*seinen Gurt aufmachen*
to extinguish cigarettes	*Zigaretten ausdrücken*
to put on a life jacket	*eine Schwimmweste anlegen*
to fasten the strap	*den Riemen festschnallen*
to inflate / a whistle / to blow	*aufblasen / eine Pfeife / pusten*
oxygen masks	*Sauerstoffmaske*
an emergency / emergency lighting	*ein Notfall / Notlichter*
escape routes	*Notausgänge*

THE TAKE OFF	*STARTEN*
the runway	*das Rollfeld*
to taxi	*rollen*
to accelerate	*beschleunigen*
to take off / to lift off / to climb	*starten / abheben / steigen*
My ears hurt.	*Meine Ohren tun weh.*
Would you like to suck a sweet?	*Möchtest Du ein Bonbon lutschen*
the altitude / the speed	*die Höhe / die Geschwindigkeit*
to look out of the window	*aus dem Fenster schauen*
to get a good view	*eine gute Aussicht haben*
the clouds / turbulence	*die Wolken / Turbulenzen*

THE DESCENT	*DER ABSTIEG*
the touch down	*das Aufsetzen*
to land / a good landing	*landen / eine gute Landung*
to remain in your seats until the plane has stopped	*in den Sitzen bleiben bis das Flugzeug angehalten hat.*
to disembark	*von Bord gehen*

TRAVELLING BY AIR cont.   *MIT DEM FLUGZEUG REISEN Forts.*

BAGGAGE RECLAIM	GEPÄCKAUSGABE
to collect your luggage	*sein Gepäck holen*
a carousel	*ein Gepäckförderband*
Can you see your suitcase?	*Kannst Du Deinen Koffer sehen?*
There's mine.	*Dort ist meiner.*
How many cases do you have?	*Wieviele Koffer hast Du?*
Is that everything?	*Ist das alles?*
a trolley	*ein Gepäckwagen*
to push / to steer / to brake	*schieben / lenken / bremsen*

CUSTOMS	ZOLL
to go through customs	*durch den Zoll gehen*
the green / red channel	*der grüne / rote Durchgang*
to have nothing to declare	*nichts zu verzollen haben*
to have something to declare	*etwas zu verzollen haben*
Have you anything to declare?	*Haben Sie etwas zu verzollen?*
to have your baggage searched	*seine Tasche durchsucht bekommen*

TRAVELLING BY FERRY
MIT DER FÄHRE REISEN

to go by ferry	*mit der Fähre fahren*
to take the Cross Channel ferry	*die Kanalfähre nehmen*

THE PARTS OF THE FERRY
DIE BEREICHE DER FÄHRE

THE RAMP	*DIE RAMPE*
to queue	*anstellen*
to wait	*warten*
to drive up the ramp	*auf die Rampe fahren*
to drive down	*runterfahren*
to embark	*einschiffen*
to disembark	*ausschiffen*

THE VEHICLE DECK	*DAS AUTODECK*
to follow the car in front	*hinterherfahren*
to go right up to the bumper	*bis zur Stoßstange fahren*
to park	*parken*
to take important things with you	*Wichtige Sachen mitnehmen*
to lock the car / to leave the car	*das Auto verschließen / verlassen*
to remember where the car is parked	*merken wo man das Auto geparkt hat*

THE PASSENGER DECKS	*DAS PASSERGIERDECK*
the restaurant / the bar	*das Restaurant / die Bar*
the toilets / the telephone	*die Toiletten / das Telefon*
the lounge / the shops / the cinema	*der Aufenthaltsraum / die Läden / das Kino*
to stay inside	*drinnen bleiben*
to go outside for some air	*rausgehen um etwas Luft zu bekommen*

TRAVELLING BY FERRY cont.	*MIT DER FÄHRE REISEN Forts.*

THE SLEEPING AREA	*DER SCHLAFBEREICH*
to sit up all night	*die ganze Nacht aufbleiben*
to have a cabin booked	*eine Kabine gebucht haben*
a sleeping berth	*eine Schlafkoje*

A ROUGH CROSSING	*EINE STÜRMISCHE ÜBERFAHRT*
Do you feel seasick?	*Bist Du seekrank?*
I feel dreadful.	*Ich fühle mich furchtbar*
I am going to be sick.	*Ich muß mich übergeben.*
Would you like to take a tablet?	*Möchtest Du eine Tablette nehmen?*
I can't walk straight.	*Ich kann nicht mehr gerade laufen.*
Hold on to the handrail.	*Halt Dich am Geländer fest.*
Would you like to go outside for some fresh air?	*Möchtest Du rausgehen, um etwas frische Luft zu atmen?*
I feel cold. Can we go back inside now?	*Mir ist kalt. Können wir wieder reingehen?*
I have got wet by the spray.	*Ich bin vom Schaum naß geworden.*

SAFETY EQUIPMENT	*SICHERHEITS-AUSRÜSTUNG*
a life belt	*ein Rettungsgürtel*
a life jacket	*eine Schwimmweste*
the safety drill	*die Rettungsübung*
a siren	*eine Sirene*

TRAVELLING BY CAR *MIT DEM AUTO REISEN*

TYPES OF CAR	*AUTOMODELLE*
a saloon	*eine Limousine*
an estate car	*ein Kombi*
a hatchback	*ein Hecktürmodell*
a sportscar	*ein Sportwagen*
an open car	*ein offenes Auto*
a four wheel drive	*ein Vierradantriebs-auto*
a two door car	*ein zwei-türiges Auto*
a four door car	*ein vier-türiges Auto*
a five door car	*ein fünf-türigesAuto*
an automatic	*eine Automatik*
a hire car	*ein Mietwagen*
a racing car	*ein Rennauto*

THE PARTS OF THE CAR *DIE TEILE DES AUTOS*

THE ROOF	*DAS DACH*
a roof rack	*ein Dachgepäckträger*
to load / unload	*beladen / entladen*
to lift up	*hochheben*
to tie / to secure	*festbinden / sichern*

THE DOORS	*DIE TÜREN*
to lock / to unlock	*verschließen / aufschließen*
central locking	*Zentralverriegelung*
to open / to shut	*öffnen / schließen*
the driver's door	*die Fahrertür*
the passengers' doors	*die Mitfahrertüren*
the front / rear doors	*die Vorder- Hintertüren*

TRAVELLING BY CAR cont.   *MIT DEM AUTO REISEN Forts.*

THE PARTS OF THE CAR cont.   *DIE TEILE DES AUTOS Forts.*

THE BOOT	**DER KOFFERRAUM**
to open / to shut	*öffnen / schließen*
to put something in the boot	*etwas in den Kofferraum legen*
to get something out of the boot	*etwas aus dem Kofferraum holen*

THE SEATS	**DIE SITZE**
to adjust the seat	*die Sitze einstellen*
to alter the height	*die Höhe verstellen*
to move the seat backwards / forwards	*den Sitz nach vorne / hinten schieben*
to fold the seat forwards	*den Sitz vorklappen*
to put the seat back	*den Sitz zurückklappen*
the headrest	*die Kopfstütze*
the ashtray	*der Aschenbecher*

THE SEATBELTS	**DIE SICHERHEITSGURTE**
to fasten / to unfasten	*anschnallen / abschnallen*
Fasten your seatbelt, please.	*Schnall dich bitte an.*
How do you fasten the seatbelt?	*Wie schnallt man sich an?*
Can you help me to fasten the seatbelt?	*Kannst du mir beim Anschnallen helfen?*
I think the seatbelt is stuck under the seat.	*Ich glaube, der Gurt ist unterm Sitz verklemmt.*

TRAVELLING BY CAR cont.

MIT DEM AUTO REISEN
Forts.

THE WINDOWS	*DIE FENSTER*
to open / to shut	*öffnen / schließen*
May I open the window a little?	*Kann ich das Fenster ein wenig öffnen?*
Could you shut the window now, please?	*Kannst du bitte das Fenster wieder zumachen?*
automatic windows	*Automatische Fenster*
Press this button to open / close the windows.	*Drücke diesen Knopf um das Fenster zu öffnen / zu schließen.*
the sun roof	*das Schiebedach*

THE MAIN CONTROLS

DIE WICHTIGSTEN BEDIENUNGSELEMENTE

The ignition	*die Zündung*
to start the car	*das Auto anlassen*

The gears	*Die Gangschaltung*
the gear lever	*der Schaltknüppel*
the reverse gear	*der Rückwärtsgang*
to reverse / the clutch	*rückwärts fahren / die Kupplung*

The brakes	*Die Bremsen*
to brake	*bremsen*
to put the handbrake on	*die Handbremse anziehen*
to take the handbrake off	*die Handbremse lösen*

The accelerator	*Das Gaspedal*
to accelerate	*Gas geben*

The steering wheel	*Das Lenkrad*
to steer / to turn	*lenken / drehen*

TRAVELLING BY CAR cont.   *MIT DEM AUTO REISEN Forts.*

The indicators	*Die Blinker*
to indicate right / left	*rechts / links blinken*
to turn on the hazard lights	*das Warnblinklicht anschalten*

The horn	*Die Hupe*
to blow the horn	*die Hupe drücken*

The headlights	*Die Scheinwerfer*
to turn on / off	*an- ausschalten*
to flash your lights / full beam	*aufblinken / Fernlicht*
to dip / dipped headlights	*abblenden / abgeblendetelichter*
sidelights / fog lights	*das Standlicht / Nebelleuchten*

The windscreen	*Die Windschutzscheibe*
dirty / to clean	*dreckig / saubermachen*
windscreen wipers	*Scheibenwischer*
to turn on / off	*an- ausstellen*
to wash the screen	*die Windschutzscheibe wischen*
the rear windscreen heater	*die Heckscheibenheizung*
to get fogged up / to wipe	*beschlagen / wischen*
a duster	*ein Staubtuch*

BASIC CAR MAINTENANCE   *INSTANDHALTUNG DES AUTOS*

Petrol	*Benzin*
to need some petrol	*Benzin brauchen*
to put in petrol	*Benzin einfüllen*
to undo the filler cap	*den Tankdeckel aufschrauben*
to serve yourself / to fill it up	*selbst tanken / vollmachen*
lead free / leaded / diesel	*bleifrei / verbleit / Diesel*
two / three / four star	*Normal / Super / Superplus*

TRAVELLING BY CAR cont.	*MIT DEM AUTO REISEN Forts.*
BASIC CAR MAINTENANCE cont.	*INSTANDHALTUNG DES AUTOS forts.*

Oil and water	*Öl und Wasser*
to check the oil / the water	*das Öl / Wasser nachprüfen*
Where is the dipstick?	*Wo ist der Ölmeßstab?*
It needs more oil / water.	*Er braucht mehr Öl / Wasser.*
to pour the oil / water in	*das Öl / Wasser eingießen*

Tyres	*Reifen*
to check the tyre pressures	*den Reifendruck messen*
The tyres look a bit flat.	*die Reifen sehen etwas platt aus.*
to pump up	*aufpumpen*
to have a puncture	*einen Platten haben*
to change the wheel	*das Rad wechseln*
to fit the spare wheel	*das Ersatzrad dranmachen*

LEARNING TO DRIVE
AUTOFAHREN LERNEN

DRIVING LESSONS	***FAHRSTUNDEN***
I am having driving lessons.	*Ich nehme Fahrstunden.*
My sister / brother is learning to drive.	*Meine Schwester / mein Bruder lernt Autofahren.*
I have had six lessons.	*Ich hatte sechs Fahrstunden.*
My parents are teaching me.	*Meine Eltern bringen es mir bei.*
I am having lessons with a driving school.	*Ich nehme Fahrstunden bei einer Fahrschule.*
a dual control car	*eine Auto mit Doppelsteuerung*
a driving instructor	*ein Fahrlehrer*

THE DRIVING TEST	***DIE FAHRPRÜFUNG***
I am about to take my driving test.	*Ich mache demnächst meine Fahrprüfung.*
I have passed my test.	*Ich habe meine Prüfung bestanden.*
I passed my test..	*Ich habe die Prüfung....*
• at the first attempt	• *beim ersten Mal*
• at the second / third attempt	• *beim zweiten / dritten Mal....bestanden*
I failed my test.	*Ich bin durchgefallen.*

LEARNING HOW TO..	***LERNEN WIE MAN ....***
to do a hill start	*eine Berganfahrt macht*
to reverse	*rückwärts fährt*
to park	*parken*
to do a three point turn	*ordungsgemäß drehen*
to do an emergency stop	*eine Vollbremsung macht*
to overtake	*überholt*

LEARNING TO DRIVE cont.   *AUTOFAHREN LERNEN*
Forts.

REMEMBERING ..   *SICH MERKEN...*
to look over your shoulder	*über seine Schulter zu schauen*
to look in your rear view mirror	*in den Rückspiegel zu schauen*
to look both ways	*auf beide Seiten zu schauen*
to indicate	*zu blinken*

PROBLEMS ON THE ROAD   *PROBLEME AUF DER STRASSE*
to break down	*eine Panne haben*
to have an accident	*einen Unfall haben*
to have a puncture	*einen Platten haben*
to be delayed	*verspätet sein*
long queues	*lange Schlangen*
roadworks	*Straßenarbeiten*
a diversion	*eine Umleitung*
to run out of petrol	*kein Benzin mehr haben*

TYPES OF ROAD   *STRASSENARTEN*
a motorway	*eine Autobahn*
a dual carriageway	*eine Schnellstraße*
a ring road	*eine Umgehungsstraße*
a main road	*eine Hauptstraße*
a minor road	*eine Nebenstraße*

JUNCTIONS   *KREUZUNGEN*
a roundabout	*ein Kreisel*
Give way to the right	*die Vorfahrt von rechts beachten*
a cross roads	*eine Kreuzung*
traffic lights	*Verkehrsampeln*
a pedestrian crossing	*ein Zebrastreifen*
a level crossing	*ein Bahnübergang*

TRAVELLING BY BIKE

MIT DEM FAHRRAD / MOTORRAD REISEN

TYPES OF BIKE	*FAHRRAD UND MOTORRAD MODELLE*
a motorbike	*ein Motorrad*
a bicycle	*ein Fahrrad*
a mountain bike / a BMX	*ein Mountain Bike / ein BMX-Rad*
a tricycle / a tandem	*ein Dreirad / ein Tandem*

PARTS OF THE BIKE

FAHRRADTEILE

The handlebars	*Die Lenkstange*
drop handlebars	*ein Rennlenker*
raised handlebars	*eine gerade Lenkstange*
straight handlebars	*hochgezogene Lenke*

The brakes	*Die Bremsen*
front / back	*vorder / hinter*
to apply	*ziehen*
to brake	*bremsen*
to slow down	*abbremsen*

The gears	*Die Gänge*
a gear lever	*ein Schalthebel*
to change gear	*die Gänge wechseln*
to go up a gear / down a gear	*einen Gang hoch / runter schalten*
low / middle / top gear	*kleiner / mittlerer / großer Gang*
three / six / twelve gears	*drei / sechs / zwölf Gänge*
fifteen / eighteen / twenty one speed	*fünfzehn / achtzehn / einundzwanzig Gänge*

The frame	*Der Rahmen*
a kickstand	*ein Kickständer*

TRAVELLING BY BIKE cont.   *MIT DEM FAHRRAD / MOTORRAD REISEN forts.*

The chain	*Die Kette*
the chainguard	*der Kettenschutz*
to adjust the tension	*die Spannung einstellen*
too loose	*zu locker*

The pedals	*Die Pedale*
to pedal	*in die Pedale treten*
to back pedal	*rückwärts treten*
to free wheel	*im Freilauf fahren*

The seat	*Der Sattel*
to raise / to lower	*höher / runter stellen*
too high / too low	*zu hoch / zu niedrig*
the height adjustment	*die Höheneinstellung*
a clamp nut	*eine Flügelschraube*
to screw / to unscrew	*zuschrauben / aufschrauben*
a release lever	*ein Freisetzhebel*
to pull / to push	*ziehen / drücken*

The wheels	*Die Räder*
a mudguard	*ein Schutzblech*
the spokes	*die Speichen*

The tyres	*Die Reifen*
Your tyres are flat.	*Deine Reifen sind platt.*
Have you got a pump?	*Hast Du eine Pumpe?*
to unscrew / replace the dust cap	*aufschrauben / die Ventilkappe austauschen*
to pump up / to inflate	*aufpumpen / aufblasen*
the tyre pressure	*der Reifendruck*
I think I have a puncture.	*Ich glaube, ich habe einen Platten.*
a puncture repair kit	*Flickzeug*

TRAVELLING BY BIKE cont.   *MIT DEM FAHRRAD / MOTORRAD REISEN forts.*

The lights	*Die Lampen*
a dynamo	*ein Dynamo*
to turn on / off	*an- ausstellen*
a headlamp	*ein Vorderlicht*
a rear lamp	*ein Rücklicht*
a bulb	*eine Birne*
to replace	*austauschen*
The bulb has gone.	*Die Birne ist durchgebrannt.*
a battery	*eine Batterie*
a reflector	*ein Reflektorlicht*

EQUIPMENT	*AUSRÜSTUNG*
a bicycle lock / a key	*ein Fahrradschloß / ein Schlüssel*
to lock / to unlock	*verschließen / aufschließen*
to padlock / a padlock	*verschließen / eine Vorhängeschloß*
a crash helmet	*ein Sturzhelm*
a fluorescent strip	*ein Leuchtstreifen*
cycling shorts	*Fahrradhosen*
gloves	*Handschuhe*
sunglasses	*eine Sonnenbrille*
a pump	*eine Pumpe*
a basket	*ein Korb*
a water bottle	*eine Wasserflasche*
a child seat	*ein Kindersitz*
a seat belt	*ein Sicherheitsgurt*

TRAVELLING BY BIKE cont.   *MIT DEM FAHRRAD /*
                                      MOTORRAD REISEN forts.

USEFUL VERBS abc	*NÜTZLICHE AUSDRUCKSWEISEN*
to accelerate	*beschleunigen*
to borrow	*ausborgen*
to brake	*bremsen*
to fall off	*stürzen*
to get off	*absteigen*
to hire	*mieten*
to lend	*ausleihen*
to lock	*verschließen*
to lose your balance	*sein Gleichgewicht verlieren*
to mount	*aufsteigen*
to pedal	*in die Pedale treten*
to push	*schieben*
to ride	*fahren*
to signal	*anzeigen*
to steer	*lenken*
to wobble	*schwanken*

EMERGENCIES
NOTFÄLLE

ACCIDENTS   *UNFÄLLE*

TELEPHONING EMERGENCY SERVICES   *NOTRUF-TELEFONNUMMERN*

IN ENGLAND	*IN ENGLAND*
Police - 999	*Polizei-999*
Ambulance - 999	*Krankenwagen-999*
Fire Brigade - 999	*Feuerwehr-999*

IN GERMANY	*IN DEUTSCHLAND*
Police - 110	*Polizei-110*
Ambulance - 112	*Krankenwagen-112*
Fire Brigade - 112	*Feuerwehr-112*

CALLING OUT FOR HELP	*NACH HILFE RUFEN*
Help!	*Hilfe!*
Come quickly!	*Komm schnell / Kommen Sie schnell!*
Fire!	*Feuer!*
Bomb scare!	*Bombenalarm!*
Everybody out!	*Alle raus!*
Call the …	*Ruf / Rufen Sie...*
• fire brigade	• *die Feuerwehr*
• an ambulance	• *einen Krankenwagen*
• the police	• *die Polizei*
• a doctor	• *einen Arzt*

EMERGENCIES cont. *NOTFÄLLE Forts.*

THERE HAS BEEN AN ACCIDENT	*ES GAB EINEN UNFALL*
a traffic accident	*ein Verkehrsunfall*
a pile-up	*ein Auffahrunfall*
Warn other traffic.	*Warne / warnen Sie andere Verkehrsteilnehmer*
a warning triangle / hazard lights	*ein Warndreieck / ein Warnblinklicht*

SOMEONE HAS BEEN RUN OVER	*JEMAND WURDE ÜBERFAHREN*
They are injured,	*Sie sind verletzt*
They are conscious / unconscious.	*Sie sind bei Bewußtsein / bewußtlos.*
a broken bone	*etwas gebrochen*
He / she is bleeding.	*Er/ sie blutet.*
to give mouth to mouth resuscitation	*Mund-zu-Mund-Beatmung geben*
to administer first aid	*erste Hilfe geben*

FIRE	*FEUER*
Press the fire alarm button!	*Drücke / drücken Sie den Feueralarm.*
That's the fire bell.	*Das ist die Feuersirene*
an alarm / to go off	*ein Alarm / losgehen*
a smoke detector	*ein Feuermelder*
a fire door	*eine Feuerschutztür*
a fire exit	*ein Notausgang*
a fire blanket	*eine Feuerschutzdecke*
a fire extinguisher	*ein Feuerlöscher*
smoke / flames / to be on fire	*Rauch/ Flammen/in Brand geraten*
to burn / to put out	*brennen / löschen*
water / sand	*Wasser / Sand*

EMERGENCIES cont.   *NOTFÄLLE Forts.*

A BOMB SCARE	EIN BOMBENALARM
to clear the area	*die Gegend räumen*
to evacuate the building	*das Gebäude evakuieren*
to call the bomb squad	*den Bomben-Entschärfungstrupp rufen*
a sniffer dog	*ein Spürhund*
to cordon off the area	*die Gegend absperren*
to detonate	*detonieren*
to explode / to go off	*explodieren / hoch gehen*
a false alarm	*ein falscher Alarm*
a suspicious package	*ein verdächtiges Paket*
an abandoned package	*ein zurückgelassenes Paket*
to report a package to the police	*der Polizei ein aufgefundenes Paket melden*

ILLNESS   *KRANKHEITEN*

INITIAL SYMPTOMS	***ERSTE SYMPTOME***
to feel off colour	*bleich aussehen*
to feel ill	*sich krank fühlen*
to look ill	*krank aussehen*
to be taken ill	*erkranken*

GENERAL SYMPTOMS	***ALLGEMEINE SYMPTOME***
I am hot / cold	*Mir ist heiß / kalt.*
I feel hot and cold.	*Ich fühl' mich heiß und kalt.*
I feel shivery.	*frösteln.*
I feel faint.	*ich fühl' mich schwach.*
I am thirsty.	*Ich habe Durst.*
I am not hungry	*Ich habe keinen Hunger.*
I have no appetite.	*Ich habe keinen Appetit.*
I couldn't eat a thing.	*Ich könnte nichts essen.*
I have a slight / a high temperature	*Ich habe leichtes / hohes Fieber.*

I HAVE A HEADACHE	***ICH HABE KOPFSCHMERZEN***
I have a migraine.	*Ich habe eine Migräne.*
The light hurts my head.	*Das Licht tut meinem Kopf weh.*
Do you have any pain killers?	*Hast Du Kopfschmerztabletten?*

FAINTING	***OHNMÄCHTIG WERDEN***
I feel dizzy.	*Mir ist schwindlig.*
I think I am going to faint.	*Ich glaube, ich falle in Ohnmacht.*
Put your head between your knees.	*Leg Deinen Kopf zwischen die Knie.*
Can I lie down, please?	*Kann ich mich bitte hinlegen?*
to pass out	*in Ohnmacht fallen*

ILLNESS cont.

KRANKHEITEN Forts.

STOMACH UPSETS	*BAUCHWEH*
I have indigestion.	*Ich habe eine Magenverstimmung.*
I have heartburn.	*Ich habe Sodbrennen.*
I feel sick.	*Mir ist übel.*
I am going to be sick.	*Ich muß mich übergeben.*
I have been sick.	*Ich habe mich übergeben.*
My stomach hurts.	*Mein Bauch tut weh.*
I have diarrhoea.	*Ich habe Durchfall.*
I think it's food poisoning.	*Ich glaube, es ist eine Lebensmittelvergiftung.*
Could I have a drink of water, please?	*Kann ich bitte eine Glas Wasser haben?*
Could I have a bowl by my bed, please?	*Kann ich bitte einen Eimer neben meinem Bett haben?*

MY THROAT IS VERY SORE.	*ICH HABE HALSSCHMERZEN*
I have tonsillitis.	*Ich habe eine Mandelentzündung.*
My throat is dry.	*Meine Kehle ist trocken.*
It hurts to swallow.	*Das Schlucken tut weh.*
My glands are swollen.	*Meine Lymphdrüsen sind angeschwollen.*
to gargle	*gurgeln*
to have a hot drink	*etwas Warmes trinken*
Have you any throat sweets?	*Hast Du Halsbonbons?*
I like lemon ones / honey / menthol / eucalyptus / blackcurrant.	*Ich mag die mit Zitrone / Honig / Menthol / Eukalyptus / schwarzer Johannisbeere.*

ILLNESS cont.   *KRANKHEITEN Forts.*

I HAVE CAUGHT A COLD	*ICH HABE MIR EINE ERKÄLTUNG GEHOLT*
to sneeze / Bless you!	*niesen / Gesundheit!*
to blow your nose	*seine Nase schneuzen*
a handkerchief	*ein Stofftaschentuch*
paper handkerchiefs	*ein Papiertaschentuch*
to find it difficult to breathe	*es schwierig finden zu atmen*
a decongestant	*Nasentropfen*
a cold remedy	*ein Erkältungsmittel*

I HAVE A BAD COUGH	*ICH HABE EINEN SCHLIMMEN HUSTEN*
a tickly cough	*einen Reizhusten haben*
a dry cough	*ein trockener Husten*
a productive cough	*ein heftiger Husten*
a spasm of coughing	*ein Hustenkrampf*
to take cough medicine	*Hustenmittel nehmen*
to need antibiotics	*Antibiotika brauchen*

ASTHMA	*ASTHMA*
to suffer from asthma	*unter Asthma leiden*
to be asthmatic	*Asthmatiker sein*
to wheeze	*keuchen*
to cough a lot	*viel husten*
to control one's asthma	*sein Asthma kontrollieren*
to be allergic to..	*allergisch sein gegen...*
• dust / animals	• *Staub / Tiere*
• chest infections	• *Lungeninfektionen*
to use an inhaler	*einen Inhalierer benutzen*
• to inhale	• *inhalieren*
• steroids	• *Steroide*

ILLNESS cont. *KRANKHEITEN Forts.*

SKIN PROBLEMS *HAUTPROBLEME*

SUNBURN	*SONNENBRAND*
to be burnt	*verbrannt sein*
to be sore	*wund sein*
to peel	*schälen*
to apply after-sun lotion	*After-Sun Lotion auftragen*
calamine	*Galmei*
to rub on	*einreiben*

A RASH	*EIN AUSSCHLAG*
an allergy	*eine Allergie*
to be allergic to	*allergisch sein gegen*
nettle rash	*Nesselausschlag*
prickly heat	*Hitzepocken*
to itch / to scratch	*jucken / kratzen*
to feel sore	*wund fühlen*
antihistamine cream	*Antihistamincreme*

SPLINTERS	*SPLITTER*
I have a splinter in my foot / hand.	*Ich habe einen Splitter in meinem Fuß / meiner Hand.*
to get it out	*ihn rausholen*
a needle / tweezers	*eine Nadel / eine Pinzette*
surgical spirit / disinfectant	*Wundbenzin / Desinfektionsmittel*

MINOR INJURIES	*LEICHTE VERLETZUNGEN*
a spot	*ein Pickel*
acne	*Akne*
a scratch	*ein Kratzer*
a graze	*eine Schramme*
a cut	*eine Schnittwunde*

ILLNESS cont.   *KRANKHEITEN Forts.*

SERIOUS CUTS	*SCHWERE SCHNITTWUNDEN*
to need stitches	*genäht werden müssen*
butterfly stitches	*Schmetterlingsstiche*
local anaesthetic	*Lokalnarkose*
a bandage	*ein Verband*
an Elastoplast ®	*ein Hansaplast*
a sticking plaster	*ein Heftpflaster*
a blister	*eine Blase*

STINGS	*STICHE*
a wasp / bee sting	*ein Wespen- Bienenstich*
a mosquito bite	*ein Mückenstich*
I have been stung by something.	*Irgendetwas hat mich gestochen.*
a jelly fish sting	*ein Quallenstich*
insect repellent	*ein Insektenabwehrmittel*
antihistamine cream / tablets	*Antihistamincreme/ Tabletten*

TOILET PROBLEMS	*VERDAUUNGS- UND AUSSCHEIDUNGS-PROBLEME*
to have cystitis	*eine Blasenentzündung haben*
to have diarrhoea	*Durchfall haben*
to take kaolin and morphine	*Kaolin und Morphium nehmen*
to be constipated	*Verstopfung haben*
a laxative	*ein Abführmittel*
to eat more roughage	*mehr Ballaststoffe zu sich nehmen*
to drink more water	*mehr Wasser trinken*

ILLNESS cont.   ## KRANKHEITEN Forts.

PERIOD PROBLEMS

to have period pains
to take pain killers
My period is..

- late
- heavy
- painful
- prolongued

PROBLEME MIT DER PERIODE

Menstruationsbeschwerden haben
Schmerzmittel nehmen
Meine Periode ist....

- zu spät
- heftig
- schmerzhaft
- zu lange

INJURIES

I hurt here.
I have bruised my..
I have cut my..
I have sprained my..
I have broken my..
I have dislocated my..
I have burnt my..
I can't move my..

VERLETZUNGEN

Hier tut es mir weh.
Ich habe mir mein....angeschlagen.
Ich habe in mein....geschnitten.
Ich habe mir mein....verstaucht.
Ich habe mir mein....gebrochen.
Ich habe mir mein...ausgekugelt.
Ich habe mir mein...verbrannt.
Ich kann mein.....nicht bewegen.

PARTS OF THE BODY   ## KÖRPERTEILE

THE SKIN / DIE HAUT

dry	trocken	cracked	aufgesprungen
sore	wund	wrinkled	runzlig
burnt	verbrannt	soft / hard	weich / hart

ILLNESS cont.　　　　　　*KRANKHEITEN Forts.*

PARTS OF THE BODY cont.　　*KÖRPERTEILE Forts.*

THE HAIR		*DAS HAAR*	
straight	*gerade*	to wear it up	*es hoch tragen*
wavy	*gewellt*	to wear it loose	*es offen tragen*
curly	*lockig*	shoulder length	*schulterlang*
blonde	*blond*	balding	*schütteres Haar*
auburn	*rotbraun*	to be bald	*eine Glatze haben*
brown	*braun*	dandruff	*Schuppen*
red	*rot*	oily / dry	*fettig / trocken*
black	*schwarz*	dyed	*gefärbt*
grey	*grau*	streaked	*gesträhnt*
white	*weiß*	permed	*mit einer*
short / long	*kurz / lang*		*Dauerwelle*

THE HEAD	*DER KOPF*
the brain	*das Gehirn*
the skull	*der Schädel*
the scalp	*die Kopfhaut*

THE FACE	*DAS GESICHT*
the cheeks	*die Backen*
the cheekbones	*Backenknochen*
to blush	*erröten*

THE EYES	*DIE AUGEN*
an eye	*ein Auge*
the eyebrows	*die Augenbrauen*
the eyelid	*das Augenlid*
an eyelash	*eine Augenwimper*
the pupil	*die Pupillen*
the iris	*die Iris*

ILLNESS cont.

KRANKHEITEN Forts.

PARTS OF THE BODY cont.

KÖRPERTEILE Forts.

THE EYESIGHT	*DAS SEHVERMÖGEN*
to wear glasses / contact lenses	*eine Brille / Kontaktlinsen tragen*
to be short / long sighted	*kurzsichtig / weitsichtig sein*
to have good eyesight	*gute Augen haben*
to have an eye test	*einen Augentest machen*
to wear sunglasses	*eine Sonnenbrille tragen*
to be partially sighted	*sehbehindert sein*
to be blind / a white stick	*blind sein / ein Blindenstock*
a guide dog	*ein Blindenhund*

THE NOSE	*DIE NASE*
a nostril	*ein Nasenloch*
to blow the nose	*die Nase schneuzen*

THE MOUTH	*DER MUND*
the lips	*die Lippen*
the tongue	*die Zunge*
the jaw	*der Kiefer*
the throat	*der Rachen / die Kehle*
the tonsils	*die Mandeln*

THE TEETH	*DIE ZÄHNE*
a molar / a canine	*ein Backenzahn / ein Eckzahn*
an incisor / a wisdom tooth	*ein Schneidezahn / Weisheitszahn*
the gums	*das Zahnfleisch*
to clean one's teeth / to gargle	*seine Zähne putzen / gurgeln*
a toothbrush / to brush	*eine Zahnbürste / bürsten*
toothpaste / to squeeze the tube	*Zahnpasta / die Tube zusammendrücken*
to floss	*Zahnseide benutzen*
to use mouthwash	*Mundwasser benutzen*

ILLNESS cont.   *KRANKHEITEN Forts.*

PARTS OF THE BODY cont.   *KÖRPERTEILE Forts.*

THE EARS	*DIE OHREN*
the ear lobe	*das Ohrläppchen*
the outer ear / the middle ear	*das Außenohr / das Mittelohr*
the ear drum	*das Trommelfell*
earwax	*Ohrenschmalz*
an ear infection	*eine Ohrenentzündung*
to be unable to hear properly	*nicht richtig hören können*
to be deaf	*taub sein*
a hearing aid	*ein Hörgerät*

THE BEARD	*DER BART*
clean shaven	*sauber rasiert*
to grow a beard	*einen Bart wachsen lassen*
to shave (See page 60)	*rasieren*
a moustache	*ein Schnurrbart*
sideburns	*Koteletten*
a chin	*ein Kinnbart*

THE BODY	*DER KÖRPER*		
the neck	*der Hals*	a rib	*eine Rippe*
the shoulder	*die Schulter*	the rib cage	*der Brustkorb*
the back	*der Rücken*	the waist	*die Taille*
the spine	*das Rückgrat / die Wirbelsäule*	the hip	*die Hüfte*
the bottom	*der Po*	the stomach	*der Bauch*
the chest	*die Brust*	the abdomen	*der Unterleib*

ILLNESS cont.   *KRANKHEITEN Forts.*

PARTS OF THE BODY cont.   *KÖRPERTEILE Forts.*

THE ARM	*DIE ARME*
the upper arm	*der Oberarm*
the forearm	*der Unterarm*
the elbow	*der Ellbogen*
the funny bone	*der Musikantenknochen*
the wrist	*das Handgelenk*

THE HANDS	*DIE HÄNDE*
the palm / the back of the hand	*die Handfläche / der Handrücken*
the knuckles	*die Fingerknöchel*
the fingers / the thumbs	*die Finger / die Daumen*
left / right	*linke / rechte*
a fingernail	*ein Fingernagel*
a cuticle / cuticle remover	*Nagelhaut / ein Nagelhautentferner*
a manicure / to manicure	*eine Maniküre / maniküren*
an emery board / a nail file	*eine Papiernagelfeile / eine Nagelfeile*
nail varnish / nail varnish remover	*Nagellack / Nackellackentferner*

THE LEGS	*DIE BEINE*
the thigh	*die Oberschenkel*
the knee	*das Knie*
the calf	*die Wade*
the shin	*das Schienbein*
the ankle	*der Knöchel*

ILLNESS cont.   *KRANKHEITEN Forts.*

PARTS OF THE BODY cont.   *KÖRPERTEILE Forts.*

THE FEET	*DIE FÜSSE*
a foot	*ein Fuß*
the heel / the sole	*die Ferse / die Sohle*
the toes / the big toe / the little toe	*die Zehen / der große Zeh / der kleine Zeh*
a toenail	*ein Fußnagel*
to cut the toenails	*die Fußnägel schneiden*
nail scissors / nail clippers	*eine Nagelschere / ein Nagelzwicker*
hard skin / bunions	*harte Haut / Ballen*
a pumice stone	*ein Bimsstein*

THE MAIN INTERNAL ORGANS		*DIE WICHTIGSTEN INNEREN ORGANE*	
the digestive system		*das Verdauungs-system*	
the lungs	*die Lungen*	the intestines	*der Darm*
the heart	*das Herz*	the bowel	*die Eingeweide*
the liver	*die Leber*	the bladder	*die Blase*
the kidney	*die Niere*		

THE CIRCULATION	*DER BLUTKREISLAUF*
the blood	*das Blut*
to be anaemic	*unter Blutarmut leiden*
an artery / a vein	*eine Arterie / eine Ader*
to bleed	*bluten*
to haemorrhage	*unter Blutungen leiden*
to bruise	*verletzen*
to clot / to form a scab	*gerinnen / Schorf bilden*

ILLNESS cont.   *KRANKHEITEN Forts.*

PARTS OF THE BODY cont.   *KÖRPERTEILE Forts.*

THE MAIN MUSCLES	*DIE WICHTIGSTEN MUSKELN*
the biceps / the triceps	*die Bizeps / die Trizeps*
the pectorals	*die Brustmuskeln*
the ham string	*die Kniesehne*
the Achilles tendon	*die Achillessehne*

THE MAIN BONES	*DIE WICHTIGSTEN KNOCHEN*
the skeleton / the skull	*das Skelett / der Schädel*
the collar bone	*das Schlüsselbein*
the spine	*das Rückgrat / die Wirbelsäule*
the vertebrae / the coccyx	*der Rückenwirbel / das Steißbein*
the shoulder blade	*das Schulterblatt*
the ribs / the hip bone	*die Rippen / der Hüftknochen*
the thigh bone	*der Oberschenkelknochen*
the shin bone	*das Schienbein*
the knee cap	*das Kniegelenk*

THE CENTRAL NERVOUS SYSTEM	*DAS ZENTRALNERVENSYSTEM*
the cerebellum	*das Kleinhirn*
the spinal chord	*das Rückenmark*
the nerves	*die Nerven*

MALE / FEMALE CHARACTERISTICS	*MÄNNLICHE / WEIBLICHE MERKMALE*
the penis / the testicles	*der Penis / die Hoden*
a broken voice	*ein Stimmenbruch*
the breasts / the nipples	*die Brüste / die Warzen*
the womb / the vagina	*die Gebärmutter / die Scheide*

THE BODY cont.   *DER KÖRPER Forts.*

PREGNANCY	*SCHWANGERSCHAFT*
to do a pregnancy test	*einen Schwangerschaftstest machen*
positive / negative / to be pregnant	*positiv / negativ / schwanger sein*
to be three months pregnant	*im dritten Monat schwanger sein*
to be at full term	*hochschwanger*
to go into labour	*die Wehen bekommen*
to have a baby	*ein Baby bekommen*
the embryo / the foetus	*das Embryo / der Fötus*

THE FIVE SENSES   *DIE FÜNF SINNE*

TOUCH		*TASTSINN*	
to touch	*berühren*	rough	*rauh*
hot	*heiß*	smooth	*zart*
cold	*kalt*	painful	*schmerzhaft*

TASTE		*GESCHMACK*	
to taste	*schmecken*	sour	*sauer*
bitter	*bitter*	savoury	*lecker*
sweet	*süß*		

SMELL		*GERUCH*	
to smell	*riechen*	unpleasant	*unangenehm*
pleasant	*angenehm*	to stink	*stinken*

HEARING		*HÖREN*	
to hear	*hören*	noisy	*geräuschvoll*
loud	*laut*	quiet	*leise*

SIGHT		*SEHEN*	
to see	*sehen*	blurred	*verschwommen*
to focus	*scharf sehen*	clear	*klar*

ILLNESS cont.   *KRANKHEITEN Forts.*

GETTING TREATMENT   *IN BEHANDLUNG GEHEN*
Shall I call..?   *Soll ich...anrufen?*
Can I make an appointment to   *Kann ich einen Termin haben*
see ..?   *mit....*
- the doctor / the nurse   • *dem Doktor / der Schwester*
- the dentist   • *dem Zahnarzt*
- the hospital   • *dem Krankenhaus*

THE DOCTOR'S SURGERY   *DIE ARZTPRAXIS*
the waiting room   *das Wartezimmer*
to sit down / to wait   *sitzen / warten*
to read a magazine   *eine Zeitschrift lesen*
I have an appointment to see.. *Einen Termin mit....haben.*

THE CONSULTATION   *DIE UNTERSUCHUNG*
I am going to ..   *Ich werde...*
- to take your blood pressure. • *Ihren Blutdruck messen*
- to take your pulse.   • *Ihren Puls messen*
- to take a blood sample.   • *einen Bluttest machen*
- to do a urine test.   • *eine Urinuntersuchung machen*
- to listen to your heart / chest. • *Ihr Herz / Ihre Lunge abhören*
- to look down your throat.   • *in Ihren Rachen schauen*
- to look in your ear.   • *in Ihre Ohren schauen*
- to test your reflexes.   • *Ihre Reflexe testen*

ILLNESS cont.   *KRANKHEITEN Forts.*

COULD YOU..	KÖNNTEN SIE.....
• roll up your sleeve.	• *Ihre Ärmel hochkrempeln.*
• undo your jacket.	• *Ihre Jacke aufmachen.*
• lift up your shirt.	• *Ihr Hemd hochziehen.*
• take off your clothes.	• *Ihre Kleidung ausziehen.*
• take everything off except your pants.	• *alles ausziehen außer ihre Unterhose.*
• put this gown on.	• *diesen Kittel anziehen.*
• lie down.	• *hinlegen.*
• put this blanket over you	• *diese Decke überlegen.*
• open your mouth wide	• *Ihren Mund weit öffnen.*
• do a urine / stool sample	• *eine Urin / Stuhprobe machen.*

SAYING WHERE YOU HURT	SAGE WO ES WEH TUT
Where does it hurt?	*Wo tut es weh?*
Show me where it hurts.	*Zeigen Sie mir wo es weh tut.*
Does it hurt...	*Tut das...*
• badly?	• *schlimm*
• much?	• *sehr ...weh?*
• when I touch it?	• *Tut das weh, wenn ich es berühre?*
• when you move it?	• *Tut das weh, wenn Sie es bewegen?*
Can you move your... (See parts of the body - pages 411-417)	*Können Sie Ihr.....bewegen?*

420

ILLNESS cont.   *KRANKHEITEN Forts.*

THE DOCTOR'S INSTRUCTIONS
DIE ANWEISUNGEN DES ARZTES

You should stay in bed.	*Sie sollten im Bett bleiben.*
You should not go to work / school / travel.	*Sie sollten nicht zur Arbeit / in die Schule / auf Reisen gehen.*
I would like to do further tests.	*Ich möchte gerne noch ein paar weitere Untersuchungen machen.*
You need an X-ray.	*Sie müssen eine Röntgenaufnahme machen lassen.*
You need a scan.	*Sie müssen eine Ultraschallaufnahme machen lassen.*
I will make an appointment at the hospital for you.	*Ich werde einen Termin im Krankenhaus für Sie machen.*
I would like a second opinion.	*Ich würde gerne noch eine zweite Meinung hören.*
It is nothing serious.	*Es ist nichts Ernstes.*
You will be better soon.	*Es wird Ihnen bald besser gehen.*
Are you allergic to anything?	*Sind Sie gegen irgendetwas allergisch?*

THE TREATMENT
DIE BEHANDLUNG

a prescription	*ein Rezept*
Take it to the chemists.	*Bringen Sie es zur Apotheke.*
to get the prescription made up	*das Rezept gemacht bekommen.*
antibiotics / penicillin	*Antibiotika / Penizillin*
a tablet / a capsule	*eine Tablette / eine Kapsel*
medicine / linctus	*Medizin (m)*
a five millilitre spoon	*ein Fünf-Millimeter-Meßlöffel*
the dosage	*die Dosis*
to swallow / to take	*schlucken / nehmen*
Shake the bottle before use.	*Vor Gebrauch die Flasche schütteln.*

ILLNESS - THE TREATMENT cont.

KRANKHEITEN - DIE BEHANDLUNG Forts.

MEDICINE cont.

MEDIZIN Forts.

three times a day	*dreimal am Tag*
before / after meals	*vor den / nach den Mahlzeiten*
Take with food.	*Zu einer Mahlzeit einnehmen.*
Take on an empty stomach.	*Auf leeren Magen nehmen.*
Do not drink alcohol.	*Keinen Alkohol trinken.*
Do not mix with other tablets.	*Nicht mit anderen Tabletten einnehmen.*
Do not take if pregnant.	*Nicht bei einer Schwangerschaft einnehmen.*
a suppository	*ein Zäpfchen*
an inhaler	*ein Inhalierer*
antihistamine cream	*Antihistamincreme*
antiseptic cream	*eine antiseptische Creme*
ointment / to rub on	*eine Salbe / einreiben*
aspirin / paracetamol	*Aspirin / Paracetamol*

GOING TO HOSPITAL	*INS KRANKENHAUS GEHEN*
an ambulance	*ein Krankenwagen*
a stretcher	*eine Bahre*
the outpatients' department	*die Ambulanz*
casualty	*Unfallstation*
the enquiry desk	*der Auskunftsschalter*

ILLNESS - GOING TO HOSPITAL cont.	*KRANKHEITEN - INS KRANKENHAUS GEHEN*

BEING ADMITTED	***EINGELIEFERT WERDEN***
Can you fill in this form, please?	*Können Sie bitte dieses Formular ausfüllen?*
Can I take your details, please?	*Kann ich bitte Ihre persönlichen Daten aufnehmen*
• Surname	*Nachname*
• Christian Name	*Vorname*
• Age	*Alter*
• Date of Birth	*Geburtsdatum*
• Place of Birth	*Geburtsort*
• Nationality	*Herkunftsland / Nationalität*
• Address / Telephone Number	*Adresse / Telefonnummer*
• Next of Kin	*nächste Verwandte*
• Medical History	*Krankengeschichte*
• Details of previous operations	*Angaben zu vorherigen Operationen*
• Serious illnesses.	*Ernsthafte Erkrankungen*
• Allergies	*Allergien*
• Have you ever had any of the following illnesses?	*Hatten Sie jemals eine der folgenden Krankheiten?*

THE FRACTURE CLINIC	***DIE KNOCHENCHIRURGIE***
to be assessed / examined	*beurteilt / untersucht werden*
to have an X-ray	*geröntgt werden*
to have one's arm in a sling	*seinen Arm in einer Schlinge tragen*
to be bandaged up	*verbunden werden*
to be given a plaster cast	*einen Gipsverband bekommen*
to have a splint	*einen Splitter haben*
to walk with crutches / to hop	*mit Krücken gehen / hüpfen*
to lean on someone	*sich auf jemanden stützen*
to use a wheelchair	*einen Rollstuhl benutzen*
to push / to steer	*schieben / lenken*

ILLNESS - GOING TO HOSPITAL cont.

KRANKHEITEN - INS KRANKENHAUS GEHEN Forts.

PHYSIOTHERAPY — *PHYSIOTHERAPIE*

a physiotherapist	*ein Physiotherapeut*
to do exercises	*Übungen machen*
to increase mobility	*seine Beweglichkeit vergrößern*
to use an ice pack	*einen Eisbeutel benutzen*
to use a bag of frozen peas	*eine tiefgekühlte Erbsenpackung benutzen*
to wrap in a towel	*in ein Handtuch einwickeln*
to reduce the swelling	*die Schwellung verringern*
to reduce the inflammation	*die Entzündung verringern*
to use a heat compress	*eine Wärmekompresse benutzen*
to have ultrasound treatment	*eine Ultraschallbehandlung bekommen*
to do exercises every hour	*jede Stunde Übungen machen*
three times a day	*dreimal am Tag*
to push / to pull	*schieben / ziehen*
to squeeze	*drücken*
to lift / a weight	*heben / ein Gewicht*
to raise / to lower	*anheben / herunterlassen*
to massage	*eine Massage geben*

OPERATIONS — *OPERATIONEN*

to have nothing to eat or drink	*nichts zu Essen und zu Trinken haben*
to sign a consent form	*ein Einwilligungsbestätigung unterschreiben*
to put on an operating gown	*einen Operationskittel anziehen*
to be given a pre-med	*eine Beruhigungsspritze bekommen*
to feel drowsy	*sich benommen fühlen*
to have a local anaesthetic	*eine lokale Narkose haben*

ILLNESS - GOING TO HOSPITAL cont.	KRANKHEITEN - INS KRANKENHAUS GEHEN Forts.
OPERATIONS cont.	**OPERATIONEN Forts.**

to be numb	betäubt sein
an injection	eine Injektion
to be given gas and air	Gas und Sauerstoff bekommen
a mask	eine Maske
to dull the pain	den Schmerz betäuben
to cover your nose and mouth	seine Nase und Mund bedecken
to breathe in	einatmen
to have a general anaesthetic	eine Vollnarkose haben
to come round	wieder zu sich kommen
to have a sip of water	einen Schluck Wasser haben
to have your pulse checked	seinen Puls überprüft bekommen
to have your temperature taken	seine Temperatur gemessen bekommen
to listen to your heart	sein Herz hören
to call the nurse	die Schwester rufen
Can I get you anything?	Kann ich Ihnen etwas bringen?
Is anything wrong?	Stimmt was nicht?
to ask for a bed pan	nach einer Bettpfanne fragen
to ask for a drink	nach etwas zu Trinken fragen
visiting hours	Besuchszeiten
to have a visitor	Besuch haben
to be given flowers	Blumen bekommen
to receive Get Well cards	Karten mit Genesungswünschen bekommen

DENTAL TREATMENT   *ZAHNBEHANDLUNG*

THE DENTIST	*DER ZAHNARZT*
to make an appointment	*einen Termin ausmachen*
to sit in the waiting room	*im Warteraum sitzen*
to go into the surgery	*ins Untersuchungszimmer gehen*
the dentist's chair	*der Zahnarztstuhl*
My tooth hurts.	*Mein Zahn tut weh.*
My filling has come out.	*Meine Füllung ist rausgefallen.*
My tooth was knocked out.	*Mein Zahn wurde ausgeschlagen.*

DENTAL TREATMENT	*ZAHNBEHANDLUNG*
to have a look	*nachschauen*
to put a bib on	*einen Latz anziehen*
Open your mouth wide.	*Machen Sie Ihren Mund weit auf.*
Does that hurt?	*Tut das weh?*
Which tooth hurts?	*Welcher Zahn tut weh?*
to be given a local anaesthetic	*eine lokale Betäubung bekommen*
an injection	*eine Injektion*
Is it numb now?	*Ist es schon taub?*
to drill a tooth	*ein Loch bohren*
to extract a tooth	*einen Zahn herausziehen*
a laser beam	*ein Laserstrahl*
to put a filling in	*eine Füllung reintun*
to bite one's teeth together gently	*leicht seine Zähne zusammenbeißen*
to polish the teeth	*die Zähne säubern*
to wash / rinse the mouth out	*auswaschen / den Mund ausspülen*
to spit	*spucken*
a tissue / to dry one's mouth	*ein Papiertuch / sich den Mund abtrocknen*
to dribble	*tropfen*
to find it difficult to talk / to drink	*es schwierig finden zu sprechen / zu trinken*
Don't eat anything for a couple of hours.	*Essen Sie nichts für ein paar Stunden*

THE OPTICIANS *DER AUGENOPTIKER*

My glasses have broken.	*Meine Brille ist zerbrochen*
Could you mend them for me?	*Können Sie sie wieder ganz machen?*
I have lost a contact lens.	*Ich habe eine Kontaktlinse verloren.*
Could I try to get a replacement?	*Kann ich versuchen, eine neue zu bekommen?*
I can't see very clearly.	*Ich kann nicht sehr klar sehen.*
I have double vision.	*Ich sehe doppelt.*
I keep getting headaches.	*Ich bekomme ständig Kopfschmerzen.*
Could I get my eyes tested, please?	*Könnten Sie bitte meine Augen untersuchen?*
A screw has come out of my glasses.	*Eine Schraube ist aus meiner Brille herausgefallen.*
Can you mend my glasses for me?	*Können Sie mir meine Brille wieder ganz machen?*
Will you have to send them away somewhere?	*Müssen Sie sie irgendwohin schicken?*
How long will it take to repair them?	*Wie lange wird die Reperatur dauern?*
I am going back to England in five days.	*in fünf Tagen fahre ich nach England zurück.*
Will they be ready by then?	*Wird sie bis dahin fertig sein?*

EYE SIGHT TESTS	***AUGENTEST***
Do sit down.	*Setzen Sie sich doch.*
Look over there.	*Schauen Sie dorthin.*
Look at the writing.	*Schauen Sie sich das Geschriebene an.*
Read as much as you can.	*Lesen Sie so viel Sie können.*
Can you read the next row down?	*Können Sie die nächste untere Reihe lesen?*

EYE SIGHT TESTS cont.	*AUGENTEST Forts.*
Take your glasses off.	*Ziehen Sie ihre Brille aus.*
I am going to try different lenses.	*Ich probiere verschiedene Gläser aus.*
Does it look clearer like this or like this?	*Ist es so oder so schärfer?*
Clearer with this lens or without it?	*Schärfer mit oder ohne Glas?*
I am going to look in your eye with a torch.	*Ich werde jetzt mit einer Taschenlampe in Ihr Auge gucken.*
Look up / down / left / right / straight ahead.	*Nach oben schauen / nach unten / links / rechts / geradeaus.*
You can put your glasses on again now.	*Sie können Ihre Brille wieder aufsetzen.*

PREVENTIVE MEDICINE
VORBEUGENDE MEDIZIN

RELAXATION	*ENTSPANNUNG*
to avoid stress	*Streß vermeiden*
to practise relaxation	*sich entspannen üben*
to relieve tension	*Anspannungen abbauen*
to do breathing exercises	*Atemübungen machen*
to meditate	*meditieren*
to practise meditation	*Meditationsübungen machen*

EXERCISE	*BEWEGUNG*
to take enough exercise	*ausreichende Bewegung haben*
to walk more / to keep fit	*mehr laufen / in Form halten*
to go to keep fit classes	*In Fitness-Klassen gehen*
to go jogging / swimming	*Joggen / Schwimmen gehen*
aerobic / anaerobic	*Aerobic / Anaerobic*
to warm up / to stretch	*aufwärmen / dehnen*
suppleness exercises	*Beweglichkeitsübungen*

PREVENTIVE MEDICINE - EXERCISE cont.	*VORBEUGENDE MEDIZIN - BEWEGUNG Forts.*
weight lifting / to work up a sweat	*Gewichtheben / schwitzen*
to get breathless	*außer Atem kommen*
to exercise three times a week	*sich dreimal in der Woche körperlich bewegen*
to exercise for at least twenty minutes	*sich mindestens zwanzig Minuten lang körperlich bewegen*

SLEEP	*SCHLAFEN*
to get a good night's sleep	*einen guten Schlaf haben*
to need eight hours' sleep	*acht Stunden Schlaf brauchen*
to lie in / to go to bed late	*im Bett bleiben/spät ins Bett gehen*
to get up early	*früh aufstehen*
to dream / to have nightmares	*träumen / Alpträume haben*
to suffer from insomnia	*unter Schlaflosigkeit leiden*
to take sleeping tablets	*Schlaftabletten nehmen*

DIET	*ERNÄHRUNGSWEISEN UND DIÄTEN*
to eat a balanced diet	*eine ausgewogene Ernährung*
to eat sensibly	*sich vernünftig ernähren*
vitamins / minerals	*Vitamine / Mineralien*
carbohydrates	*Kohlenhydrate*
protein	*Protein*
fibre	*Faser*
vegetarian / vegan	*Vegetarier / Vegan*
to drink too much caffeine	*zu viel Koffein trinken*
to count calories	*Kalorien zählen*
to cut down	*einschränken*
to have small portions	*kleine Portionen nehmen*
to have a little of everything	*wenig von allem haben*
a calorie controlled diet	*eine Kalorien-Kontroll-Diät*

PREVENTIVE MEDICINE	*VORBEUGENDE MEDIZIN*
DIET cont.	*ERNÄHRUNGSWEISEN UND DIÄTEN Forts.*

a strict diet	*eine strenge Diät*
a diabetic diet	*eine Diabetiker-Diät*
to binge	*fressen*
anorexia nervosa	*Magersucht*
bulimia	*Bulimie*
to lose / gain weight	*zunehmen / abnehmen*
to lower one's cholesterol level	*seinen Cholesterinspiegel senken*
to be a desirable weight	*ein wünschenswertes Gewicht haben*
to be a little overweight	*etwas Übergewicht haben*
to be underweight	*Untergewicht haben*
to be obese	*fettleibig sein*

ALCOHOL CONSUMPTION	*ALKOHOLKONSUM*
to drink sensibly	*vernünftig trinken*
a unit of alcohol	*eine alkoholische Einheit*
to be a social drinker	*ein Gesellschaftstrinker sein*
to drink too much	*zu viel trinken*
to get drunk	*sich betrinken*
to have a hangover	*einen Kater haben*
to be dehydrated	*ausgetrocknet sein*
to be an alcoholic	*ein Alkoholiker sein*

SMOKING	*RAUCHEN*
cigarettes / cigars / a pipe	*Zigaretten / Zigarren / eine Pfeife*
tobacco / nicotine / tar content	*Tabak / Nikotin / Teergehalt*
How many do you smoke a day?	*Wieviele rauchst Du am Tag?*
to try to cut down / to be addicted	*versuchen es einzuschränken / abhängig sein*
to inhale / lung cancer	*inhalieren / Lungenkrebs*

DRUGS

DROGEN

soft / hard drugs / to smoke	*weiche / harte Drogen / rauchen*
stimulants	*Anregungsmittel*
cannabis	*Cannabis*
ecstasy / an E	*Ecstasy / "E"*
a tablet	*eine Tablette*
to inject	*spritzen*
a pusher	*ein Drücker*
illegal	*illegal*
I think he / she has taken some drugs.	*Ich glaube er / sie hat Drogen genommen.*
Do you know what he took?	*Weißt Du was er/sie genommen hat?*
to be unconscious	*nicht bei Bewußtsein sein*
I think we should get help.	*Ich glaube, wir sollten Hilfe holen.*
He / she is drinking a lot of water.	*Er / Sie trinkt viel Wasser.*

ALTERNATIVE THERAPIES

ALTERNATIVE THERAPIEFORMEN

AROMATHERAPY	***AROMATHERAPIE***
essential oils / a drop	*ätherische Öle / ein Tropfen*
to blend / a carrier oil	*vermischen / Verbindungsöl*
to massage / a massage	*massieren / eine Massage*
to inhale	*inhalieren*
an essential oil burner	*ein Brenner für ätherische Öle*
to put in the bath	*ins Bad geben*
a compress	*ein Umschlag*

HERBALISM	***KRÄUTERHEILKUNDE***
a herbalist	*ein Heilkräuterexperte*
a herb / to gather / to store	*Kräuter / sammeln / aufbewahren*
an infusion / a decoction	*ein Kräutertee / ein Kräutersud*
a tincture / a compress	*eine Tinktur / ein Umschlag*

ALTERNATIVE THERAPIES cont.

ALTERNATIVE THERAPIEFORMEN Forts.

HOMOEOPATHY	*HOMÖOPATHIE*
a homoeopath	*ein Homöopath*
a remedy	*ein Heilmittel*
constitutional treatment	*konstitutionelle Behandlung*
the potency	*die Potenz*
the dose	*die Dosierung*

CHIROPRACTIC AND OSTEOPATHY	*CHIROPRAXIS UND OSTEOPATHIE*
a chiropractor	*ein Chiropraktiker*
an osteopath	*ein Osteopath*
to manipulate	*manipulieren*
the joints	*die Gelenke*

CRIME   *KRIMINALITÄT*

THEFT	***DIEBSTAHL***
I've been robbed.	*Ich bin ausgeraubt worden.*
Someone has taken my..	***Jemand hat mir...***
• bag / wallet	*meine Tasche / Brieftasche*
• purse / money	*mein Portemonnaie / Geld*
• credit card	*meine Kreditkarte*
• watch	*meine Uhr*
• jewellery	*meinen Schmuck......gestohlen.*
a thief / a pickpocket	*ein Dieb / ein Taschendieb*
a car thief / a joyrider	*ein Autodieb / ein Joyrider*
to break into	*einbrechen*
to steal / to snatch	*stehlen / klauen*
to mug	*überfallen*
to rob a bank	*eine Bank ausrauben*
to steal from the till	*aus der Kasse stehlen*
to shoplift / a shoplifter	*einen Ladendiebstahl begehen / ein Ladendieb*
a hijacking / to hijack	*eine Entführung / entführen*
a kidnapping / to kidnap	*ein Kidnapping / kidnappen*
to demand a ransom	*ein Lösegeld verlangen*
to take a hostage / terrorism	*eine Geisel nehmen / Terrorismus*
to hold up / a hold-up	*überfallen / ein Überfall*
a murder / to murder	*ein Mord / ermorden*
to kick / to stab	*treten / stechen*
to thump	*eine verpassen*
to cosh	*jemandem eins überziehen*
to knock someone out	*jemanden bewußtlos schlagen*
to strangle / to suffocate	*würgen / ersticken*
rape / to rape / to be raped / a rapist	*Vergewaltigung/vergewaltigen/vergewaltigt werden/ein Vergewaltiger*

CRIME cont. *KRIMINALITÄT Forts.*

HELPING THE POLICE	*DER POLIZEI HELFEN*
a witness / to witness	*ein Zeuge / Zeuge sein*
to say what happened	*sagen, was passiert ist*
to recognize	*erkennen*
to identify	*identifizieren*
a suspect	*eine verdächtige Person / ein Verdacht*
to be cautioned	*verwarnt werden*
to be taken into custody	*in Gewahrsam genommen werden*
to be arrested	*eingesperrt werden*
to be let out on bail	*aus der Haft entlassen werden*
to be innocent	*unschuldig sein*
to be guilty	*schuldig sein*

LOSING OR DAMAGING IMPORTANT POSSESSIONS

WICHTIGES EIGENTUM VERLIEREN ODER BESCHÄDIGEN

I'VE LOST MY...(abc)	*ICH HABE ....*
• bag	• *meine Tasche*
• briefcase	• *meine Aktentasche*
• bus pass	• *meinen Busausweis*
• camera	• *meine Kamera*
• cheque book	• *mein Scheckheft*
• cheque card	• *meine Scheckkarte*
• contact lens	• *meine Kontaktlinse*
• credit cards	• *meine Kreditkarte*
• diary	• *meinen Terminkalender*
• foreign currency	• *mein ausländisches Geld*
• glasses / spectacles	• *meine Brille / meine Brille*
• handbag	• *meine Handtasche*
• Identity card	• *meinen Personalausweis*
• key / keyring	• *meine Schlüssel / meinen Schlüsselbund*
• money	• *mein Geld*
• passport	• *meinen Paß*
• purse	• *mein Portemonnaie*
• rail pass	• *meinen Bahnausweis*
• rucksack	• *meinen Rucksack*
• shoulder bag	• *meine Umhängetasche*
• suitcase	• *meinen Koffer*
• ticket	• *meine Fahrkarte / meine Eintrittskarte*
• travellers cheques	• *meine Reiseschecks*
• wallet	• *meine Brieftasche*
• watch	• *meine Uhr..... . **VERLOREN***

LOSING OR DAMAGING IMPORTANT POSSESSIONS

WICHTIGES EIGENTUM VERLIEREN ODER BESCHÄDIGEN

I'VE BROKEN MY..

- camera
- contact lens
- glasses / spectacles
- watch

I'm sorry but I have broken your...

I will pay for it.
My parents will get you another...

ICH HABE MEINE....

- *Kamera*
- *Kontaktlinse*
- *Brille*
- *Uhr..* **KAPUTT GEMACHT.**

Tut mir leid, aber ich habe Dein / Deine.....kaputt gemacht.

Ich werde dafür bezahlen.
Meine Eltern werden Dir ein neues / eine neue besorgen.

I'VE TORN MY..
trousers / skirt / coat / dress / shirt

Could you mend it for me, please?
I've lost a button.
My button has come off.
Could I sew it back on, please?
Have you a needle and thread I could use?
My zip has broken.

Do you have a safety pin?

MIR IST ....
meine Hose / mein Rock / mein Mantel / mein Kleid / mein Hemd **...ZERRISSEN**.

Könnten Sie es bitte flicken?
Ich habe einen Knopf verloren.
Mein Knopf ist abgegangen.
Kann ich ihn wieder annähen?
Könnte ich eine Nadel und einen Faden haben?
Mein Reißverschluß ist kaputt gegangen.
Haben Sie eine Sicherheitsnadel?

FORM FILLING / PERSONAL INFORMATION

FORMULARE AUSFÜLLEN / PERSÖNLICHE INFORMATIONEN

Could you fill in this form, please?	***Könnten Sie bitte dieses Formular ausfüllen?***
in block capitals	*in Großbuchstaben*
Please print clearly.	*Bitte schreiben Sie deutlich.*
Please use pen or biro.	*Bitte benutzen Sie einen Füllfederhalter oder einen Kugelschreiber.*
Have you a pen I could borrow, please?	*Kann ich mir Ihren Füllfederhalter ausleihen?*
Please put one letter in each square.	*Bitte jeweils nur einen Buchstabe in jedes Viereck.*
Please sign and date the form at the end.	*Bitte unterschreiben Sie zum Schluß und setzen das Datum ein.*

Personal details	***Persönliche Angaben***
Title	*Anrede / Titel*
Surname / Christian names	*Nachname / Vornamen*
Date of Birth	*Geburtsdatum*
Place of Birth	*Geburtsort*
Age	*Alter*
Gender / Sex	*Geschlecht*
Marital Status	*Familienstand*

ADDRESS	***ADRESSE***
House name / number	*Hausnummer*
Street	*Straße*
Town / City	*Ort / Stadt*
County / Area / Postal Code	*Bundesland / Bezirk / Postleitzahl*
Country	*Land*
Where are you staying at the moment?	*Wo wohnen Sie momentan?*
Where do you live?	*Wo leben Sie?*

FORM FILLING / PERSONAL INFORMATION
FORMULARE AUSFÜLLEN / PERSÖNLICHE INFORMATIONEN

TELEPHONE NUMBER	*TELEFONNUMMERN*
Country code	*Internationale Vorwahlnummern*
Area code	*örtliche Vorwahlnummern*
Work telephone number	*Berufliche Telefonnummer*
Home telephone number	*Privatnummer*
Mobile telephone number	*Mobilfunknummer*
FAX number	*FAX-Nummer*

GETTING THINGS TO WORK	*DINGE ZUM FUNKTIONIEREN BRINGEN*
How does this work?	*Wie funktioniert das?*
Can you show me how to use this?	*Kannst Du mir zeigen, wie es funktioniert?*
This isn't working properly.	*Das funktioniert nicht richtig.*
Is there something wrong with it?	*Funktioniert etwas nicht richtig?*
Am I doing something wrong with this?	*Mach´ ich irgend etwas falsch?*
Can I watch you use it?	*Kann ich dabei zugucken, wie es funktioniert ?*
Can I try to use it now?	*Kann ich es jetzt nochmal versuchen?*
How did you do that?	*Wie hast Du das gemacht?*

Your German Exchange

Index

Your German Exchange